ON SELF-TRANSLATION

Also by Ilan Stavans

Fiction *The Disappearance* * *The One-Handed Pianist and Other Stories*

Nonfiction *The Riddle of Cantinflas* * *Dictionary Days* * *On Borrowed Words* * *Spanglish* * *The Hispanic Condition* * *Art and Anger* * *Resurrecting Hebrew* * *A Critic's Journey* * *The Inveterate Dreamer* * *Octavio Paz: A Meditation* * *Imagining Columbus* * *Bandido* * *¡Lotería!* (with Teresa Villegas) * *José Vasconcelos: The Prophet of Race* * *Return to Centro Histórico* * *Singer's Typewriter and Mine* * *Gabriel García Márquez: The Early Years, 1929–1970* * *The United States of Mestizo* * *Reclaiming Travel* (with Joshua Ellison) * *Quixote: The Novel and the World* * *Borges, the Jew* * *I Love My Selfie* (with Adál) * *Sor Juana*

Play *The Oven*

Conversations *Knowledge and Censorship* (with Verónica Albin) * *What Is la hispanidad?* (with Iván Jaksić) * *Ilan Stavans: Eight Conversations* (with Neal Sokol) * *With All Thine Heart* (with Mordecai Drache) * *Conversations with Ilan Stavans* * *Love and Language* (with Verónica Albin) * *¡Muy Pop!* (with Frederick Aldama) * *Thirteen Ways of Looking at Latino Art* (with Jorge J. E. Gracia) * *Laughing Matters* (with Frederick Aldama)

Children's Book *Golemito* (with Teresa Villegas)

Anthologies *The Norton Anthology of Latino Literature* * *Tropical Synagogues* * *The Oxford Book of Latin American Essays* * *The Schocken Book of Modern Sephardic Literature* * *Lengua Fresca* (with Harold Augenbraum) * *Wáchale!* * *The Scroll and the Cross* * *The Oxford Book of Jewish Stories* * *Mutual Impressions* * *Growing Up Latino* (with Harold Augenbraum) * *The FSG Books of Twentieth Century Latin American Poetry* * *Oy, Caramba!*

Poetry *The Wall*

Graphic Novels *Latino USA* (with Lalo Alcaraz) * *Mr. Spic Goes to Washington* (with Roberto Weil) * *Once @ 9:53 am* (with Marcelo Brodsky) * *El Iluminado* (with Steve Sheinkin) * *A Most Imperfect Union* (with Lalo Alcaraz) * *Angelitos* (with Santiago Cohen)

Translations *Sentimental Songs*, by Felipe Alfau * *The Plain in Flames*, by Juan Rulfo (with Harold Augenbraum) * *The Underdogs*, by Mariano Azuela (with Anna More) * *Lazarillo de Tormes* * *El Little Príncipe*, by Antoine de Saint Exupéry

Editions *Cesar Vallejo: Spain, Take This Chalice from Me* * *The Poetry of Pablo Neruda* * *Encyclopedia Latina* (4 volumes) * *Pablo Neruda: I Explain a Few Things* * *The Collected Stories of Calvert Casey* * *Isaac Bashevis Singer: Collected Stories* (3 volumes) * *Cesar Chavez: An Organizer's Tale* * *Rubén Darío: Selected Writings* * *Pablo Neruda: All the Odes* * *Latin Music* (2 volumes)

General *The Essential Ilan Stavans*

ON SELF-TRANSLATION
Meditations on Language

ILAN STAVANS

STATE UNIVERSITY OF NEW YORK PRESS

Published by
STATE UNIVERSITY OF NEW YORK PRESS, ALBANY

© 2018 State University of New York

All rights reserved

Printed in the United States of America

No part of this book may be used or reproduced in any manner whatsoever without written permission. No part of this book may be stored in a retrieval system or transmitted in any form or by any means including electronic, electrostatic, magnetic tape, mechanical, photocopying, recording, or otherwise without the prior permission in writing of the publisher.

For information, contact
State University of New York Press, Albany, NY
www.sunypress.edu

Library of Congress Cataloging-in-Publication Data

Names: Stavans, Ilan, author.
Title: On self-translation : meditations on language / Ilan Stavans.
Description: Albany : State University of New York, [2018] | Series: SUNY series in Latin America and Iberian thought and culture | Includes bibliographical references and index
Identifiers: LCCN 2017054959 | ISBN 9781438471495 (hardcover : alk. paper) | ISBN 9781438471488 (pbk. : alk. paper) | ISBN 9781438471501 (ebook)
Subjects: LCSH: Self-translation.
Classification: LCC P306.97.S45 S728 2018 | DDC 418/.02—dc23
LC record available at https://lccn.loc.gov/2017054959

10 9 8 7 6 5 4 3 2 1

"If thought corrupts language, language can also corrupt thought."

—George Orwell, *1984*

CONTENTS

Preface   ix

PART I: MEETING THE "I"

On Self-Translation   3

PART II: MEDITATIONS

Alphabetizing   13
As It Were   15
Parable of Don Quixote   19
Finger Snapping   21
The Tenure Code   23
Transadaptation   27
Ellipses and I   31
On Clarity   35
Auto-Corrected   39

PART III: BEYOND WORDS

On Being Misunderstood   45
Against Representation: A Note on Borges's Aleph   53
The Monkey Grammarian   59
Midrash on Truth   65
Don Quixote in Schlemieland   71
Dying in Hebrew   75
The Reading Life of Ricardo Piglia   89
Adiós, Chespirito   95

PART IV: ON *FÚTBOL*

"Sudden Death"	101
Van Persie's Goal	105
Box of Resonance	107

PART V: LANGUAGE AND POLITICS

Trump and the Wall	111
Why Doesn't English Have an Academy?	115
Shakespeare in Prison	119
The Spanish Language in Latin America since Independence	123
Against "Diversity"	135
Rolling One's R's	139

PART VI: CONVERSATIONS

The Poet's Alchemy (with Richard Wilbur)	145
On Silence (with Charles Hatfield)	157
Translating Cervantes (with Diana de Armas Wilson)	167
The Color of Existence (with Ryan Mihaly)	181
The Downpour of Inspiration (with *Asymptote*)	193
The Translingual Sensibility (with Steven G. Kellman)	197
Rescuing the Classics (with Lydia Davis)	211

PART VII: ONTO SPANGLISH

Un Walker en Nuyol	219
Hamlet, Acto 2, Scene Dos [fragment] and Acto 3, Scene Uno	229
El Little Príncipe, Chapters I–IV	239
Don Quixote, Parte II, Chapter 72	245
Spanglish and the Royal Academy	251

About the Author	253
Index	255

PREFACE

In *Paterson* (1946), William Carlos Williams eloquently writes:

> We sit and talk,
> quietly, with long lapses of silence
> and I am aware of the stream
> that has no language, coursing
> beneath the quiet heaven of
> your eyes
> which has no speech

"The stream that has no language" is an ongoing obsession of mine. Are the words we have at our disposal enough to convey the complexity of life? Why do some languages have more words than others? And how do we say what cannot be said?

The essays and conversations in this volume, which I have collectively called meditations, require no further elucidation. They were prompted by invitation of an assortment of editors. I have tried to organize them cohesively around a series of themes.

The exploration of self-translation is autobiographical in that it delves into the conundrum of my multilingual self. Am I one or more persons, each in a different tongue? The pieces in Part II discuss how the alphabet is becoming a casualty of modern technology and other hindrances, the meaning of finger snapping, translation as adaptation and vice versa, the secretive language of tenure, and what we say through ellipses. They also delve into the limits of clarity and auto-correction. "Beyond Words" is about being misunderstood, about words as friends, and about the limits of representation. Part IV seeks to elicit the poetry of sports. "Language and Politics" reacts to the impoverishment of language in the political sphere, which is neither new nor terminal. It also explores the way language is a depository of memory. Part VI is made of dialogues with poets and scholars;

they are mostly about the classics and about the possibility, as the *Sefer ha-Zohar* suggests, that before the world was created words were already around. And "Onto Spanglish" returns to lifelong concerns of mine: linguistic pollution and the birth of language.

I end with a confession: I'm an inveterate lover of the essay form, particularly in English. It is succinct, feisty, and decisive. I enjoy the fact that the word "essay" derives from the French "*essayer*," to rehearse, and from the Latin "*exagium*," meaning weighing, and *exigere*, to ascertain. To write an essay is for me to rehearse a line of argument. Invariably, I don't know what I think until my thoughts acquire form on the page. To reach that point, I ponder, I meander, and I establish. It is all a dialogue, of course, with myself and with others.

To think is to live. And to live is to let out the stream of words and silences that is us. A single day without writing is a day lost in time.

—July 12, 2018

PART I

MEETING THE "I"

ON SELF-TRANSLATION

"It's like opening one's mouth and hearing someone else's voice emerge."

—Iris Murdoch

In 2001 I published *On Borrowed Words: A Memoir of Language*, in which I reflected on the lives I had lived in Yiddish, Spanish, Hebrew, and English. In the years since, I have often reflected on those reflections, as well as on various facets of my experience that I couldn't fully address in the book. I want to concentrate here on one of those facets—namely, on self-translation. But I will have to begin more generally, by exploring the link between language and epistemology.

    I firmly believe that how one perceives the world in any given moment depends on the language in which that moment is experienced. Take Yiddish, which is, at its root, a Germanic language, but is strongly influenced by Hebrew. It also features Slavic inclusions. These distinct elements give the language a taste, an idiosyncrasy. The life I lived in Yiddish was defined by the rhyme, the cadence of the sentences I used to process and describe it. But this wasn't my only life. I was born in 1961 in Mexico City into an immigrant enclave of Eastern European Jews, and so began speaking Spanish right alongside Yiddish. I have two mother tongues—*di mame loshn* and *la lengua maternal*. Both shape my viewpoint. Eating in Spanish—dreaming, loving, and deriving meaning from life in that language—all these actions differ from their counterparts in Yiddish. The taste of things is determined by the words used to express it.

    It wasn't until I left Mexico—that is, left Spanish and Yiddish—and switched first to Hebrew while living in Israel in 1979, then to English after immigrating to New York City in the mid-eighties, that I was inspired

---

First published in *The Los Angeles Review of Books*, August 23, 2016.

to write a linguistic autobiography. I had read a number of memoirs in the same vein. Among the accounts that influenced me most were Eva Hoffman's *Lost in Translation,* Joseph Conrad's *A Personal Record,* Vladimir Nabokov's *Speak, Memory,* Andre Aciman's *Out of Egypt,* Edward Said's *Out of Place,* Ariel Dorfman's *Heading South, Looking North,* and Jorge Luis Borges's "An Autobiographical Essay," cowritten with Norman Thomas di Giovanni and first published in the *New Yorker.*

While I frequently saw myself mirrored in these authors' odysseys, I felt that, in some cases, they didn't quite do justice to the polyglot's sense of having multiple dimensions, each manifesting itself in a different tongue. For me, this experience could even be seen as a splitting of selves. I empathized with the protagonist, or protagonists, of Robert Louis Stevenson's *Strange Case of Doctor Jekyll and Mister Hyde.* This Victorian parable inspired me to conceive of my linguistic division as a deeper psychological rift. Each language symbolized another sphere: in Yiddish and Spanish I felt I was closer to a raw, primal aspect of my being, whereas in English, which to me is more methodical, I could act like a cosmopolite. These, of course, are just fictions of the mind. Still, a polyglot switching languages does more than simply substitute one code for another. The shift is also physical. Whenever I use Spanish, for instance, I am aware of a freer, more agile movement of my arms, and even of a different grammar in terms of facial expressions. English forces me to be more rigid, maybe even uptight. Yiddish, I feel, is the best, most humorous tongue to swear in. And Hebrew is more liturgical as well as theological; to me, it is the language of the divine and of the afterlife.

In conceiving *On Borrowed Words,* one of my original intentions was to write each of its lengthy chapters in the tongue in which I experienced the relevant phase of my life, but that plan was obviously impractical. Truth is, I was suffering from writer's block, a malady that rarely affects me. Meditating on the past is one thing, but turning those musings into a readable story is another. Tired of waiting, my editor at Viking, Don Fehr, decided to pay me a visit. After lunch, we took a long, contemplative walk on a nearby bicycle path. At one point, after finally confessing my anxiety, my inability to "open the faucet," a metaphor I liked using at the time, Fehr came up with an intriguing idea: he suggested I write—or, at least, attempt to write—my memoir as if I were still living through it. That is, that I look at my past as a continuous present.

It was an exciting proposal, but I wanted to take it even further. I wanted to explain the depth of what "the present" meant in its own terms.

It was then that I told Fehr my thought of drafting each of the chapters not only in the present but also in the tongue in which it had been lived. He laughed and reminded me that I had signed up to write a memoir in English.

"What if I write the chapters in their respective languages and then translate them into English?" I asked. That drew a smile. We discussed the difference between reading a book in the original and reading it in translation. I related two metaphors for translation that I like enormously: in *Don Quixote*, Cervantes writes that reading a book in translation is like looking at a Flemish tapestry from the back; and the Hebrew poet Chaim Nahman Bialik once said that translation is like kissing a bride through a veil. "As long as the quality of the prose is as solid as it is likely to be in the chapter written in English, I'm game . . ."

He was—but I wasn't. My approach was shrewd yet cumbersome. It would entail becoming a different writer in each section. I had been active as a writer in every linguistic period of my life: I wrote plays and stories in Yiddish, and letters and essays in Hebrew; in Manhattan, I regularly filed newspaper columns and reviews in Spanish to newspapers in Mexico, Argentina, Colombia, and Spain; and now I was married and had a child and wrote for the *New York Times* in English. Now I would have to become a native or a near-native speaker in all these tongues at the same time. To become such a speaker, it isn't enough to learn a language; one must internalize it, make it fully one's own. We internalize a language when we organize the world around us based on its parameters. It isn't that we know words to describe things, but that things come to us through their respective words. This is only achieved through time, by letting oneself be absorbed (and, maybe, *absolved*) by a language's metabolism.

A polyglot may be proficient in several languages at once or may be more active and engaged in some and less so in others. Some languages are more deeply ingrained in one's soul. I was able to switch from Spanish to English and back with ease. If prompted, I could switch to Yiddish, but I felt rusty, even inept, as if I had abandoned a lover years ago and now suddenly wanted to return to her embrace. She knew well I no longer cared for her as I once had. She knew also that other lovers had come along. The same with Hebrew. In fact, a few years later I would write a book precisely on this topic, *Resurrecting Hebrew* (2008). It had two parallel narratives: one concerned my attempt to regain my footing in the sacred tongue after years of neglect, and the other concerned Eliezer ben Yehuda, the great linguistic renovator who had made the biblical tongue modern as part of the Zionist project.

Similarly, each of the chapters of *On Borrowed Words* is devoted to a significant person in my life: my paternal grandmother, *Bobe* Bela; my father, Abraham Stavans, a Mexican actor; my brother, Darian, a musician; and, finally, me. These chapters are anchored by an object connected to the person at their center: a pistol, a set of keys, an old photograph . . . Each chapter starts in the present, as the object, to which I refer in detail, prompts a flashback. Each chapter navigates from past to present and back, giving the impression that each story is still unfolding, that one's reminiscences help one understand what is taking place today, right now.

If I were going to write the book in languages other than English, there was never any doubt in my mind that I, and nobody else, would also do the translation. The translator would become the protagonist of the book, not only in terms of content, but also in terms of form. In the end, I decided to write the entire autobiography *in translation without an original*, that is, to give my English a variety of accents. And so, for example, I wrote about the *Yidishe Schule in Mexike* where I studied as a child in English, but used a Yiddish cadence, a rhythm that makes it appear, to invoke Bialik's metaphor, as if one were accessing that period "through a veil." The same goes for my experiences in Israel, where I worked at a kibbutz. I wanted the reader to get the impression that something was awkward, slightly amiss—that the lens through which my odyssey was seen was somewhat warped.

Over the twelve months I spent writing the book, doubling languages as well as temporalities, I suffered from constant doubts about the accuracy of my recollections and the authenticity of my voice, and I was haunted by lucid, peculiar dreams; seeing my memoir in print gave me a sudden, overwhelming sense of being an impostor, of having usurped someone else's identity. I recall receiving the first copy by mail and thinking, well, this is who I am now. Or better, this is who I have chosen to be. This was the narrative by which others would know me . . . I also remember thinking, my life is certifiably in English now. It was as if there had been a linguistic race inside me, and English had won it. All other languages, all other versions of me would now be appended to it.

Unsurprisingly, when translations of *On Borrowed Words* began to appear, I found them nothing short of bizarre. Spanish was a special case. Lety Barrera, a talented translator and the wife of a friend, titled her rendition of the book *Palabras prestadas: Autobiografía* (2013). As she worked, she periodically sent me sections for review and approval. This was a surprisingly unsettling experience. I saw right away that the work was first-rate, but it didn't feel like *my* Spanish. At first I was tempted to revise it, to make it sound like the Spanish-language me. But I knew that would be wrong. This was Barrera's translation, not mine. I didn't want to be an intrusive author.

The publisher had originally asked me to do the Spanish version myself. I declined: it would have taken enormous psychological effort to redress the narrative, which I had fashioned with such care, in another language. It would have essentially meant rewriting the book, and repetition is one of my lifelong phobias. Besides, why redo the autobiography when I could employ my energy in other ventures?

But the very prospect invited me to think about self-translation more thoroughly. What happens when translating one's own work? To what degree is the exercise more than the traditional endeavor of rendering a text in another language? Often enough, a translator approaches the source text as immobile, perhaps even sacred. Of course, every translation is an appropriation that involves changes, but there is often a sense that one must, in one way or another, remain faithful to the original, however flawed it may be. In self-translation, on the other hand, there is an unavoidable temptation—indeed, a compulsion—to rewrite the original, to improve upon the source.

In rare instances, of course, an author may feel compelled to improve the original when working with another translator. Case in point: Norman Thomas di Giovanni, one of Borges's many English translators, met the author of "The Aleph" in Cambridge, Massachusetts, when Borges was already a figure of worldwide renown. Di Giovanni offered to translate the Argentine master's stories and even managed to secure a multibook contract with Doubleday. Then he moved to Buenos Aires to be closer to Borges so that he could seek his help in the translation process. They would meet in Borges's office and go over specific texts. Eventually, as the Doubleday books began to appear, the two men grew closer, and di Giovanni started to exert power over Borges. When a particular section of the translation that departed from the original met with Borges's approval, di Giovanni would urge the author to change the original the next time it was reprinted in Spanish. Thus, the translation became the original. This continued for some time, until Borges phoned di Giovanni and informed him that he no longer wished to collaborate.

Another curious example is that of Isaac Bashevis Singer, who emigrated from Poland to the United States in 1935. All his stories and novels—and he wrote plenty—were written in Yiddish. Yet he himself was often involved in their translation into English. A few of the books were rendered by his nephew, Joseph Singer. But many others were translated by women such as Dorothea Strauss and Elaine Gottlieb. An infamous womanizer, Bashevis Singer would invite a female companion out for coffee or to his apartment and would propose that she become one of his translators. Sometimes these women were fluent Yiddish speakers; on other occasions, they knew no Yiddish at all. The session would start with him reading the original Yiddish and translating it orally into English while the woman took notes. Once they reached the end of the piece, she would take her notes home and edit them; she would then return to Bashevis Singer's apartment and, between sessions of lovemaking, they would work on an acceptable English version. Bashevis Singer called these English versions "the second (or else, the other) original."

Other authors are less susceptible to pressure. Nabokov, who was unhappy with early translations of his work by other hands, became his own translator. He wrote his autobiography, *Speak, Memory*, in English, translated it into Russian, and then engaged in a "re-Englishing of a Russian re-vision" for the final edition. Sholem Aleichem, author of *Tevye's Daughters*, better known in the English-speaking world as the source of the Broadway musical *Fiddler on the Roof*, first wrote in Hebrew and then turned to Yiddish. He himself translated some of his Hebrew works into Yiddish to make them accessible to an audience of poor, semiliterate Jewish shtetl dwellers.

A writer may be prompted to self-translate for a number of reasons. It might have to do with the reach of his or her different languages. Writing a piece in Hebrew, for instance, automatically frames it within a certain context: political, historical, cultural, and aesthetic. The number of secular readers of Yiddish in the twenty-first century is minuscule. There is a growing audience of Hassidic Jews, but their concerns and mine are quite dissimilar; I am a secular Jew interested in global culture. Writing in Spanish would place me in the tradition of Latin American literature, where I only half-belong; after all, I live in the United States, and I speak, read, and write in English on a daily basis. In short, a language is always more than a code of communication. Languages come packaged with cultural memories and literary traditions. Those of us who have a choice of languages are fortunate, but our situation is complicated. The chief benefit is a sense of freedom, of infinite possibility. The chief drawback is a sense of being up in the air, of belonging nowhere in particular.

I want to talk now about the satisfactions and misgivings of translation and self-translation by discussing my own experience. Over the years

I have produced numerous translations in various genres, including novels (*The Underdogs*) and memoirs (*Lazarillo de Tormes*) from the Spanish, *Don Quixote* into Spanglish), essays (Borges from the Spanish, Cynthia Ozick from the English), poetry (Pablo Neruda from the Spanish, Yehuda Halevi from the Hebrew, Emily Dickinson and Elizabeth Bishop from the English), and stories (Juan Rulfo from the Spanish, Isaac Bashevis Singer from the Yiddish). I have even tried my hand at what is known as reverse translation. Working alone and with colleagues, I made two attempts to bring Ángel-Luis Pujante's 1995 Spanish translation of Shakespeare's *Macbeth* back into English; one version employed an Elizabethan style, the other modernized the text.

And, in spite of my reluctance, I have also done an occasional self-translation. One of my stories, "Xerox Man," which was included in *The Disappearance: A Novella and Stories* (2006), was originally commissioned by the BBC in 1998 to be read on air. I was living in London then, and the piece—which is set in Manhattan and concerns an Orthodox Jewish book thief—was composed in English. Then a couple of friends, Edmundo Paz Soldán and Alberto Fuguet, asked to include the story in their anthology *Se habla español*. A translator rendered it into Spanish. I was unhappy with the result—the rhythm felt off—and redid it myself. I hesitated, because earlier in my career I had gone in the other direction, translating of my short stories from Spanish into English, and had found it extraordinarily difficult.

I am talking about a series of stories in *The One-Handed Pianist* (2007)—namely, the title piece, "The Death of Yankos"; "Three Nightmares"; and "A Heaven without Crows." Rendering them into English, I felt the temptation to toy with the language, to add characters, and even to change the endings. In truth, I was engaged in the act—the art—of rewriting. I felt untruthful, and preferred to pass on the job to translators such as Amy Prince, David Unger, Harry Morales, and Dick Gerdes. The only self-translation I kept was "The Death of Yankos," and the Spanish and English versions differ dramatically.

Then there was the bilingual experiment of "Morirse está en hebreo," a story that served as the basis for the movie *My Mexican Shivah* (2007). The idea was given to me by the director, Alejandro Springall, who had heard it from a friend: an elderly man plots his own death, then his dysfunctional family comes together for the wake and, without really wanting to, sorts out its conflicts. Springall and I spent a sleepless night talking about the plot from numerous perspectives. I subsequently wrote the story in English. Springall adapted it into a Spanish-language screenplay, which he sent to me. Reading his draft inspired me to change certain aspects of the piece, again in English. This effort at self-translation didn't just entail navigating between languages, but also moving from one genre to another. Eventually, the story was also included in *The Disappearance*. In 2012 it finally appeared in Spanish in the personal anthology *Lengua Fresca*, rendered by the outstanding Argentine translator Felipe Yiriart.

For me—and, I suspect, for most other authors—what begins as self-translation always ends in a more elaborate rewriting. This brings me back to where I started: the existence, in various languages, of different versions of ourselves.

I find it far easier to work with translators who bring my work into "my" languages, even when I fail to recognize myself fully in the results. I have learned to live with the awkwardness of this situation. It has taught me that I have many selves, and that I negotiate these selves every time I choose to express myself in Spanish, Yiddish, Hebrew, or English. While writing *On Borrowed Words*, I came to believe that I lived in translation without an original. In the past decade and a half, I have come to refine that view: I exist in an echo chamber of self-translated voices, all of them my own.

PART II

MEDITATIONS

ALPHABETIZING

Our ABCs seem to have changed dramatically before our very eyes, and no one is making a fuss. Not that it would matter.

It used to be that the alphabet was a sequence of twenty-six letters from A to Z. The letter A came first for reasons that are arbitrary. Other than historical loyalty, there is no explanation—neither phonetic nor graphic—for why it is at the beginning. The *aleph* in Hebrew starts the alphabet, and other Middle Eastern alphabets, such as the Phoenician, also had similar-sounding letters opening their writing systems. The B, the *bet* in Hebrew, could have led the pack, but it ended up second.

Looked at en toto, the list of twenty-six letters in the Roman alphabet is beautiful yet haphazard: A, B, C, D, E, F, G, H, I, J, K, L, M, N, O, P, Q, R, S, T, U, V, W, X, Y, Z, and not M, I, F, W, T, Z, Y, H, B, K, C, O, V, R, Q, L, U, S, E, A, X, N, D, G, J, P, or any other arrangement you please.

Digital technology has made that sequence obsolete. Proof of it is the awkwardness with which the average teenager experiences a printed dictionary. He or she looks at it with utter amazement. Asked to find anything spelled with a W, paralysis takes over. Look up the word *chameleon*? He looks under K, then C, until he connects C and H. The word *phosphorescent*? He starts with F. This strategy comes from sounding letters and is only tangential to my argument. But for these students, the fact that C is before K and F is before P is meaningless. That succession has been made irrelevant by technology. In online lexicons, C doesn't come before K; instead, the letters are concurrent.

By this I mean simultaneous, not chronological but synchronic. In the online version of Merriam-Webster, the order of letters matters little. The key to locating a definition is knowing the first few the letters of a word; the rest is done automatically by the search engine.

First published in *The Chronicle of Higher Education*, May 31, 2014.

Grasping the idea of an alphabet that is simultaneous and not sequential is challenging to the mind because language is structured by a before and after. In the word *language*, L antecedes G; it doesn't coincide with it. It is as if in natural evolution, the transformation from a *Clepsydra* to a butterfly happened not gradually, in sequence, but all at the same time. Or if, in our understanding of history, the conquest of Mexico and Lincoln's delivery of the Gettysburg Address overlapped.

(Maybe they did. . . . No doubt everything always happens in the present. The past exists because we have a way to refer to it, although not necessarily a verbal conjugation, because some languages don't have a past tense, yet their speakers are capable of referring to events that occur before and after.)

The dictionary, in printed form, is an endangered species. I predict that it will cease to exist in the next few years. There is really no need for it, just as encyclopedias have no reason to exist as physical books; online resources have deemed them redundant. And with them will go the concept of alphabetizing as a sequential, not as a concurrent, endeavor.

Of course one could feel nostalgic about this transformation in cultural mores. Technology affects human behavior in subtle yet decisive ways. Reading time on traditional clocks made with a longer and shorter hand is troubling to adolescents; they prefer using ascending Arabic numbers. Likewise, organizing items with Roman numerals is cumbersome for them: finding Part IV, Proposition LVII, in Spinoza's *The Ethics* (*Ethica Ordine Geometrico Demonstrata*), which asserts that "the proud man delights in the company of flatterers and parasites, but hates the company of the highminded," is harder than locating Part 4, Proposition 57.

Children today still memorize, in melodic form, their ABCs. In the future, that effort is likely to remain intact, except that, for all it matters, they could learn it as BAC or any other random configuration.

AS IT WERE

The other day I came across a hilarious *New Yorker* poem by Fred R. Miller. It was published in the August 26, 1961, issue. As its title, "A Madrigal, As It Were, of Modifiers," suggests, it is packed with modifiers, a term used by Miller specifically to denote not an adjective or a noun used attributively ("a happy vacation trip"), but a phrase that purports to add information to a sentence when, in fact, it is utterly useless.

Indeed, Miller's poem ridicules this particular type of strategy, displayed often by pretentious English-language speakers, which allows them to show off a certain self-fashioned panache by accumulating needless recursions within a phrase. These kinds of utterances are normal—maybe even innocuous—in Britain (people no longer say "Great" before the country's name) because the Queen's English tends toward formality. In the United States, they sound pretentious.

These are the first of three stanzas in Miller's madrigal:

> Although, unhappily, it would appear,
> That, like it or not, the trend,
> Which, taking one fact with another, the sheer
> Weight of the evidence, whatever the mere
> Look of the thing, contravening, as here
> The improbable, so to speak, end,
> Must tend,
> By force of its logic, to wend—

"Like it or not," "true enough," "in effect," "taking one fact after another," "so to speak," "we must concede" . . . The list of modifiers in the poem is delicious and also deliberately arduous. In fact, it could be said that the

---

First published in *The Boston Globe*, September 1, 2016.

entire piece is nothing but appended clauses. This abundance, needless to say (here I go, inserting one such modifier!), is something for which the old *New Yorker* was known, which obviously makes Miller's an exercise in self-mockery.

I confess: as I am a non-native English speaker (from Mexico, to boot), these unpleasant expressions drive me nuts. They feel like fluff. Although it's impossible to avoid them, I prefer succinctness, simplicity, and directness.

One modifier to which I react with more discomfort is "as it were." After more than three decades in the United States, I'm still unsure exactly of its usage. Maybe this is as it should be, to make those of us coming to English from its periphery feel marginal, unsynchronized with its rhythm.

"As it were" is an idiom used after a figurative, when the speaker is not meaning what she appears to mean. Take the sentence "If María is ready, she could pay for the present, as it were." The speaker is unsure of María's action, thus the modifier. "As it were" could be replaced by similar modifiers, such as "by and large," "so to say," "in a manner of speaking," "in a way," "to some extent," and so forth.

Merriam-Webster offers this definition: "— used to say that a statement is true or accurate in a certain way even if it is not literally or completely true." Notice that the dictionary doesn't attach the terms "modifier" or "idiom." It simply puts a —, leaving it to the reader to guess. The dictionary follows its statement with what appears to me a joyful example: "His retirement was, as it were, the beginning of his real career." (The true personality of a lexicon comes across not only in its definitions but also in its examples. Proof is Doctor Johnson's marvelous *A Dictionary of the English Language* from 1755.)

Of course, "as it were" is entirely useless because the sentence is conditional, meaning that "could" denotes possibility. That implies that María has several options, one of which is to pay for the present, and that her action is open to chance, and, thus, meaning isn't set.

To insert "as it were" in the sentence is therefore to subscribe to two options. The first is to enlarge the role of chance. (María might not be unready to pay for the present, but she is possibly hesitating about that option.) The second option is mere fat. The sentence is perfectly clear when annunciated this way: "If María is ready, she could pay for the present." Nothing else is needed. In other words, the expression "as it were" neither adds nor takes an iota. Yet by inserting it, the speaker is boasting linguistic sapience, that is, adding a needless layer of butter to the toast.

The whole thing reminds me of the paralyzing virus of "likes" from which upper-middle class Americans youths, especially girls, already suffering from it for a couple of decades, seem incapable of getting themselves cured. "Like" might be used as a preposition ("there were other Mexicans like me," where like" is the equivalent of "just as"), a conjunction ("I felt like an alien"), an adjective ("I reacted in like manner"), and an adverb ("The singer sang bird-like"). However, the virus I'm referring to employs "like" as a tag word, as in, "And I wanted, like, to scream!"

The use of "like" in this circumstance isn't a modifier per se. It needlessly prolongs the enunciated idea, interrupting it with an obnoxious pause. Imagine it now with "as it were" instead of "like": "And I wanted, as it were, to scream." Or else, with "so to speak," "true enough," and "in a way." The essence is the same but not the tone, much less the attitude.

In the case of American girls, the profusion of "likes" is much worse than this example implies. Habitually in the same sentence there might be four, six, maybe even more intrusions. "Like, my girlfriend was shopping for like an hour and I was like, what's going on, and she said, like, I told you I would needed stuff, like, didn't we agree to go to the mall, like, for the afternoon?" By contrast, "as it were" is deliberately featured more sparingly, given that cautionary, well-orchestrated grammar is a sign of erudition.

The last four lines of Fred R. Miller's madrigal—which, by the way, is a short, lyrical song in several voices, emulating a Renaissance tradition, thriving in the enjoyment of counterpoint—are suitable to conclude my brief meditation on verbal bluff:

> . . . once the pattern, unsought,
> Is envisaged, or, rather, since what has been wrought
> With such, by and large, opaque art,
> Is smart,
> Leaves us just where we were at the start.

PARABLE OF DON QUIXOTE

Because nothing human lasts forever, Don Quixote, on his deathbed, briefly relapsed into Alonso Quijano before passing away of natural causes. Cervantes did this wishing (Second Part, LXXIV) to preclude the possibility of any author falsely bringing the knight back to life.

"For me alone was Don Quixote born," Cervantes announced, "and I for him; it was his to act, mine to write; we two together make but one."

Yet no sooner did Don Quixote see, shortly after, that Cervantes died too and was buried in a nameless pit than he set out in search of another adventure, first through the arid landscape of a declining Spain, then through the ascending colonial fortunes of what would become Mexico and Peru. He was immediately surprised by people dressing up in festivals like him and his squire, Sancho Panza, thinking these were doubles—and doubles of doubles—created by the faked Tordesillesque writer; he met a prince whose simplicity and open-hearted goodness made others believe he was an idiot; he came across a bored housewife about whom it was said that she was him in skirts and a *pelado* comedian speaking on behalf of the downtrodden; he read chapters about his odyssey purportedly forgotten by Cervantes; and he debated a French plagiarist whose claim to fame was to rewrite a portion (First Part, Chapter IX) in seventeenth-century Spanish that on the surface sounded archaic but was infused with symbolism.

Don Quixote was dumbfounded by an invention that projected shadows on a large white screen, which reminded him of Plato's cave; by dancers on slippers fighting against windmills; by marionettes recreating Maese Pedro's puppet show; by picture books and markets displaying enormous piñatas of his enchanted head.

Introduction to *Quixotica: Poems East of La Mancha*, edited by Juan José Morales, Tammy Ho Lai-Ming, David McKirdy, and Germán Muñoz (Hong Kong: Chameleon Press, 2016).

Emphatically, he attempted to count a vast number of translations ("Flemish tapestries") of his narrative into unimaginable languages but, fatigued, gave up the effort.

As is stated, little had he and Cervantes suspected, as the end drew near, that his fragile profile in the theater of La Mancha would become, in the future, as poetic as Sinbad's haunts. And so Don Quixote winked: it was still his act, for thousands of others to write.

Time had given him gravitas: he no longer belonged to Cervantes; in fact, he, an inveterate reader and unredeemed impostor, belonged to no one and to everyone.

FINGER SNAPPING

I have recently encountered an endearing trend among high school and college students, informally as well as in classrooms and in larger gatherings: collective finger snapping. Once, in the middle of a lecture I delivered at the University of Oxford, someone began expressing approval by snapping her fingers, and within seconds the entire hall followed her. The same thing has happened in class discussions about varieties of love and ways of expressing them. At first the sound was distracting, but it quickly became evident that its purpose was congratulatory.

The tradition seems to me connected with spoken-word poetry. I've been at slam-poetry events where finger snapping is the most visible way the audience connects with performers.

During the Occupy Wall Street movement, all sorts of hand signals were used to communicate, including "twinkles" (both hands raised with fingers pointing up and wiggling to indicate agreement) and finger snapping as a sign of accord.

Sign language of this type, specific to a particular group, was also used during street marches and other organized community efforts, like the anti-austerity movement in Spain (also called Movimiento 15-M); public gatherings in Tahrir Square in Egypt; and after the *Charlie Hebdo* massacre in France. In ancient Rome, the *pollice verso* was a type of hand sign used in gladiator fights to offer judgment on a defeated combatant. Exactly what the sign was is still unknown.

I've made an effort to study the finger-snapping behavior, and I've reached an early conclusion: finger snapping is done delicately, respectfully, democratically, always in the middle of an event, whereas hand clapping, which is by definition louder and more disruptive, is invariably reserved for the end. Also, finger snapping, when done this way, always lasts, *in totto*, only a few seconds and is generally repeated three times in a row.

First published in *The Chronicle of Higher Education*, October 22, 2015.

Most people use their thumb with their middle finger, and only very few their thumb, index, and middle finger. I've seen only one person using the ring finger. Maybe there is a difference between finger snapping done individually and in unison with others.

When I was growing up in Mexico, snapping one's fingers was an action inevitably connected with class and, occasionally, with gender and ethnicity—and, unfortunately, it still is. The image that comes to my mind is of a patron in a restaurant snapping his fingers to get the attention of the waiter. The pattern is perceived culturally as a sign of arrogance: the haves feel they can get the have-nots to do as they wish, when they wish, through this automatic gesture. Often, though not always, the patron is Caucasian, and the waiter is female and mestizo. I can't for the life of me invoke in my mind the reverse: a mestiza snapping her fingers to get a Caucasian's attention.

Finger snapping is occasionally linked to tics, especially in people with Tourette's syndrome and other chronic tic disorders.

As a behavior, it is, of course, as old as life itself. It was connected with dance and music in ancient Greece (the word is *apokroteo*). In Mediterranean music—in flamenco, for example—finger snapping, or *pitos*, is an essential component that is used in syncopated fashion, adding not only to the rhythm but also to the magic. It is usually done on the offbeat, on 2 and 4. In glee clubs, it shows up frequently. In fact, I've heard the joke that among certain glee groups, snapping is popular because you can't clap and hold a beer at the same time.

To me, finger snapping is connected with a popular expression I hear often these days: "Oh, snap!" Popularized by comedians like Tracy Morgan on *Saturday Night Life*, it denotes surprise, even bewilderment. I make the connection because several students of mine, as well as their friends, often say it, most recently during a conversation in my office, while snapping their fingers, as if to apologize for an error: "Oh, sorry. My bad! I've messed up!" Otherwise, it occurs in countless other manifestations of pop culture. Think of Thing in *The Addams Family*. In the comics, Robin of *Batman and Robin* often snaps his fingers when an idea comes to him.

I love the way finger snapping has acquired this new quality of joy to express understated, restrained public endorsement. I love when it is done by the young in an event I participate in: it creates a sense of community. I love its spontaneity, the way it serves as traction, involving the public in the performance, bringing sound and movement to silence and stasis.

THE TENURE CODE

At Amherst College, where I've taught for more twenty years (*oy, gevalt!*), a tenure case was brought down a couple of years ago in part because of the word "solid." I've put it in quote marks in part because tenure cases are multiheaded monsters: they rise or fall as a result of countless factors. In this particular one, one of the factors—and, ultimately, a stumbling block—was this much-contested word.

An outside reviewer had used it to describe a candidate's publications record. It became a subject of debate between the Committee of Six and the department supporting the candidate.

Here I need to offer a quick crash course through the college's hierarchical structure, or at least a portion of it. The Committee of Six, a judicial body of elected faculty whose job it is to legislate on a large number of issues, is in charge of reviewing tenure cases once the candidate's department has offered its recommendations. For these cases, the C6 looks at, among other things, every student evaluation, every letter from peers, and every outside review with utmost dedication. In other words, it is a painful, meticulous process of what I call logocrasy: a Kafkaesque labyrinth of language. The president then endorses or rejects the C6 tenure recommendation.

"Solid," a colleague with past experience in C6 affairs told me, is code for flaccid, uncooked. She added another no-no: strong. An institution of our statue, she said, only wants—only should want—the best, the brightest. In short, the brilliant.

But if everybody is brilliant, then nobody really is, for brilliance isn't about norm. This, clearly, is a conundrum, for three reasons. Reason no. 1: members of the C6 come from various fields, from the sciences to the humanities. Their capacity to judge candidates from fields other than their

---

First published in *The Chronicle of Higher Education*, February 3, 2014.

own in at least half the cases is based on goodwill, not on intimate knowledge of the discipline. Reason no. 2: to be elected to the C6, they must have spent about a decade making themselves known in the community, which in turn makes them electable. By this time, the demands for tenure have changed from when *they* went for tenure. So they often demand of a candidate's record more—much more—than their own records are able to display. This means that by their own implausible standards, they wouldn't receive tenure themselves. And Reason no. 3: the drive for exceptionalism is a long and winding road.

Reason no. 3 concerns me the most. Amherst College, like other institutions at the top of the food chain, sees itself as superior. It wants only top students, top faculty, and top administrators. But what does "top" imply? Do we get top people or do we make them? Isn't that what our mission is? By way of example, I know countless B and even C students whose originality is unsurpassed by their fellow A counterparts. Likewise with faculty: how does one become a strong teacher? Answer: talent + experience + DNA. As for administrators, I leave their qualifications to others with better discernment.

Exceptionalism at Amherst is such that the C6 expects—and the college community expects the C6 to expect—outside reviewers to use only exceptional language in tenure letters. If a candidate isn't "superb," "extraordinary," "unparalleled," "remarkable," and "at the top of her field," then the assessment is coded with mediocrity: good isn't good enough.

The rush for superlatives is distressing. Departmental letters for tenure are narratives as long as 15,000 words festered with adjectives as cartoonish as they are improbable. Outside letters follow the same fetish. The composite portrait isn't of real-life people but of utopian characters. This exceptionalism, this sense that we are above the crowd, better even than our closest competitors, allows the C6, and the rest of us, to be proud of our aloofness, though it gets lonely at the top.

Do outside reviewers know about this tenure code? They do. Or, at the very least, they use the codes they've learned in the culture of their own institutions. For every institution has a code. Too bad these letters are confidential; otherwise, someone could do a longitudinal analysis.

Personally, I get an average of between six and eight tenure-evaluation requests a semester. Such is the volume, let alone my other commitments, that I regularly decline, often to all, unless the candidate is a former student of mine, because each of these letters takes weeks to prepare: They involve attentive, meditative reading of the candidate's dossier, comparison with equals in the field, and, more than anything else, a cavalier approach. One's readership is minuscule, yet it has an outsized degree of power in its hands. Everyone knows the formula: academics + power = mendacity.

I'm told that in some institutions, declining such invitations amounts to a rejection ending up in the candidate's files. For that reason, I do what I most dislike but others have suggested as the pertinent approach: I don't respond.

What I don't know, where I'm in the dark (as other outside reviewers surely are, too), is in regard to particular institutional codes. Will "wonderful" be "sorrowful" at the University of Fredonia? Is "perfect" really "imperfect" at Yoknapatawpha College? I could blanket my letter with exceptional language, but it would be a travesty: things are what they are, not as we wish them to be.

By the way, I like teaching at an exceptional place. It's rock solid, especially the students.

TRANSADAPTATION

Efforts to translate a text within the same language, from, say, the French of Molière to the present-day language of immigrants in Paris, are common today. Not long ago, I got a copy of Andrés Trapiello's faithful modernization of the entire *Don Quixote*, all 126 chapters. His argument is that today's readers, especially young ones, no longer read Cervantes's novel. Because its antiquated language might be one of the causes, why not render it in twenty-first-century Iberian Spanish?

Even more common is what has come to be known as "transadaptation," the effort to freely re-create an established narrative in a new context. I cherish, for example, my copies of *William Shakespeare's Star Wars* by Ian Doescher. (You can look it up on Wookieepedia.) In one of the episodes, Luke Skywalker, holding a stormtrooper's helmet, announces: "Alas, poor stormtrooper, I knew ye not, / yet have I taken both uniform and life / From thee. What manner of a man wert thou? / A man of inf'nite jest or cruelty? / A man with helpmate and with children too? / A man who hath his Empire serv'd with pride? / A man, perhaps, who wish'd for perfect peace? / What'er thou wert, goodman, thy pardon grant / Unto the one who took thy place: e'en me."

I don't like the word itself: *transadaptation*. But I've come to accept it because neither *translation* nor *adaptation* explains the phenomenon on its own. Of course, this is an ancient practice, repackaged for our derivative, self-referential, merchandise-driven times. Throughout *Don Quixote*, the narrator frequently says that the story of the Manchego hidalgo who lost his wits to become a knight errant has been told in numerous ways, yet his is the real thing. Something similar might be said of Shakespeare. Some among his thirty-seven solo plays might be described as transadaptations of a sort. *King Lear* is based on an ancient folk tale, of which a number

---

First published in *The Chronicle of Higher Education*, April 24, 2016.

of versions are available, including *The True Chronicle History of King Leir and His Three Daughters*. *Romeo and Juliet* is also a transadaptation of an Italian tale translated by Arthur Brooke into verse in 1562 as *The Tragical History of Romeus and Juliet*, then rewritten in prose by William Painter in 1566 as *Palace of Pleasure*.

In other words, the fine line between creativity and inspirational source is treacherous. Plagiarism isn't too far away. Then again, basing one's work on previous sources was common in the Renaissance, and a kind of homage. Originality is a tricky business.

In "Translating the Classics," a course I am co-teaching this semester, we invited the students to reimagine, from a more contemporary perspective, Macbeth's famous soliloquy, "She should have died hereafter" (Act 5, Scene 5, lines 17–28), delivered as he learns of the death of Lady Macbeth, with the English troops under the command of Macduff and Malcolm fast approaching the castle:

> She should have died hereafter;
> There would have been a time for such a word.
> —To-morrow, and to-morrow, and to-morrow,
> Creeps in this petty pace from day to day,
> To the last syllable of recorded time;
> And all our yesterdays have lighted fools
> The way to dusty death. Out, out, brief candle!
> Life's but a walking shadow, a poor player
> That struts and frets his hour upon the stage
> And then is heard no more. It is a tale
> Told by an idiot, full of sound and fury
> Signifying nothing.

The echoes of this soliloquy are infinite, from William Faulkner to Robert Frost to Kurt Vonnegut to the Broadway musical *Hamilton*.

Toying with the idea of transadaptation (and maybe also ventriloquism), one student, Robert Croll, who for his senior thesis completed a new full translation of Julio Cortázar's collection of stories *Secret Weapons*, reimagined Macbeth's soliloquy in nineteenth-century New England—as a poem by Emily Dickinson.

> It's like a Walking Shadow—Life—
> A Player—poor—who struts,
> And frets away his hour

> Upon the Stage,
> And then is heard—no more—
> It's like an Idiot's Story—full—
> Of Sound—and Fury yet,
> Devoid of Meaning in—
> The End—

The layers create an enchanting effect: Dickinson's idiosyncratic punctuation, her uppercase nouns, the syncopated rhythm of the poem, the cathartic end, and her philosophical—perhaps epileptic—delves into the infinite are all here. So are Shakespeare's words, and his ethos.

A parody, a rereading, an adaptation, a reinvention, a tribute.

ELLIPSES AND I

I have been thinking about the changing nature of the ellipsis as a grammatical device.

A few days ago, I was going over a draft of a graphic novel I am about to send to the publisher. It is called *Angelitos*, and it is about a Mexican priest who devotes his life to protecting homeless children. I had written two versions, one in Spanish and the other in English, about a year ago. I had put them aside to simmer. When I looked at them again, I was struck by the abundance of ellipses in the two versions.

The protagonist is a passionate yet hesitating young man. In the dialogue I used the ellipses to convey his uncertainty. Now I had doubts about my strategy.

I realized, first, that the ellipsis is a relatively recent phenomenon (there are none in the Hebrew Bible, for instance, although contemporary Hebrew does use them), and, second, that different languages, verbal and numerical, use ellipses in different ways.

In Chinese, for instance, they are made of six dots divided into two subgroups of three, although sometimes, to shorten communication, people resort to only one subgroup. In mathematics, the ellipsis can be used to mean "and so on," communicating the repetition of a pattern. And then there is literature, where the ellipsis often conveys omission, as in "The region . . . is full of unicorns."

In the two versions of *Angelitos*, my ellipses were consistent with Spanish usage. Called *puntos suspensivos* (suspension points) in Spanish, the device, as in French, implies doubt, is synonymous with "et cetera," or suggests either silence or speechlessness.

In comparing the Spanish and English versions of *Angelitos*, it became clear to me that I didn't know to what extent English followed those rules.

First published in *The Chronicle of Higher Education*, June 26, 2016.

Because I have lived in the United States since the mid-eighties, this discovery made me feel as if the road of assimilation, which has transformed me deeply as a person, is really never ending. Although I'm a teacher and have published a plethora of books—several of them translations—I had never stopped to think about the nuances of the meaning of the ellipsis in the two languages.

So I embarked on a comparative study.

What I found out was enlightening. According to the language historian Anne Toner, in her book *Ellipsis in English Literature: Signs of Omission*, the first appearance of the ellipsis in English dates back to 1588, in a translation by Maurice Kyffin of Terence's adaptation of the Greek play *Andria*. Toner makes this point forcefully, but to me it seems like finding a needle in a haystack. Equally difficult to explain, other than blaming it on Darwinian evolution, is how, by the nineteenth century, the three little dots had become a fixture of the Queen's English.

The word *ellipsis* comes from Ancient Greek ἔλλειψις, *élleipsis*. In English nowadays, an ellipsis might appear in the beginning, middle, or end of a sentence. It can be preceded by a period or appear as four dots with added space between them. It shows up with spaces before and after the three dots or without them. The *MLA* and *Chicago Manual of Style* offer dissenting views on its usage. You may find it in parentheses or in between brackets. In other words, its use is elastic: it might suggest further thought, condense a list or quotation, or simply mean blah-blah-blah.

It looks to me as if the biggest difference with Spanish is that in English the ellipsis doesn't connote doubt . . . or does it?

One of the most intriguing components of my study pertains to social media: in texting, the ellipsis is used to hold one's attention; that is, to announce that there's more is to come, to politely change topics, or to emphasize anger, disagreement, or bewilderment.

And of course, there are myriad ways of misusing ellipsis in texting. Some of these, it goes without saying, are a sign of the user's age. This was made irrevocably clear to me when my twenty-year-old son, Isaiah (who goes by Zai), a student at Kenyon College, told me recently that my texts are both too formal and too idiosyncratic.

To prove his point, he showed me an exchange between his friends Z and D: Z had just bought two tickets for a soccer game and invited D to the event. But D had more in her mind than a simple no: "are u comin" Z asked. "Maybe . . ." responded D.

"You follow, Pa?" Zai asked.

I said not quite.

"Look, when texting you can use ellipses to mean a thought is unfinished. But people inject tone to that unfinishedness. In the example I showed you there is a difference between 'maybe' and 'maybe . . .' The former denotes doubt, even uncertainty: D is unsure of her schedule. The latter is a step further: D is withholding specific information. The 'maybe' is actually an 'I have something better to do.'"

Zai went on: "You, Pa, write a text that says, 'I need to think about it . . .' Nobody else texts that way anymore. It's enough to say 'I need to think about it' without even a period at the end because the period itself might entail anger. You only put an ellipsis if you're keeping something to yourself, some strategic information you don't want your correspondent to have. Get it?"

Well, sort of. Honestly, I was more confused than ever. Later, when I got back to the English version of *Angelitos*, every ellipsis, no matter its placement, suddenly seemed suspicious. There are stark differences between Spanish and English rules, I kept saying, but languages are by definition fluid, and rules are created to be broken.

Life is what happens outside an ellipsis. In any case, I ended up scratching out about 90 percent of the ellipses in the graphic novel, maybe more, in both the English and the Spanish versions. Why leave that much room to uncertainty, to speechlessness, to bewilderment?

My protagonist was now more certain of himself than before.

ON CLARITY

One cannot but be dismayed by the extent to which pollution of thought is endemic in our culture.

The illness is ubiquitous: in Washington, in academe, on the radio and TV, among activists. Being clear, explaining oneself lucidly, seems to be an endangered form of human behavior. Was clarity ever better regarded? Or is the current attitude toward it a constant in history? One could blame the educational system, seldom pushing students to express themselves neatly, in clean and tidy ways. But that's an easy target. After all, we are what we teach and vice versa.

In any case, I want to offer here an ode to clarity, to make a call for its worthiness—and to do it clearly. As a word, *clarity* isn't just beautiful but also elegant, even peaceful. Like the word *moon* (in Spanish, it is even more melodious: *luna*), it enchants me, it makes me surrender to its sound. Merriam-Webster defines *clarity* somewhat unclearly, as "the quality of being expressed, remembered, understood, etc., in a very exact way." That *etc.* is unneeded. The same idea could have been expressed more economically, without the accumulation of passive verbs followed by obnoxious commas.

And what exactly does *very exact* mean? Exactness is a synonym of *accuracy*, so *very exact* must mean very accurate, that is, with anal-retentive precision. I, for one, am not talking about such extremes. Clarity is the capacity to be simple, unambiguous, on target, without blubber. It is about the freedom to choose the right thoughts and, in succession, just the correct words to express them.

That the purpose of language in general is to communicate isn't debatable. The question, as I'm suggesting here, is about the quality of that communication. When a sentence is unclear, is the problem at the level of language or is it at the level of thought? After all, language is thought articulated in words.

First published in *The Chronicle of Higher Education*, April 18, 2014.

Amy Tan, in her essay "Mother Tongue," describes her surprise at people's responses to her mother's broken English. As an immigrant from China, her mother struggled, upon arriving to the United States, with forming syntactically correct sentences. The reaction was, in the eyes of others, that not only her language but also her thoughts were broken. That is preposterous, of course, for Tan's mother was perfectly capable of expressing herself in Mandarin.

But the language of immigrants distracts from my thesis, which is that clear thoughts foster clear language. By this I mean that clarity might be an attribute of language only after our thoughts have been built rigorously—or, in the topography of Merriam-Webster, *very exactly*. And how does one reach clarity of thought? After a long process of careful, meticulous refinement. That, and nothing else, is what the life of the mind should be about: refinement of thought.

I consider the work of George Orwell models of clarity. Take Orwell's sentence from "Shooting an Elephant": "I perceived at this moment that when the white man turns tyrant it is his own freedom that he destroys." The whole of imperialism is sharply encapsulated in it.

In expressing themselves, children tend to be enviably clear, perhaps because their verbal reservoir is limited but also because they have little patience for ornamentation. What they want, they are eager to get: refinement of purpose implies sharpness of tongue.

Grown-ups are at the opposite end. Might the problem be that, unlike children, adults don't always know what they want? Or else that we want too much, all at the same time?

When in need of laughter, my wife and I often do one of two things: watch a Marx Brothers movie (I am one of those who can recite entire sections of *Duck Soup,* and I start one of my courses, "Impostors," with the mirror scene between Groucho and Harpo—or, better, between Pinky and Firefly) or read Derrida. They take a diametrically different approach: the former is consciously hilarious, whereas laughter comes about in the latter by accident, among those who, like me, live outside the Derrida cult.

The following paragraph comes from "Of Grammatology" (1967):

The science of writing should therefore look for its object at the roots of scientificity. The history of writing should turn back toward the origin of historicity. A science of the possibility of science? A science of science which would no longer have the form of logic but that of grammatics? A history of the possibility of history which would no longer be an archaeology, a philosophy of history or a history of philosophy?

Does dense, complex thought require dense, complex language? No! Wittgenstein, in *Tractatus Logico-Philosophicus*, states that "what can be said at all can be said clearly; and what we cannot talk about we must pass over in silence."

It is rather easy to ridicule the Derrida quote. That ridicule doesn't come from taking it out of context but from the inscrutability of its construction. Scientificity? Grammatics? Historicity?

In *Don Quixote* (Part I, Chapter I), Cervantes, deriding the fluffiness of chivalry novels, delivers one of the novel's famous sentences (translated by John Ormsby): "the reason of the unreason with which my reason is afflicted so weakens my reason that with reason I murmur at your beauty." Now that, unlike Derrida's grammatocalifragilisticology, is a clear refutation of the unclear.

Maybe Derrida, secretly, is mocking understanding. I say *maybe* because I'm not sure. Or perhaps, a clown at heart, he seeks to undermine clarity, and, proving Wittgenstein wrong, to show that what can be said at all can also be said obfuscatingly. But does that mean it is deeper?

Again, no! Depth of thought doesn't bring about linguistic malfunction.

I have a philosopher friend who teaches at a university in upstate New York. Not long ago, he told me that philosophers thrive on the feeling of intellectual superiority. They look down at the rest of the mortals as mentally limited. The fact that women are hardly represented in philosophy departments has much to do, in his view, with this macho approach: to be a philosopher is to be able to communicate in coded (e.g., befuddling) language.

The whole thing is baloney!

But I don't want to turn this into a diatribe against philosophers. Lack of clarity is everywhere. Can you follow Rachel Maddow's labyrinthine sentences? How about those of Speaker of the House John Boehner? His statements are usually short but seldom clear.

Shouldn't we hold our politicians accountable when their ideas are blurred? Wouldn't it be constructive to fire TV newscasters who don't make sense, who talk in a spiral? Isn't the classroom the place to teach clarity to the young?

Talking about the young, here is one more thought (which relates to Amy Tan's mother): speaking in dialect doesn't mean one is hazy. The other day, I heard a girl on a Brooklyn street say, "I can't take nobody no more." A common complaint that ain't pretty but is clear.

Language changes, clarity doesn't.

AUTO-CORRECTED

"Can I be spermed?" a student asked in an email last year, requesting to forgo an extra assignment. I laughed. At the bottom of the message, it read: "Sent from my iPhone."

In less than five minutes, the student wrote back. "Apologies, Prof. It wasn't me but A-C. I really meant 'spared.'" And she added: "It won't happy again."

This time I just smiled.

The complications brought on by technology are countless. And in them, the opportunities for Freudian slips never stop. Are we in charge, or has a coup d'état taken place, leaving the id in full control? Is the maxim "I don't know what I mean until I see what I say" still true when we usually forgo the opportunity to reread what we typed?

Needless to say, in the academy, students aren't the only ones falling into this imbroglio. I do too, all the time. A week ago after class, I was asked by someone what I meant by the text "Yes, go ahead and festoon." What did I mean, indeed? (By the way, there's a website called Crazy Things Parents TEXT.)

My email exchanges with students are frequent. I encourage them to write to me after class with lingering comments on the material. I also ask them to shape their arguments for the final project through an e-dialogue. Sometimes the message I send them back is as long as two thousand words. More often, it is telegraphic: "Meet me at 3:30pm," "Brilliant!," and "Your draft, I'm afraid, is as flat as a pita."

These messages might originate from my iPad, the use of which allows me to think a bit longer than when I respond from my iPhone, where sloppiness is more likely to prevail. Still, what matters, I tell myself, is that I'm in communication with them. That to me is why teaching is such

---

First published in *The Chronicle of Higher Education*, December 13, 2013.

pleasure: because I witness the making of a thinking mind, and, to some degree, I'm responsible for it.

In other words, I'm supposed to be the students' guide. I have authority bestowed upon me to improve their language, to push them to new heights. In doing so, I sharpen my own mental processes, too.

But a phantom has inserted itself into our daily lives: the Corrector. It is meant to speed things up when in truth it causes havoc. Before a word is fully spelled, the phantom guesses our intention, finishing it in front of our eyes. A mere second is required to confirm the right spelling . . . but who has a second to spare?

The funny thing is that the phantom, in the Apple kingdom, is known as "Auto-Correct." (That's what my student meant by A.-C.) Auto-Correct, I take it, is synonymous with Self-Correct. It is the sender who is in control, even though the phantom, like a poltergeist, is doing the work. But are Auto- and Self- really the same thing here? And do we need such police inside our iPhones? Have we surrendered our liberty to the device? Do we need to be second-guessed? Some people don't buy iPhones for this very reason: outside Apple, they have more linguistic control.

And will the time come when the Corrector is available in oral communication? Well, that orality is already a fact, as one can dictate, not type, a text message.

Usually, when a student lets the Corrector take over, I ignore it—and I hope the same happens in the opposite direction. Or else I play along. For instance, not long ago a Spanish-language student, after receiving an assignment prompt, replied to me: "*Vale, estic d'acord amb tu* :)"

Mmmm . . . Inscrutable! Because *vale* is used in Spain as OK, I assumed he was in agreement with me and simply disregarded the rest. But then I decided to respond in gibberish, on purpose: "*Lind a stú* . . ."

I was proud to have usurped the role of the Corrector, choosing to be equally clumsy. My next thought was that, should this exchange continue, the two of us would be creating an entirely new language. Yet I stopped. Education is built on communication: intelligible, decipherable, and logical. I told myself that the gestation of an alternative, maybe parallel code should be left for another—a special—occasion.

Then again, the phantom might be part of a cohort of darker forces. For one thing, I can't forget the statement "Can I be spermed?" Assuming, as one should, that the student typed "Can I be spared?," The Corrector would have changed it to—what? Sperm isn't a verb in English; that is, Auto-Correct wouldn't choose "spermed" as a replacement for "spared."

Have our iPhones embraced dyslexia? Anyway, I'm glad it won't happy again.

Addendum: A few days ago, I was part of a three-way email conversation with two colleagues, both women, one an editor at Norton, the other a professor at UCLA. They had been pondering some scheduling issue and wanted my response, but I had been busy all day delivering a series of lectures in a studio. Finally having time to reply, I meant to send a message that said, "Sorry, I've been taping all day." Except that my dyslexic device (or I myself?), instead of *taping*, wrote *raping*. I didn't realize it until one of them asked, "Ilan, did you mean taping?" and, within minutes, the other wondered, "I thought you meant rapping." I was embarrassed. Maybe I should have written *napping*.

PART III

BEYOND WORDS

ON BEING MISUNDERSTOOD

In June 2012 I delivered a lecture titled "Translation and Hypocrisy" at the Changshu Institute of Technology, a university on the Yangtze River Delta, near Suzhou, in the eastern coastal province of Jiangsu, China. The lecture was in front of hundreds of people, the majority of them students, although a hefty number of scholars, teachers, and translators were in the audience as well. I received a loud, enthusiastic applause. Still, no sooner had I finished and even before people were allowed to ask questions, I was overwhelmed by a strange feeling: the feeling of having been misunderstood.

PART I: THE LECTURE

I am honored by the invitation to speak in front of you today. My minimal knowledge of Chinese literature is reduced to classic poetry, in particular to the *Wangchuan ji*. I have also read translations done by Kenneth Rexroth. The poems I have become acquainted with have come to me in English. Because one of my first—I shall call it "original"—languages is Spanish, my access to this literature involves a degree of removal. That removal is not only the result of the natural loss that comes with translation. It comes to me from accessing the poems in languages I have learned along the way, in this case English.

I want to delve into another realm: espionage. To be a translator is to be a double agent. A double agent serves two masters: he spies on a group on behalf of another but is a full member of that second group. That membership enables him to have an insider's knowledge, to convey information that is precious because of his status within the target group. That dual loyalty means that double agents are hypocrites. A hypocrite puts on false appearances. He acts—and becomes an artist—in contradiction. Double agents live a double life.

First published in *Translation Journal* 84, no. 1 (2012).

To call translators hypocrites is demeaning. I am a translator myself and know what it means to live in two worlds, to serve two masters, to squeeze meaning out of a sentence. I often feel like a hypocrite when I translate. Nevertheless, I apologize if this gives you the impression that some translators are unpleasant people. Sometimes they are, sometimes they aren't. At any rate, the translator does not thrive in contradiction, even though contradiction is at the heart of the translation endeavor.

To translate is to build a bridge between two linguistic habitats, each of which represents a different culture. That bridge brings these cultures together. But the togetherness is not without sacrifice, and the translator, to be successful, needs to know how to maneuver that sacrifice. Because the two linguistic habitats are by definition different, a statement in one is different in the other.

To convey the essence of that statement in the target language, the translator needs to falsify, to reconfigure, to rewrite. That rewriting involves the loss I mentioned before. That is, an aspect of the original language will not be conveyed in the target language. What needs to be sacrificed and how to make the meaning fulsome are difficult questions. The translator needs a full-fledged knowledge of the two linguistic habitats, although knowledge in the original language is less essential, more "foreign" than the knowledge in the target language. Seldom does the translator feel at ease going back and forth between the two habitats, because one of these habitats always dominates.

The Italians have a saying: *traduttore, traditore*. This is only partially true. To be accurate, the translator needs to be ready to betray the original language. But treason gives the impression of sedition, of a willingness to betray trust. The translator depends on trust. His translation hopes to make the reader not only comfortable but also committed to the idea that what is said in the original language is also conveyed in the target language. This is an impossible idea; thus the feeling of betrayal. Ironically, the betrayal is achieved insofar as trust is established.

Hypocrisy is eminently histrionic. A hypocrite pretends. A hypocrite feigns to believe what he does not. He wants others to believe in him based on his appearance. Yet his appearance is a lie, an impostorship. Hypocrites are condemned by society as despicable because they are said to be untrue to others. And by being untrue to others, the consensus is that spies are untrue—that is, inauthentic—to themselves.

Again, strictly speaking, the translator is not a hypocrite because translation is about being truthful to the meaning of the original language. But because that truthfulness is unattainable in full, a degree of untruthfulness, of inauthenticity, is inevitable in a translation. It follows that hypocrisy, not as an action but as a condition, is part of translation. To either minimize or maximize the hypocrisy, the translator makes conscious a couple of strategies: either his translation will seek to be as natural as possible, therefore making the reader feel that the translation is another original text, or the artifice of the endeavor will be emphasized, hence reminding the reader that what is in front of him is concocted, rearranged, remixed.

No matter what strategy is taken, it is important for the translator to be aware of his status as double agent. It is important for him to know he is a traitor, a hypocrite. This awareness is the equivalent of a teacher realizing that complete knowledge of anything is impossible yet striving to provide his students with the right tools to harvest complete knowledge of any aspect of the universe.

As you can see, my view of translation is of an activity full of danger. I have spent many inspiring hours attempting to bring writers from one language to another. For instance, I have tried to make Pablo Neruda, the Chilean poet who wrote *Canto General*, comfortable in the English language. That comfort, I recognize, is a mirage. Neruda lives in Spanish. In fact, his poetry has made the Spanish language less stilted, more elastic. He will never be as good in English as he is in Spanish. This recognition cannot stop us from trying to make him also *live* in English or in any other language. Not trying would be an acknowledgment of defeat. Every translation is a falsification. Every translation is a defeat. Every translation is imperfect. Still, it is important to try to the best of our capacity. Otherwise we would live in a solipsistic universe where dialogue across cultures would not exist.

I have translated Emily Dickinson in the opposite direction, from English into Spanish. The effort has been rewarding yet maddening. Dickinson's elusive themes, her idiosyncratic punctuation, are an integral part of English. As a translator, my hope is to come up with the most suitable approximation.

Yes, an approximation is a betrayal, but a betrayal I am willing to attach my name to.

Once more, I apologize if these rambling notes have given you the impression that I see translation as a negative endeavor. Perhaps you will get this impression because hypocrites, traitors, and double agents are condemned by society. Truth is, even when you are not a translator, there is an element of betrayal in everything humans do. In order to function, we betray our instincts, we betray our dreams, we betray those around us. The life of the mind is prone to these types of contradictions.

That is why spies are always interesting people.

Thank you for the patience you have shown in listening to me. I dream of one day reading a classic Chinese poem of the Tang dynasty in its original language. I doubt this dream will be granted to me because I know how difficult it is to learn another language late in life. Still, regardless of how old one gets, the capacity to dream is constantly with us.

PART II: THE RESPONSE

Why had I apologized in my lecture? Was I unsure of my argument about translators being histrionic, about them being double agents? Did I deliberately seek misunderstanding?

Actually, misunderstanding is what translators deal with all the time. Sometimes the message in the original language is convoluted; on other occasions, the translator might be at fault, having failed to find the right words to say what was clear in the original. But the feeling I experienced that afternoon entailed a different kind of misunderstanding. Was the audience I had before me, whose pulse I didn't know, the right one to reflect with on issues such as loyalty? What do I know about hypocrisy and betrayal in China?

I had been invited to the country to promote the translation of volume 1 of my biography of Gabriel García Márquez and to talk about topics related to him and Latin American literature, in particular about "El Boom." On other occasions during my trip I had spoken about *One Hundred Years of Solitude* (1967), about its author's early career, about Borges and Neruda. Here the host wanted something different. I chose the double life of a translator because I had recently finished translating Juan Rulfo's *The Plain in Flames* as well as Neruda's odes.

The communication method I used, one I recur to when in a country where I don't speak the language, was to read a paragraph, then allow an interpreter to do the same. For this particular time, my interpreter was a vivacious student in his thirties who happened to be the host's son. To work on it, the interpreter had requested to see the text of my lecture more than a month in advance. When I met him, a few days before my lecture, he told me he had translated my words into a type of Chinese that employed some archaisms.

In any case, I was not prepared for the dynamite the Q&A session included. In general, the questions I got from the public were gracious, insightful, even thought provoking, but they dealt only marginally with the topic I had explored in my lecture. The audience was well acquainted with my interest in multilingualism. My memoir *On Borrowed Words* (2001) had been discussed beforehand in various academic settings. So were my ideas on Spanglish.

Yet not everyone was nice. The first question I got was outright accusatory. I remember it less clearly than the furious tone in which it was delivered. The speaker was beside himself. My lecture had offended him. He wanted to speak out not only for himself but also on behalf of the translation community in general and for Chinese translators in particular. Translators aren't spies, he stated in no uncertain terms. In fact, he was sure translators are loyal, devoted, and professional folks, by which he meant—he said—trustworthy. Yes, it is the business of translators to be trusted. In the speaker's view, it was a shame that the Changshu Institute of Technology had invited me to come because my lecture was dangerous in that it polluted the minds of the students in the auditorium. It would confuse the countless listeners who would listen to me online.

I smiled, struck by the speaker's lack of desire to debate my ideas, to ponder their value whatever it might be. What he wanted was to quarantine my ideas. I responded that ideas are only dangerous when we attach danger to them. Instead, we can see them as part of a marketplace, one in which they rise or fall depending on the resonance they have on the environment.

I explained that I had used abstract, figurative, symbolic language in my lecture to get at the heart of the translator's quest. By equating translators with spies, what I was alluding to was the double track a translation must live in, serving two masters, knowing the betrayal of one signifies (or at least might suggest) the success of the other. I invoked an actual spy who had been a translator: La Malinche, Hernán Cortés's Aztec mistress. She was courted by him not only because of her beauty but also because of her intellectual savvy. According to lore, the downfall of the Aztec Empire in the seventeenth century came about, to some extent, because of La Malinche's betrayal of her own people.

In Mexico we have a word for what she did: *malinchismo*, defined either as a lover's course or perhaps as a translator's kiss.

My accuser took to the microphone again and persisted in his attack. It was clear to him that I didn't empathize with translators, even if I myself was a translator. He predicted that I would never be able to understand the

Chinese mind. Months after the exchange occurred, I'm still bewildered by his latter point. After the lecture, I was told that in Chinese the connotation of the word *spy* is far stronger than in English. Plus, my inexperienced translator had used ancient terms in interpreting my lecture, which might have sent some unintended historical echoes to my listeners.

And I was told by a colleague that speaking of spies in contemporary China is explosive. Indeed, a few weeks prior, a scandal had erupted in which the wife of a high-ranking member of the Chinese Communist Party who was in line to become the country's leader was accused of plotting the killing of a British citizen. The politician and his wife were arrested. They were also stripped of everything they owned.

A thought crossed my mind. Was there something in the language I had used in my lecture that was close in spirit to the literary genre of parody? I had not meant to be humorous. Nor had I wanted to ridicule translators. My objective had been to sense the rawness of the translator's task: to imagine the translator being sinful, even treacherous. I had not been exposed to parody while in China.

In fact, as I reached back into my readings of foreign literature, I suddenly realized I had never been exposed to a novel by a Chinese author whose purpose was to satirize, in the spirit of Rabelais, Cervantes, and Laurence Sterne making a parody of their surroundings. Are some cultures prone to parody while others aren't? Is abstract, symbolic language culturally defined?

Puzzled by the speaker's attack, the host encouraged other questions from the audience. It was at that point that the conversation moved to another explosive topic: jargon and hybrid speech in contemporary China. A student wanted to know why Spanglish is seen as politically empowering Latinos in the United States. Another was eager to find out the extent to which this form of communication is an emblem of creativity. I put the issue in context, describing how English isn't threatened by jargons formed in its midst, but, on the contrary, its fabric is reinforced by them.

The inevitable next question was about the similarities between Spanglish and Chinglish.

Specifically, a scholar wanted to know if the latter should be encouraged among China's youth. Given the overwhelming presence of American pop culture in the country, she stated, as well as the embrace of English as the primary foreign language taught in Chinese schools, a new generation is coming of age switching between English and Chinese and, in doing so, being caught in the crossfire. She wanted to know if this is good or bad.

I responded in the affirmative: yes, unquestionably it is good! There were loud cheers in the auditorium, followed by piercing boos. Obviously, I had touched a nerve. As the Q&A continued, I realized the opposing sides were divided across generation lines: I was embraced by the young, who perceived me as a champion of Chinglish, because I welcome its mistakes as a sign of improvisational joie de vivre. And there were the not-so-young, for whom my opinions were anathema. Was I encouraging a dialogue between them or simply getting these two views further apart?

I then stressed that while on the surface similar, Spanglish, Chinglish, and other "mix tongues" respond to distinct cultural phenomena. As a result of globalization, English is a ubiquitous presence everywhere in the world, although each encounter it has with another language needs to be seen on its own terms. I said that as the largest minority, Latinos in the United States are undergoing a process of *mestizaje* that amounts to the formation of a new civilization, neither Hispanic nor Anglo. While other immigrant groups (Jews, Germans, Italians . . .) brought their native languages, Spanglish is unlike Yinglish, for instance, in that English and Yiddish cohabited as an amalgamated language only for a short period of time. Instead, Spanglish, as a crossbreed, has been in use at least for a century and a half, as historical and literary sources testify.

Chinglish, on the other hand, doesn't emerge, at least in China, from the minority–majority dichotomy. Rather than being limited to an ethnic group or location, it is about making intelligible in one tongue what is uttered in another. The abyss between standard Chinese and English is enormous. Chinese characters are logographs that contain all sorts of phonetic composites. A word acquires meaning depending on phonemic tones.

English is concrete. It uses an alphabet. The sound of certain letters depends on their position in a word.

For a nation like China, where language remained astonishingly stable for centuries, this transformation is generating a deep social rift. Indeed, a few days earlier a Chinese colleague had told me there are movies done in China today where generous chunks of the dialogue are in English. While one must appreciate the mechanisms a standard language activates to protect its integrity, change is not only inevitable but essential to make a people contemporaneous with the rest of the world. I don't believe the Chinese youth should be antagonized for its use of Chinglish.

In my mind, I recalled an anecdote a Cuban friend had told me. During a train ride from Beijing to Shanghai he sat next to a young Chinese woman who spoke broken English. He didn't speak more than a handful of words in Chinese, so they communicated in whatever way they could. He asked her about places to visit, food to eat, and so on. There was no attraction between them. They were simply two travelers chitchatting.

When the time came for my friend to leave the train, he said goodbye and approached the exit door. He then saw a man who had been sitting behind them all along stand up, approach the young woman, and slap her in the face several times, admonishing her in Chinese that speaking to a Westerner in that way, and doing so in English, a language few adults in the train understood, was shameful. My friend looked at the scene from afar. Devastated, he wanted to run back, to defend the young woman. But she made a gesture implying that it was better that way, that he shouldn't come back, that she deserved the punishment.

I didn't relate this anecdote. "It is too risqué," I convinced myself. Instead, I told the audience that as a visitor from an English-speaking habitat, the Chinglish signs I came across in Beijing, Shanghai, and elsewhere were hilarious. To me, laughter was the least interesting response, though. What I was attracted to wasn't what such "false translations" conveyed but why they said it in that particular way.

I repeated that I dreamed of mastering the Chinese language one day, in part to be able to study more closely a few of these Chinese statements.

I mentioned one particular case. In the bathroom of my Beijing hotel room, there were all sorts of hygienic tools: toothbrushes, shampoos, shower caps, and so on. There was also—and in my long life as a traveler, I had never seen one like this given to every guest as part of the room apparel—a sex kit. Out of curiosity, I opened it: the user's instructions were among the funniest I've ever read.

I apologized for not being able to go into specifics.

Again, I had apologized. Why? My comment on the sexual kit agitated the audience even more.

What I now had in front of me was a raucous crowd. There was laughter as well as discomfort. Had I gone too far? Was the sex kit beyond protocol in China in public forums like this one I had been invited to participate in? Were my words about Chinglish understood as criticism of Chinese hospitality, which I in no way had intended? At this point, I had the impression I was talking not about translation but about national security. Suddenly, I was happy being misunderstood. Quite happy! I liked the sensation of not being in control of my message. I liked knowing there was a cultural abyss separating me from my audience.

It was sheer exhilaration. That abyss granted me freedom.

AGAINST REPRESENTATION

A Note on Borges's Aleph

"I saw the unimaginable universe."

I have a vast collection of editions, in multiple languages, of Jorge Luis Borges's book *El Aleph* (1949). In general, there are four types of covers. One type, allergic to representation, is limited to a conventional pattern on which appears the author's name and title. This second depicts some sort of labyrinth. And the third resorts to details of Hieronymus Bosch's *The Garden of Earthly Delights*. Or else it uses one of a variety of woodcuts, lithographs, and mezzotints by Dutch artist E. M. Escher, to whom Borges is frequently linked.

The fourth type appears in the original Editorial Losada cover, published in Buenos Aires three years after the end of the Second World War. It reproduces, with some adornment (invoking the work of Argentine artist and Borges's friend Oscar Agustín Alejandro Schulz Solari, aka Xul Solar), the first letter of the Hebrew alphabet, which refers to the story "El Aleph," first published in the September 1945 issue of Victoria Ocampo's magazine *Sur*. There are a total of seventeen texts in the volume, including "Emma Zunz" and "*Deutsches Requiem*." Obviously, the fact that this letter is featured on the cover emphasizes the story's importance. In the story, the letter also serves as the name of the magical object Borges, the narrator, describes as he descends into the cellar of Carlos Argentino Daneri's house, where the bulk of the action takes place.

A number of Borges's "*ficciones*," among them "The Library of Babel," "Tlön Uqbar, *Orbis Tertius*," and "The Garden of Forking Paths," have been illustrated, a few as graphic novels, others as hypertexts. The quality,

---

First published in *Studies in 20th and 21st Century Literature*, vol. 42, issue 1 (2017).

though not homogenous, is estimable. Others have been adapted to the screen, large and small, such as *The Spider's Stratagem*, directed by Bernardo Bertolucci, based on "Theme of the Traitor and the Hero." In my estimation, they are all subpar.

"The Aleph" too is an image machine, but it is unrepresentable. To me this is, in and of itself, what the story is about.

An homage to Dante's *Divine Comedy*, with Beatriz as an elusive object of adoration, the plot is about the ephemerality of love. One of its two epigraphs is from *Hamlet*, Act II, Scene 2: "O God! I could be bounded in a nutshell, and count myself a King of infinite space . . ." The other is from Hobbes's *Leviathan*.

The fact that the object Borges discovers in Daneri's basement ("somewhat of a pit") is impossible to pin down is stated in the following paragraph. Arguably the best Borges ever wrote, it comes toward the end, when, after counting off nineteen steps, the narrator is finally face to face with the Aleph:

> Cada cosa (la luna del espejo, digamos) era infinitas cosas, porque yo claramente la veía desde todos los puntos del universo. Vi el populoso mar, vi el alba y la tarde, vi las muchedumbres de América, vi una plateada telaraña en el centro de una negra pirámide, vi un laberinto roto (era Londres), vi interminables ojos inmediatos escrutándose en mí como en un espejo, vi todos los espejos del planeta y ninguno me reflejó, vi en un traspatio de la calle Soler las mismas baldosas que hace treinta años vi en el zaguán de una casa en Fray Bentos, vi racimos, nieve, tabaco, vetas de metal, vapor de agua, vi convexos desiertos ecuatoriales y cada uno de sus granos de arena, vi en Inverness a una mujer que no olvidaré, vi la violenta cabellera, el altivo cuerpo, vi un cáncer en el pecho, vi un círculo de tierra seca en una vereda, donde antes hubo un árbol, vi una quinta de Adrogué, un ejemplar de la primera versión inglesa de Plinio, la de Philemon Holland, vi a un tiempo cada letra de cada página (de chico, yo solía maravillarme de que las letras de un volumen cerrado no se mezclaran y perdieran en el decurso de la noche), vi la noche y el día contemporáneo, vi un poniente en Querétaro que parecía reflejar el color de una rosa en Bengala, vi mi dormitorio sin nadie, vi en un gabinete de Alkmaar un globo terráqueo entre dos espejos que lo multiplican sin fin, vi

caballos de crin arremolinada, en una playa del Mar Caspio en el alba, vi la delicada osatura de una mano, vi a los sobrevivientes de una batalla, enviando tarjetas postales, vi en un escaparate de Mirzapur una baraja española, vi las sombras oblicuas de unos helechos en el suelo de un invernáculo, vi tigres, émbolos, bisontes, marejadas y ejércitos, vi todas las hormigas que hay en la tierra, vi un astrolabio persa, vi en un cajón del escritorio (y la letra me hizo temblar) cartas obscenas, increíbles, precisas, que Beatriz había dirigido a Carlos Argentino, vi un adorado monumento en la Chacarita, vi la reliquia atroz de lo que deliciosamente había sido Beatriz Viterbo, vi la circulación de mi oscura sangre, vi el engranaje del amor y la modificación de la muerte, vi el Aleph, desde todos los puntos, vi en el Aleph la tierra, y en la tierra otra vez el Aleph y en el Aleph la tierra, vi mi cara y mis vísceras, vi tu cara, y sentí vértigo y lloré, porque mis ojos habían visto ese objeto secreto y conjetural, cuyo nombre usurpan los hombres, pero que ningún hombre ha mirado: el inconcebible universo.

This is an English translation by Norman Thomas Di Giovanni and the author:

Each thing (a mirror's face, let us say) was infinite things, since I distinctly saw it from every angle of the universe. I saw the teeming sea; I saw daybreak and nightfall; I saw the multitudes of America; I saw a silvery cobweb in the center of a black pyramid; I saw a splintered labyrinth (it was London); I saw, close up, unending eyes watching themselves in me as in a mirror; I saw all the mirrors on earth and none of them reflected me; I saw in a backyard of Soler Street the same tiles that thirty years before I'd seen in the entrance of a house in Fray Bentos; I saw bunches of grapes, snow, tobacco, lodes of metal, steam; I saw convex equatorial deserts and each one of their grains of sand; I saw a woman in Inverness whom I shall never forget; I saw her tangled hair, her tall figure, I saw the cancer in her breast; I saw a ring of baked mud in a sidewalk, where before there had been a tree; I saw a summer house in Adrogué and a copy of the first English translation of Pliny—Philemon Holland's—and all at the same time saw each letter on each page (as a boy, I used to marvel that the letters in a closed book did not get scrambled and lost overnight); I saw a sunset in Querétaro that seemed to reflect the colour of a rose in Bengal; I saw my empty bedroom; I saw in a closet in Alkmaar a terrestrial globe between two mirrors that multiplied it endlessly; I saw horses with flowing manes on a shore of the Caspian Sea at dawn; I saw the delicate bone structure of a hand; I saw the survivors of a battle sending out picture postcards; I saw in a showcase in Mirzapur a pack of Spanish playing cards; I saw the slanting shadows of ferns on a greenhouse floor; I saw tigers, pistons, bison, tides, and armies; I saw all the ants on the planet; I saw a Persian astrolabe; I saw in the drawer of a writing table (and the handwriting made me tremble) unbelievable, obscene, detailed letters, which Beatriz had written to Carlos Argentino; I saw a monument I worshipped in the Chacarita cemetery; I saw the rotted dust and bones that had once deliciously been Beatriz Viterbo; I saw the circulation of my own dark blood; I saw the coupling of love and the modification of death; I saw the Aleph from every point and angle, and in the Aleph I saw the earth and in the earth the Aleph and in the Aleph the earth; I saw my own face and my own bowels; I saw your face; and I felt dizzy and wept, for my eyes had seen that secret and conjectured object whose name is common to all men but which no man has looked upon—the unimaginable universe.

Borges's first reaction is "a shock of panic, which I tried to pin to my uncomfortable position and not to the effect of a drug." He sees the Aleph in the darkness, on the back part of the step, "a small iridescent sphere of almost unbearable brilliance." His first impression is that it is revolving. Then he realizes that the movement is "an illusion created by the dizzying world it bounded." He adds: "The Aleph's diameter was probably little more than an inch, but all space was there, actual and undiminished."

As he is about to describe what his eyes notice, Borges is paralyzed: "I arrive now at the ineffable core of my story. And here begins my despair as a writer. All language is a set of symbols whose use among its speakers assumes a shared past. How, then, can I translate into words the limitless Aleph, which my floundering mind can scarcely encompass?" The paralysis is emblematic because the Aleph contains all language, yet it is also beyond language.

One possibility is to see the Aleph as a TV. Black-and-white television appeared in the 1920s. Although the invention did not reach Buenos Aires until 1951, Borges, already suffering from a partial form of blindness, made notice of its arrival in Europe in the forties. More adventurously, the object he describes is imaginable as a version *avant la lettre* of the Internet: all information at once and the semblance of the entire universe at one's fingertips.

However, what we see on TV is not reality but a reflection. And the Internet is not the universe either.

That Borges attempts a description of what he perceives is proof of his literary mind. He succumbs because he is aware that any representation of what his eyes register is about the tapering of perception. William Blake put it thus in *The Marriage of Heaven and Hell* (1793): "For man has closed himself up, till he sees all things thro' narrow chinks of his cavern."

In short, no representation of the Aleph is possible because any illustration must follow a syntax, which de facto pigeonholes the universe into a fixed language. Human language is about falsification.

THE MONKEY GRAMMARIAN

"As if you could kill time without injuring eternity."

—Henry David Thoreau

In 1951, Octavio Paz, then a thirty-seven-year-old mid-level diplomat at the Mexican embassy in Paris, received the news of his official transfer to India. Mexico had recently established relations with the newly independent nation, which shortly before had made peace with Pakistan and Nepal. British colonialism had been brought to its knees, and the entire world was greeting the events with enthusiasm, even after the Gandhi assassination.

Jawaharial Nehru was prime minister. Paz arrived in Bombay a few months later, in 1952. He stayed in India until 1968, a total of fourteen years, the last six as ambassador. He resigned from this post in protest of the student massacre in Mexico City's Tlatelolco Square, a repressive response by the Mexican government to the growing dissatisfaction against its long-standing autocratic policies. By then his seminal book *The Labyrinth of Solitude* (1950), where he reflected on how Mexico had half-heartedly become a modern nation, had become a classic.

The encounter with India was transformative. Paz read broadly and traveled widely. There he met his second wife, Marie José, who became his indefatigable companion. His inquisitive spirit was in constant stimulation, reinvigorating him as a poet and essayist and opening new vistas not only to the world (he had already lived in Berkeley, New York, and Paris) but also to understanding his native Mexico. He also wrote profusely. Years later, already close to his death in 1998, Paz published a memoir-cum-disquisition on religion, politics, and society about that crucial period called *Vislumbres de la India* (1994). Fittingly, the English translation is titled *In Praise of India*.

Introduction to *The Monkey Grammarian*, by Octavio Paz (New York: Arcade, 2017).

One of the things he learned was that in spite of their enormous differences, India and Mexico had much in common, starting with the geographic vastness, the depth and multifacetedness of syncretic religious devotion, and the rich pantheon of deities. Paz found points in common with regard to cuisine and fashion. He was fascinated by the frantic drive toward urbanization in which the two countries were engaged. In other words, it seems as if this period was an invitation to consider the qualities of his own home.

Of course, Paz came across essential differences, too. For instance, India understood time as cyclical, whereas Mexico saw it as a straight line. Likewise, Hinduism and other Eastern religions approached eroticism as liberating, while the influence of Catholicism in Mexico made sexuality constraining, even stultifying.

The Monkey Grammarian (1970) might be the book by Paz that best showcases the way his worldview was reshaped. Although he completed it while he was already at Cambridge, England, a couple of years after his resignation as ambassador to India, everything in it is marked by his time on the Indian subcontinent. It was written explicitly for the series *Les Sentiers de la Creation* (The Paths of Creation), edited in France by Swiss publisher Albert Skira and French essayist and art critic Gaëtan Picon. A meeting place for important artists and intellectuals, the series included works by influential figures like Louis Aragon, Michel Butor, Eugene Ionesco, and Henri Michaux. In a *postscriptum* Paz inserted in volume 11 of his own *Obras Completas* (1996), which includes *The Monkey Grammarian*, he stated that in this book he sought to use the title of the Skira and Picon series as a guiding metaphor: he wanted to produce a meditation that was as much about the impressions India had left in him as a real place as it was about the discombobulating emotions he absorbed in the treks he took while there. That is, India as a reality and an abstraction.

The result is ambitious. The plot, if *The Monkey Grammarian* might be said to have one, is a quest to reach a specific place: Galta, a small town—and the ruins in it—near Jaipur, the capital and largest city (with a population at the time of around 1.7 million) of the northern state of Rajasthan.

As Paz goes to Galta for a visit, he discovers he is revisiting the different chambers of his self. Galta soon becomes an excuse for him to talk about the fugitiveness of time and the impossibility of seizing it. It is also about the task of language to capture the dilemma of being conscious about our own action and thought. Does that consciousness take away from the experience itself?

The style Paz uses is a hybrid. The book is neither a full-fledged poem nor a cohesive essay. Paz loved this type of experimentation. He was fond of breaking barriers. This comes from his appreciation of opposites—the proverbial yin and yang—as being promiscuous in their liaison. What we perceive, he argued, is deceptive: male and female, young and old, black and white, truth and falsehood are only superficial antipodes; in fact, each of these polarities carries in itself its own opposite. And we do too, for the Western concept of individuality is a mirage. Even when we are alone, we are always with others; and although we recognize ourselves as unique, we are, as Walt Whitman suggested, a sum of parts: a multitude.

Paz came of age in the 1930s, when the Surrealist movement in Europe, which emphasized the artificial separation between dreams and wakefulness, was at its height. His aesthetic views were influenced by it. Throughout his oeuvre, he sought to erase the border between sensorial knowledge and the life of the imagination. That, precisely, is what *The Monkey Grammarian* seeks to achieve: it invites the reader to look at things not as they are but as a mere stepping-stone toward a greater consciousness of the universe.

My instinct is to describe *The Monkey Grammarian* first and foremost as a travel book. But the meaning of "travel" needs to be explained. Paz embarks on a journey: to see the ruins of Galta. That, however, is only the visible aspect of it.

The journey has another side, invisible to the eye, which is about the inner thoughts contained in, and resulting from, the physical voyage. Paz regularly gives us sensorial images that accompany him: a wall in the middle of a square where "the traces of red, black, and blue paint create imaginary atlases"; children pullulating on the side of the road, begging him for money; pilgrims en route to a sanctuary and a *sādhu*, a mystic, in that sanctuary; and so on. He includes an assortment of photographs of these and other sites, perhaps to verify that those sensorial images are accurate.

At the core of the narrative is Hanumān, a popular monkey god featured in the epic saga *Rāmāyana*. He represents bravery and persistence and is a symbol of loyalty and selflessness.

Paz uses it as leitmotif. He opens with a quote from John Dowson, the noted British "Indologist" who wrote about Urdu and the history of India, and who served as editor of the still-in-print *A Classic Dictionary of Hindu Mythology* (1879). Dowson describes Hanumān as a hopping monkey who "tore up trees, carried away the Himalayas, seized the clouds and performed many other wonderful exploits. . . ." He is also "the ninth author of grammar." That double feature, the monkey's rambunctiousness and his linguistic aptitude, fascinates Paz: objectively, Hanumān travels the universe; subjectively, he sews it together through words.

Humans do the same, Paz argues. We build and destroy our environment, then use language to describe those actions. Just as our behavior in the natural world is capricious, so is our effort at articulating it verbally. Why call the color yellow *yellow*? Is the essence of Galta inside the word *Galta*? And in what sense is the sentence *The best thing to do will be to choose the path of Galta, traverse it again (invent it as I traverse it), and without realizing it, almost imperceptibly, go to the end—without being concerned with what "going to the end" means or what I meant when I wrote that sentence*, which serves as the opening of *The Monkey Grammarian*, a reasonable depiction of its intentions?

Like Hanumān, Paz, in the action recounted in the book, builds a net of signifiers that offers a portrait of his own physical odyssey. Yet that net is made of procrastinations, false starts, and countless returns. It is also made of words that lead to other words that lead to other words. . . .

Just as Paz approaches Galta, he realizes he hasn't moved an inch. All of us are trapped in the same place, our being, committed to the pursuit of simultaneously leaving and returning home. This makes Paz infer that time is a labyrinth made of a single straightforward line that gives the false impression of movement. Actually, time is about fixity, about stillness, about the joyful art of rotating around the "I." As Paz put it in *Obras Completas*, "rather than going forward, the text rotated on itself." And on each rotation the text would unfold into another spin, which was at once a translation and a transposition of the original intentions: "a spiral of repetitions and reiterations that resolves around a negation of writing as a path." To the point, he claims, that "I realized my text wasn't going anywhere, except an encounter with itself."

A text that isn't going anywhere . . . Needless to say, *The Monkey Grammarian* is a challenging text. It might be better described as a test. Indeed, I know of countless readers who have succumbed in the process of navigating it. Then again, those who do stay for the ride are handsomely rewarded.

This is a book of magical thinking and heightened awareness, one that suggests that India, just like any other place, is itself because of us: our body in it as well as our attempt to articulate in words what that body is, how it looks at the world, and how the world looks at it. "Every body," affirms Paz, "is a language that vanishes at the moment of absolute plenitude; on reaching the state of incandescence, every language reveals itself to be an unintelligible body." He concludes: "the world is a disincarnation of the world."

Also a native of Mexico, I have been a Paz devotee for decades. His deep-seated cosmopolitanism is one of the elements that pushed me to other landscapes. It was through reading his essays that I learned the pleasures and challenges of developing one's own ideas in rigorous, consistent, yet jazzy and personal ways, that ideas never exist in isolation but in constant motion, coexisting with other ideas at all times, and that the free exchange of those ideas is an indispensable component in a free, healthy, and democratic society.

In the end, encouraged by Paz's travels, I left Mexico and became a writer away from home, which granted me a unique perspective on things, including my own culture.

Perhaps the most important lesson Paz taught me is that Mexican writers should not be confined thematically to Mexico in their oeuvre. Just as Shakespeare set his plays in England as well as in Italy, Denmark, Greece, France, and other places, the scope of the Mexican writer ought to be the entire world.

But my admiration for Paz isn't without complaint. Frequently I find his writing aloof, not to say pedantic and frustratingly elusive. What made me unhappy, though (and I speak here as a member of an entire generation), is the way in which late in his career Paz embraced the very same political power he had rejected earlier on.

Having resigned his ambassadorship in India, he returned to Mexico in 1968. Two years later, he founded one of the most venerable of literary journals in the Spanish-speaking world, *Plural*. It confronted the excesses of Mexico's government with civility and acumen. When the Mexican government became impatient with its critique, it ordered the magazine shut down. Paz did not despair: he continued his endeavor in another magazine he founded, *Vuelta*, as well as in a tireless career as a public intellectual.

But slowly he became more comfortable with that government, so much so that he ended up assuming the role of its spokesperson. That embrace felt to me like a betrayal. By then Paz's writing style in my eyes had become complacent and self-congratulatory. In response, I stopped reading him.

Time has gone by—or, as Paz argues, it effectually hasn't. Perhaps it is that fixity that has prompted me to reread *The Monkey Grammarian*, which, just as it did when I first encountered it, strikes me as a stunning and unsettling rumination on evanescence.

MIDRASH ON TRUTH

The greater part of the world's troubles are due to questions of grammar.

—Michal de Montaigne

He sits down. A fly buzzes around, crossing his sight. It then disappears almost magically. He looks around. There it is: the fly has landed on the curtain, attracted by the rays of the sun. It is almost spring, and the light projects new shadows on the walls. The fly is moved by the desire for comfort.

He has sat down after much thought. He feels the urge to dissect—his son makes fun of him using the verb "to meditate"—on the truth. This isn't a voluntary effort; the urge has been pushing itself into his thoughts. Sometimes as he reads or watches TV or eats a sandwich he wanders into an intellectual sphere where he questions if there is a way of proving what we know and, therefore, if truth is knowledgeable. He wants to believe this is the case, but he is doubtful.

He is of a time in which the bombardment of information feels punishing. He turns on the radio, reads the newspaper, looks at Twitter, and browses online . . . How is one to make sense of this sensory overload? He knows—because he is over fifty—that information is not knowledge. Knowledge requires work. Knowledge is insight. And insight is always personal.

He is honest with himself, or at least he thinks he is. He doesn't have the faintest illusion that exploring what truth is might make him less of a cynic. That, in fact, seems like an impossible desire: to come closer to truth. Yet organizing his thoughts around it might grant him a sense of satisfaction.

First published in *Kenyon Review*, April 12, 2017.

Is he a cynic? He doesn't think of himself one. And is what he is after really about organizing his thoughts? He realizes that all his life he thought what the concept was about, and without warning he is at an existential precipice, without confidence. He lives in the age of skepticism. Truth in particular is a casualty: everyone invokes it, swearing it is essential, arguing that without it you just can't live a rational life. However, if you stop and ask people to define it, everyone feigns ignorance.

Obviously, he knows that truth is not a menu of facts. Sometimes he likes to imagine himself transformed into an invisible dictionary, one without boundaries, a dictionary capable of containing all aspects of language not in static form but in a state of transition. Right away he is wondering how the word "fact" is defined in it. An item that is indisputable? He isn't happy with this definition. He knows that facts are often denied, hidden, camouflaged. Yet that doesn't make them irrelevant.

Facts are facts: that's what he himself often repeats. He also knows that empiricism is a doctrine built on the premise that we receive information from the senses. Yet he has always enjoyed thinking that the imaginary life of facts is as attractive as the facts themselves. This is because he is a lover of fantasy, of things that don't exists in the world per se yet make their home in his mind.

Honestly, only when pushed does he confess to be a skeptic. More often than not, he likes to portray himself as a believer. It is good to believe, he tells himself, although he doesn't always know what to believe in. For instance, he believes in God (out of superstition, he writes it with upper-case "G") only in situations in which he finds himself in danger. Otherwise he doubts the existence of any supernatural forces, thinking it is all superstition. And he doesn't believe in ghosts, although he teases his two boys that ghosts on occasion visit him at night, conferring truths he would otherwise not know.

Truths he would otherwise not know . . . He wonders if all truths are knowledgeable. Is that what makes truth truth?

He feels annoyed by the way you are able to tune in to a network on TV to get a version of the truth, and with a simple click you can jump to another channel to get a dramatically different interpretation of the same events. Whom to believe? But he tells himself this is the wrong question, because truth isn't about belief, at least not empirical truth. It is faith that is about belief. Faith is about the unknown, about what can't be measured.

He dislikes this last thought because truth, he tells himself, is also immeasurable. How might one measure truth? How do we know that good is good and bad is bad? Perhaps by thinking that good furthers life and bad impedes it. Still, there is no way to prove such binaries. One must simply believe.

As he gets angry at himself for not being capable of furthering his thoughts into some kind of illumination, he realizes that the fly is back again in his spectrum of consciousness. It is nervously gliding from one corner to another, his desk the occasional tarmac. He becomes aware of his disquiet. More than aware, he is impatient. He wonders if the fly's aphoristic life isn't better than his own.

Is there much to be gained with this *midrash* on truth? He knows that a certain degree of certainty about truth is needed—otherwise we become savages—yet he can't quite wrap himself around the effort to explain why this is so. He now remembers what his anchor was: facts. This is how he gets into circular thinking when pondering truth. He has looked up the word in an existing lexicon and has stumbled on that most unpleasant of caveats: "thing": a thing of information that is used as evidence.

Are facts things? Oh, now he is more disoriented than before. Not only does he not know what the truth is but he has caught himself reflecting on the term "thing," which people use as an easy escape: "the thing is," "stop doing those things," and "I got a thing or two in the supermarket." Truth cannot be a thing, he is confident of that. Truth is heftier, more complex, more abstract.

The other day, he heard someone on TV talking about "alternative facts." The statement has left him inspired, to the degree that he hasn't been able to consider much else. Indeed, that's what prompted him to scrutinize the confines of truth. He tells himself: truth is not malleable; truth is truth. He doesn't like to think of himself as manipulating facts, although perhaps it is inevitable that everyone does. That's how people lie: they don't convey the whole truth, they tailor it to their own needs.

This he knows for sure: he is fascinated by lies. Not his lies, which he finds boring; rather, the lies of others. He enjoys catching people *infraganti* in the art of lying, finding out that we all know perfectly well that X is true, but all of a sudden, oops, just now it happens to have become Y. Time and again he tells himself that it is impossible to live life without lies. We lie to suit what happens to us to our own needs. Then again, is that what manipulating facts is about? And is this proof that truth is partial, subjective, biased?

He surprises himself by saying: if truth is biased, then it isn't truth.

Ever since he read Plato's *Symposium*, in his twenties, he has been an admirer of Socrates. The icon is more than a martyr to him; he is a method, a means to achieve an end. He knows that Socrates was ugly, which in his eyes makes him all the more appealing. He also knows that he was accused of perverting Athens' youth through his wisdom. Only recently he has had the courage to follow Socrates's ordeal more closely. It all started when a colleague gave him a copy of I. F. Stone's *The Trial of Socrates*. He devoured it in a matter of hours. That Stone looked at the trial from a journalist's eye was a stroke of genius.

Why exactly was Socrates condemned? It looks as if he was antidemocratic, like Plato, his pupil. And he might have been misanthropic too. In any case, Socrates placed an emphasis on the oral tradition. What we know about him comes from Plato, Aristophanes, and Xenophon, not from his own words. In that sense, Socrates was utterly elusive. It might be said that Socrates was suspicious of anything that was put in writing because the oral tradition is unfixable whereas the written word is a contract.

What he likes about Socrates as method is that one can never reach the truth directly; instead, one must work at it with the help of others. This means that truth doesn't belong to one individual alone but to everyone at the same time. He also acknowledges that truth is not fixed; it is subject to change. There are, to be sure, universal truths. These are truths belonging to everyone. And then there are particular truths, which belong to specific circumstances.

He looks further into this dichotomy and again is uncertain. Is it really true that there is a set number of universal truths? That's the position of the absolutists. As for himself, he prefers the side of the relativists, backing the position that truths change over time. Take the truism that all men are created equal. He knows this to be an absolute truth; there is not an iota of doubt inside him in this regard. Yet it only takes a second to realize that such equality is sheer illusion. In their most intimate moments, people confess that no one is equal to anyone else. The inmates in a prison are a case in point: they are criminals, meaning they are amoral, which means people build theories to keep them apart, to separate them from the rest.

Mark Twain said: "Never tell the truth to people who are not worthy of it." Ah, he likes this statement; it implies that truth is dependent on others. Is it?

He likes to conceive of what he does as "a life in letters." Letters understood not only as books but also as the letters of an alphabet. He toys with them all the time. He thinks of truths as concepts that can be narrated. Someone once portrayed him as an architect of words.

He ruminates on art as the other side of truth. The more consistent and thought-out art is, the more enchanted he is by it. However, he thinks of artists as liars, although these, as he sees it, are convenient lies. At least that's what he used to believe. As of late, he has become suspicious of the current representation of art as facilitator of truth.

According to the Talmud, which he enjoys studying every other Thursday afternoon with Rabbi David, twisting the truth is advisable on a few occasions. These occasions need to be clearly delineated. For example, it is appropriate to lie in order to honor someone. It is also right to lie to be modest or humble, or to protect someone from embarrassment or harm, or to recoup a loss. All these are permissible lies, says the Talmud. But there are exceptions (or else, exceptions to the exceptions). One of them is that one shouldn't lie on a regular basis. Another is that one shouldn't lie to children because they might grow up with a mistaken impression of what is good and evil.

And then there's the most adorable of all exceptions in the Talmud: one isn't allowed to lie about the future. Why not? Because the future is still unrealized. And because by tarnishing the future, our life expectations are questioned.

Not long ago he scribbled in the notebook he keeps in his pocket some thoughts on the difference between the truth as delivered by historians and the truth as conveyed by writers. He thinks the two target the same truth yet reach it through different means. Matthew, a dear friend, doesn't agree; Matthew stresses that these are different truths, and he prefers the writer's truth because he is an artist himself. He knows that a historian would say the same thing as Matthew while leaning in the opposite direction.

Then he considers inserting a scientist into the mix. Would anyone doubt that the scientist's truth *is* the actual truth? Not he, for sure, and not anyone with the slight bit of common sense. Yet—and this is what obsesses him—the scientist's truth in his eyes is boring. Facts are facts are facts . . . What makes the other truths appealing is that they compete with reality; that is, they add depth to our understanding of the world.

What if art is nothing but a series of alternative facts?

He hates catching himself arguing against science, because many of his friends are scientists. Still, he is convinced that science reigns today like a tyrant. And here he smiles: facts are not ends onto themselves, he tells himself, which is what scientists believe. Facts are trampolines.

He recollects reading Oscar Wilde's *The Importance of Being Earnest* in his youth. It left a lasting impression, specifically a line—the world for him is a succession of sentences—that still haunts him: "Man is least himself when he talks in his own person. Give him a mask and he will tell you the truth." The line stuck, he thinks, because, in his youthful view, truth was arduous. Over the years he hasn't quite changed his opinion. Nobody likes truth because truth makes us uncomfortable. It is easier to convey it when you hide behind a mask. Of course, that doesn't make it easier to accept it.

Unexpectedly he recalls a conversation he had with his mentor, Grace P., while the two were down in Guadalajara. The conversation was about happiness. Grace told him that happiness is the capacity to enjoy the pleasant and the unpleasant because one cannot exist without the other. Someone had told Grace that happiness is the absence of pain, but she believed that was absurd. Pain for her was also a form of happiness. You need to suffer to build character, she said, and that process of decantation makes you appreciate the pleasant aspects of life.

Maybe the same ought to be said about truth: that one specifically values truth when it is under attack, at peril, a target being delegitimized. Without truth it would be easier for dictators to do as they wish. On the other hand, dictators are the ones engineering alternative versions of the truth to fit their goals.

There it is again, the word "alternative" . . . He doesn't like it!

The fly is back again, next to him. It has landed on his left sleeve. It isn't buzzing anymore, which is a relief, because he finds that buzz annoying. He considers raising his right hand and slapping the fly, which would no doubt kill it. But he stops on its tracks as he realizes that such an action would make him a destructor of life.

He realizes that, to his dismay, while attempting to elucidate the meaning of truth, he has entered the mind-set of a killer. It is only a fly, though, he tells himself, but now he is ashamed of his thoughts.

Aggravated, he stands up and leaves the room. The fly follows his trail.

DON QUIXOTE IN SCHLEMIELAND

My first intent was to call this blog post "Schlemiel the First," because it strikes me that Don Quixote, the mythical character created by Miguel de Cervantes in 1605 (the second, and concluding, part of the novel was published in 1615, almost exactly four hundred years ago), is the source, the urtext from which all subsequent schlemiels originate. But I immediately realized that this, in and of itself, is a myth, by which I mean, in this case, a false premise. The Merriam-Webster definition of schlemiel is "an unlucky bungler." Much might be said about Don Quixote, including that he is a schemer, an impostor, even a fraud. In the long and tortured—maybe "torturous"—narrative, he goes through all sorts of ordeals through which he puts his fanciful ideals to test. But one thing is certain: he is never unlucky.

In my *yidishe kop* I've always thought (call it *pensée irrationnel*) that "Quijotismo" in Spanish is the condition of being a schlemiel. In other words, either Don Quixote isn't a schlemiel or Merriam-Webster is wrong, or both. In my Yiddish-speaking childhood home in Mexico there were heated discussions attempting to differentiate between a schlemiel and a schlimazel. The former was seen as a fool, and Don Quixote is certainly one, whereas the latter as understood to a person prone to misfortune, which is also a description of Don Quixote. He is a mix of both, then. In the discussions, someone would frequently say that you can't be a fool without being unlucky, although the opposite, you can't be unlucky without being a fool, doesn't hold true.

This conundrum—that the Knight of the Sorrowful Countenance brings these two qualities together—is untenable in my eyes. To explain why, I need to comment on various elements of Cervantes's book.

Many call it the first modern novel. It is, in my estimation, the one that, almost singlehandedly, invented modernity. Cervantes was a cautious

---

First published in *Schlemiel Theory*, September 16, 2016.

proponent of the Enlightenment in Spain. *Don Quixote* is courageous in idealizing the power of dreams, but it doesn't take the Holy Inquisition head-on, nor does it intend to. It distills some of the ideas of Erasmus of Rotterdam's *In Praise of Folly*, although, again, it isn't critical of the Catholic Church as an institution, at least not directly. What the narrative does—illustriously, no doubt—is question the concept of truth.

Should it be written with a capital "T"; that is, might it ever be seen as absolute? Cervantes's answer is a rotund no: as Schopenhauer and Bishop Berkley would argue later, everything we are exposed to, reality as a whole, exists only in our mind; it is subjective, meaning relative, biased, and partial. We are the architects of the world, for the only way to register it, the only way to represent it is through our independent perspective. One could call this approach a road to foolish, for, after all, if the stimulation we receive from the outside is invariably filtered by our own misconceptions, truth and falsehood are easily interchangeable.

Yet *Don Quixote of La Mancha* is wiser; it doesn't fall for this easy, Manichean dichotomy. Its basic premise is that reality and our imagination are intrinsically connected and, perhaps more importantly, that reason and foolishness aren't antonyms. This is why I love Cervantes's novel: because it proposes to see reason also not as absolute. A fool might be quite intelligent, even reasonable. And reasonable people are often foolish.

The reader delves into the adventures of Don Quixote and his squire Sancho with the intuition that they are a study in contrasts: one is rich and the other poor; one is thin and the other fat; one is an idealist and the other a pragmatist; and one is learned and the other illiterate. More importantly, the reader enters the novel with the conviction that one is a fool and the other is not.

The narrative quickly brings down these expectations. In fact, it fulminates them. It takes almost no time to realize that Cervantes is presenting different types of knowledge: the learned man, for instance, is often impractical. Furthermore, as the episodes accumulate, the reader witnesses an extraordinary feast: Don Quixote is "Sanchified" and Sancho Panza is "Quixotified"; that is, elements from one suddenly appear in the other and vice versa. That, after all, is what true friendship is about.

All this is done through laughter. The novel is a parody: it makes fun of chivalry literature; it also makes fun of itself, and it even makes fun of humor. It thrives on the wretched, the ridiculous, and the pathetic, an aspect, needless to say, constant in depictions of schlemiels: we laugh at and with them.

In any case, the knight isn't a bungler. He doesn't habitually bungle things. He isn't an amateur either. He is impish, clumsy, certainly inelegant, but he even often gets from people what he wants. Sancho also isn't unlucky. Actually, as recompense he is promised, early on in the plot, the governorship of an island, which will be a way for him to be paid and, along the way, to cease being poor, and toward the end of the Second Part he does get it, sort of: it is called Barataria, and after a brief tenure at its helm he realizes it is better for him not to get involved in politics. So no: the fellow is rewarded, and he learns from experience not to want to be outside his own class.

Still, Don Quixote, more than Sancho, does strike me as a schlemiel, maybe even the proto-schlemiel: the fool of fools, a wise man whose façade confounds those around him. And he is a schlimazel in that, in his quest to right all wrongs, he is regularly hit by misfortune. By the way, being hit by misfortune isn't the same as being unlucky. They are dramatically different things.

In fact, my impression is that *Don Quixote of La Mancha* inaugurates a space—call it "Schlemieland"—wherein the state of being a fool in constant misfortune becomes a feature of life in general. It is the space where dreams are attempted but fail to materialize, the dimension where everything we try ends up in failure. Cervantes's character is a success in failure. Everything he attempts ends up in collapse, yet his effort becomes a model, even a form of sustenance for others who, when, toward the end of the novel, he renounces his dreams and is ready to die as the hidalgo he once was, beg him—nah, they implore him—to remain the fool he always was.

There is a long-standing tradition in Jewish literature of celebrating, even emulating Don Quixote, discreetly or otherwise. Mendele Mokher Sforim's *Masoes Beniamin Hashlishi* (Travels of Benjamin the Third) is the most obvious example. There are Quixotic elements in Tevye, in Isaac Babel's Odessa stories, in Philip Roth, in Woody Allen, all of whom, to some degree, inhabit that liminal space invoked by Cervantes I've called Schlemieland.

The word "schlemiel" came about in the Pale of Settlement. Its birth is probably in the seventeenth century, although there are no data to prove it. Either way, I'm aware it is an anachronism to describe Don Quixote as a schlemiel and, furthermore, to image La Mancha and beyond, the universe in which he moves, as Schlemieland. Still, our language—any language—is made of a hefty dose of anachronisms. This is because every time a new concept emerges, people apply it not only to address the present but, unequivocally, to refer to the past. Not to go too far, think of the word "Quixotic," which is taken to mean a dreamer, a person who is unrealistic. Not long ago, I came across a scholarly portrayal of Moses, the biblical patriarch, as Quixotic. Talk about applying the tools of one era to understand another.

Why not? If Moses is Quixotic, then Don Quixote is Schlemiel the First.

DYING IN HEBREW

"To handle a language skillfully is to practice a kind of evocative sorcery."

—Charles Baudelaire

Some years ago, a short story I wrote—called, in Spanish, "*Morirse está en hebreo*" (2006)—was adapted into a film. The title in English was *My Mexican Shivah*. It was a comedy about a dysfunctional Jewish family forced to congregate at the wake of its patriarch. The literal translation of the title of my story is different: "Dying in Hebrew." It comes from the pronouncement by military leader Casca, in Shakespeare's *Julius Caesar*: "It was Greek to me." This is still the expression used in English to dismiss something as incomprehensible. In Spanish, people say, "It is in Chinese," or "It is in Hebrew"—*está en chino*, or *está en hebreo*. And maybe the incomprehensible is also the unknown. Think of it: whatever is expressed in a foreign language, a language we don't know or don't quite master, appears encrypted to us, a secret. The story, as well as the film, is set in Mexico, where I was born and where Jews are a minority. The occasion of the funeral brings the characters together, making them aware of their Jewishness. The film assumes the foreignness of Jewish rituals to the audience; in Mexico, with a population of approximately 115 million, only around 30,000 are Jews. Thus, I intended the title to imply that Jewishness, in the diaspora I come from, is an enigma. And I also meant it in another way: the unknown is not only beyond human comprehension but also associated with the divine.

In this essay, which speaks about Hebrew as a language that connects us simultaneously with the natural and supernatural spheres, I begin by

---

Delivered as the Samuel and Althea Stroum Lecture, University of Washington in Seattle, May 24, 2016. Printed in *Michigan Quarterly Review* 55, no. 4 (Fall 2016). Reprinted in *What We Talk About When We Talk About Hebrew*, ed. Nancy Berg and Naomi Sokoloff (Seattle: University of Washington Press, 2018).

suggesting that all languages divide the world in two: those people who know it and those who don't. An unknown foreign language alienates us: it leaves us out. To decipher it, one needs special tools. Or, better, one needs to work at procuring inside knowledge. Let me add to this an idea: I don't believe all languages are equal. Not to me; not, I think, to any one of us. Whether we want it or not. We don't love all people the same way: we love our children, our parents, our spouses, our siblings, and other relatives more closely, more intimately, more essentially than we love anyone else. And even among them there is a closer group, followed by concentric circles. At times we love our friends in even stronger, more defining ways, perhaps because we don't choose family but we do choose friends. Something similar happens with languages. They form hierarchies: some matter more because they have a larger number of speakers, or because they are more influential in cultural terms. Furthermore, their position in the hierarchy isn't permanent. Things change as culture changes. Out of the 6,500 spoken languages in the world—a few of them endangered species—I only know some half a dozen, three or four of them intimately. Even these languages, to be honest, don't mean the same to me. Toward some of them I feel reverence, even awe. Others are better for cursing than for falling in love. Yiddish, one of my two first languages, is the past to me; it is wrapped in nostalgia. English, to which I arrived in my twenties, is precise, cold, and methodical. In my view, Spanish, a Romance language, is untidy, emotional, and melodramatic. French is pretentious. Portuguese is mysterious. And German is frightening. These are my personal connections. They are filtered through emotion, not through reason. And Hebrew? Hebrew is a special case.

 I have written about the theme of Hebrew in a couple of books: *Resurrecting Hebrew* (2008) and, as it relates to the Bible, in a series of conversations I held with Canadian journalist Mordechai Drache called *With All Thy Heart* (2010). I still feel I haven't exhausted the topic, and, thus, I return to it now with a coda that in due time might entail further reflections. Hebrew for me symbolizes the marriage of the earthly and the divine. I love the language profusely because it is larger than anything human: it is part of nature, and also it is what we make of it. Hebrew is a fixture of the universe, a mystery, a friend, although now I invoke Mark Twain's dictum about the moon: all of us are like it, with a dark side we hide away. Hebrew has a dark side as well, which some of us might prefer to hide away.

 I spoke fluent Hebrew when I was a young man. I read Bialik and Agnon in the original. And then I pushed the language aside (I went through what I've described as "language withdrawal") in favor of other tongues: English, most prominently. My connection to Hebrew is allegoric, like a story capable of revealing hidden meaning. How to comprehend the infinite permutations of the same twenty-two letters in the sounds of a buzzing supermarket, the disputations of the houses of Hillel and Shammai, a girl surreptitiously learning the *alef-bet* in Warsaw, a silver shekel used by Bar Kochba's rebellious army? In what way to understand the language Franz Rosenzweig heard in the fateful Kol Nidre in Berlin, a political march in Tel Aviv, the hallucinations of Isaac Luria in Safed in the Galilee region of Ottoman Syria, Grover in *Rechov Sumsum*, a stuttering Moses as he faces his own inefficacies, the buried prayer books under the AMIA ruins in 1994 in Buenos Aires, the misspelled *Tetragrammaton* tattooed on a waitress's arm, the duties of Bahya ibn Paquda's heart, a soldier inside a tank performing his army duties in Gaza, and an old Russian immigrant riding on a bus in Haifa? In what way is it possible to convey the fluidity of a language that at times is humble and unassuming and at others strident and presumptuous? I shall resign myself to a handful of imperfect ruminations.

Words, as everyone knows, are pregnant not only with meaning but also with memory. When we speak, we bring along in our conversation the ancestors who preceded us and the successors who will follow us. Each sentence is a vessel with coded information that travels through time. For languages are memory palaces. We are invited to enter them and explore their labyrinthine pathways, their multiplying chambers, their ancestral décor . . . They don't belong to us. Rather, we are their transient visitors. In our relationship with them, we make them come alive, adding to their history, expanding on their treasure trove of memories. At the same time, languages become our friends and companions through life. Through them we apprehend the world, establishing our place in it. And they themselves are self-sufficient universes. It is through words, in that sense, that we connect to the here and now as well as to the hereafter, that we build bridges between what is internal and external.

Along these lines, it is important to establish that all languages except Hebrew are purely horizontal in that all languages are by-products of human ingenuity. In the debate on the origins of language, I think Chomsky is partially right: language does precede us before birth. However, it isn't only that linguistic patterns are already imprinted in our DNA. In the case of Hebrew, it was there before humankind came to be on the planet. I am using poetic imagery here, borrowed from Jewish mysticism, endorsed by the Talmud, which holds that the Hebrew alphabet was created by God before anything else. The twenty-two letters competed for divine attention in the nothingness before the universe emerged. The letter *aleph*, the letter *bet*, and so on wanted to know their purpose, the reason for their existence. In addition, they also struggled to be the first in the alphabet. God, understandably, needed to compromise because, in spite of his omnipotence, only one letter can start the list. And of those, while aleph is the first, bet is the one at the beginning of *Breshit*, Genesis, the first chapter of the Hebrew Bible.

The idea of the alphabet awaiting our arrival and not the other way around is beautiful: language precedes human consciousness; it also precedes human communication. Modern scientific thought acknowledges that human language is the result of evolution, but the Talmud suggests that before Genesis 1:1, "*Breshit bara elohim et hashamaim v'et ha'aretz*" (In the beginning God created the heaven and the earth); God spoke language to himself. Consequently, there is "*lashon ha'kodesh*" and "*lashon b'nei adam*," a divine language and a human language. The divine language might be said to be solipsistic: God uses it for his own endeavors. It is incomprehensible to humans. Human language, or let's say it plural, human languages, are, obviously, a vehicle for humans to communicate with each other. Hebrew has both functions. Moreover, among the human languages, there are some irrevocable differences, because God also needs to be in dialogue with us. To achieve this dialogue, God doesn't use just any language: God uses Hebrew, the vertical language, the language that doesn't only go from east to west and north to south and vice versa, but also goes from top to bottom and from bottom to top. In other words, Hebrew isn't only useful for people to communicate with each other. It is also the conduit through which we relate to the divine.

The mystical book *Sefer ha-Bahir* posits that Hebrew appeared complete, unadulterated, fully formed, for it emanated from the divine. This means it didn't go through a natural process of evolution, bouncing and hopping depending on the circumstance. However, in fact, the language of the Hebrew Bible is sprinkled with Aramaic and other linguistic provenances. In other words, it isn't pure. That to me is an essential quality: the *lashon b'nei adam* is polluted, imperfect, human. Although Hebrew is known as a sacred language, in today's world we understand it to be the by-product of thousands of years of distillation. The lexicon used in Genesis morphs as the narrative of the scriptures progresses.

Hebrew is among the world's oldest languages. It is referred to in the Torah in myriad ways: "the language of Canaan," as well as Judean and

Judahite (Isaiah 19:18 and 2 Kings 18:26). In contrast, the historian Flavius Josephus, in his book *Antiquities*, calls it *Hebraios* and *Hebraïsti*. The *Mishna* (*Treatise Gittin* 9:8) instead describes it as *Halashon Ivrit*. As a Semitic language, Hebrew developed in the Near East, between the Jordan River and the Mediterranean Sea, in the late second and first millennia BCE. The earliest archeological item available, the Gezer Calendar, discovered by schoolchildren in 1880 and preserved in Istanbul's Museum of Antiquities, is from the tenth century BCE, in the time of Kings David and Solomon. Its six lines are a record of the labor connected to the construction of a tunnel at the time of King Hezekiah, mentioned in 2 Kings 20:20 and 2 Chronicles 32:3 and 33:14.

Unquestionably, the most astounding document in the history of Hebrew is that which begins with *Breshit*, that is, the *Five Books of Moses*. These books offer a compelling story—or better, a fragmented narrative made of an almost infinite number of stories—from the beginnings of creation to the moment Abraham and his descendants are chosen by God to become a light to other nations, and continuing up to the kingdom of Jehoahaz in approximately 821–805 BC. This content is what defines us as Jews: the narrative of Israelites becoming a nation. But the content of the Bible is equally defined by the vehicle through which it is delivered. That vehicle is its language, and that language evolves and changes in contact with other languages. The earliest material is the poetry, such as Genesis chapter 49, Exodus 15, and Deuteronomy 32. Even though it is clear that subsequent editors have manipulated the Hebrew in these sections, it is still possible to trace influences of neighboring dialects used in the northern region of Canaan. For the most part, the prose in the Bible dates to the period of King David, when a national language appeared to have been used in Jerusalem. It was used in court and among the educated elite. As a canonized anthology, the Torah probably began to be compiled in the mid-fifth century BC, at the request of the priestly scribe Ezra. Having led about five thousand Israelites in exile from Babylon back to their home in Jerusalem, Ezra orchestrated the editing of the five books. The process of expanding, modifying, and adjusting the text continued unabated for centuries. It also left behind material judged by the various editors to be unacceptable. These books came to be known as *Apocrypha* and *Pseudo-Epigrapha*. It is possible to discern an archaic modality used until the Babylonian exile, the Hebrew used in the Babylonian exile, and a late type used between the sixth and fourth centuries corresponding to the Persian period. The stabilizing of the content seems to have been completed by the second century CE—a long time, by all accounts. Until then, the language as it appears in the Bible is in constant flux.

Subsequently, Hebrew continued to come in contact with and interact with other languages throughout the many years of the Jewish diaspora. All languages emerge out of necessity, and they are always the result of cross-fertilization. There are close to thirty different Jewish languages, including Judeo-Arabic (Yahudic), Judeo-Aramaic (Kurdit, Hulaulá, Tárgum, Kurdishic), Ladino (Djudezmo, Haketiya, Judeo-Spanish), Judeo-Greek (Hellenic, Yevanic), Judeo-Persian (Dzidi, Jidi, Parsic), and Yiddish (Judeo-German). Each of these Jewish languages is the result of diasporic needs and is based on a fusion of Hebrew elements with other languages. Some are existent, others extinct. Each conveys a collective memory, for language doesn't exist in a vacuum. The endurance of some of these Jewish languages represents the survival of their memory, although, as we all know and as Jorge Luis Borges and Yosef Hayim Yerushalmi have admonished us, to remember is not the same as not to forget: to know a language doesn't mean we are familiar with it as a depository of heritage. One needs to live in that language, to let oneself be permeated by it in full, to achieve that undertaking.

In thinking of the difference between biblical and Modern Hebrew, it is impossible to avoid the question of redemption. And in thinking about redemption, we cannot help thinking about death. Redemption is about being saved from fate. For millennia, Hebrew existed in a void, kept alive by a few devout speakers, thus enduring against the odds. After the destruction of the Second Temple in the year 70 CE, it entered a kind of deep freeze. It was used in Talmudic discussion, in the shaping of the Gemara, and in liturgy. But it lost footing in the real world. It wasn't until the second half of the nineteenth century, with the emergence of nationalism, that the idea of a revival took shape. Bringing back a language that has long been on ice is an astonishing task. Can you imagine defrosting Latin, the language of Virgil, Horace, and Catullus, to rebuild the *Imperium Romanum* (which flourished roughly between Julius Caesar's rise to power in 44 BC to the fall of its western part in 476) in, say, Cantabria, Italy? The effort would require what appears like almost insurmountable resources, not only financial but also physical and emotional. Even more important, it would need an ideology to justify it and a movement to execute it. That, precisely, is what occurred in the nineteenth century, the age of nationalism, in the Pale of Settlement, under the lead—though by no means in a solo act—of Eliezer Ben Yehuda. Years ago I retraced, for an extended period of time, Ben

Yehuda's journey. It was at once exhilarating and disheartening. I reread his oeuvre, I visited the places he lived in, I looked at his unfinished lexicon, I put a stone on his tomb, and I talked to an endless number of characters (scholars, Talmudists, grammarians, prostitutes, translators, diplomats, novelists, kibbutzniks, and so on) about his legacy, in Israel and the diaspora. A taxi driver assured me he was a street in Tel Aviv. A librarian in New York said Ben Yehuda was a medieval philosopher. A friend in Marseille thought Ben Yehuda was a fundamentalist in the Occupied Territories. And a couple of orthodox Jews in Jerusalem fervently cursed his name.

Ben Yehuda's essay "The Burning Question"—"*She'elah Lohatah*" in Hebrew—positions Hebrew at the heart of modern Jewish redemption. It argues that the revival of Jewish nationalism and the resurrection of the biblical tongue went hand in hand. Historians of the State of Israel see the essay, and the series of letters he wrote to contend with its response, as a cornerstone in the history of Zionism. But when Ben Yehuda sent the essay to magazines, he swiftly received rejections. It wasn't until he mailed it to *Hashachar* (The Dawn), a periodical edited between 1868 and 1885 by another Lithuanian, Peretz Smolenskin, that the message fell on attentive ears. In the piece he offered the rationale for the revival of Hebrew as an integral part of the Zionist quest. Smolenskin published it, along with his own rebuttal. The essay was then read widely and generated much controversy among Jewish thinkers. It started an epistolary debate between Ben Yehuda and Smolenskin. In one letter dated 29 Kislev 5641 (1880), Ben Yehuda wrote:

> It is plain for all to see, sir, that our youth is abandoning our language—but why? Because in their eyes it is a dead and useless tongue . . . Only a Hebrew Ben Yehuda's synonym for Jew with a Hebrew heart will understand this, and such a man will understand even without our urging. Let us therefore make the language live again! Let us teach our young to speak it and then they will never betray it!
>
> But we will be able to revive the Hebrew tongue only in a country in which the number of Hebrew inhabitants exceeds the number of gentiles. Therefore, let us increase the number of Jews in our desolate land [in Palestine]; let the remnant of our people return to the land of their fathers; *let us revive the nation and its tongue will be revived, too!*

For Ben Yehuda, the land was a stepping-stone for linguistic redemption—a way of moving into the modern future and back to Sinai at the same time. And he was zealous; he forbade his children from speaking any other languages and even from listening to the singing of birds, lest this song pollute their Hebrew. This puritanical ethos defined early generations of modern Hebrew speakers.

In contrast, Hebrew today is a post-Zionist language. Were Ben Yehuda to wander around the globe now, no doubt he would be shocked by the reach of his effort: the language isn't only alive and well, it is actually quite different from what he envisioned. It borrows easily from English, Russian, and Arabic. It has done the same with Yiddish, which, by the way, Ben Yehuda thoroughly despised, because in his mind it represented the awkward, primitive, undesirable side of Jewishness: diasporic, that is, non-national. Yet, in stunning ways, Hebrew, spoken by 8.5 million in Israel, including Arabs, and about four million elsewhere, is diasporic. It is spoken in the world, not only in Israel; it is without boundaries.

At the same time, the number of Hebrew speakers remains minuscule by all accounts. Mandarin, for instance, is the language of one billion. Hebrew is not even widespread enough to be the Jewish language par excellence nowadays, because Jews, by some estimates, amount to fifteen million. Is it nonetheless the tongue shared by most Jews today? My instinct tells me English holds that place. This debate on demographics is, inevitably, also a debate on ownership. Who among mortals owns the Hebrew language? The answer depends on whom you ask. To some religious fanatics, it is theirs and theirs alone. Eighteen percent of Arabs in Israel list Arabic as their native—and primary—language, and they total almost a million, although 60 percent of them have a good understanding of Hebrew. Anton Shammas and A. B. Yehoshua were part of a heated discussion rotating around a simple question: Who owns the Hebrew language? The answer, in my view, is straightforward: its speakers, whoever and wherever they might be—including, of course, Israeli Arabs. I need to emphasize this because xenophobia in Israel comes in many shapes. Shammas, the author of *Arabesques*, is Agnonian in style, and Agnon abounds in biblical and Talmudic references, so I'm talking about echoes of echoes of echoes . . . One also hears Hebrew in Buenos Aires, Riyadh, and Los Angeles, often among natives, always among tourists. The same might be said for English: Who owns it? Not only Shakespeare, not only Samuel Johnson, not only George Bernard Shaw, but anyone who wants to use it—even those people who abuse the language, including the millions of non-native speakers who, in an effort to communicate, turn its morphology upside down.

Granted, Hebrew occupies a bizarre place in the contemporary imagination, and here I am referring to that quotation by Mark Twain I mentioned earlier about the dark side of the moon. Not only for non-Jews but for Jews as well, Hebrew invokes an assortment of emotions: disgust as well as admiration. It is ugly in that it is associated with destruction, devastation, and death. Israeli soldiers, let us never forget, use it as a language of occupation. Its sounds are the cause of suffering. I remember reading an opinion piece in the *New York Times* by Hans Magnus Enzensberger in which he described the shock he felt upon realizing the perceptions Americans had of the German language. This was in the 1990s, some fifty years after the end of the Second World War. Turning on the TV, Enzensberger invariably came across depictions of Nazis giving orders in a merciless guttural tone. Although German and Germany had evolved dramatically since 1945, in popular culture the German language remained somehow fossilized in the war period. My impression of what has happened to Hebrew is along the same lines. Ubiquitous almost everywhere in the world, Hebrew is frequently present on TV screens as the language in the mouths of faceless Israeli soldiers killing enraged Palestinians, as well as the language of hard-hearted politicians justifying those actions. In other words, Hebrew is the language of grief, anguish, and misery, the language that executes commands resulting in murder.

When I followed Ben Yehuda's odyssey, I came across this view of Hebrew, and not only among Arabs. Honestly, I don't know if there is an antidote to it: Israel is at once a polarized and a polarizing nation. Nothing in it or about it comes easy. Not to speak out against xenophobia, against oppression, against destruction is to be complicit. For many non-Hebrew speakers around the globe, Hebrew is perceived as lethal. They latch onto widely disseminated images of violent Israeli soldiers. These aren't only the images propagated by Hamas, Hezbollah, Al-Qaeda, and Isis. I am talking also of scenes of Palestinians disenfranchised with Israeli society. And yet it is, as I mentioned before, the attitude of "Like Greek to me." It is a pity that this media stimulation, real as it is, doesn't allow for a counter side. For Hebrew is also the vehicle of Shaul Tchernichovsky, Yehuda Amichai, David Grossman, Ronit Elkabetz, and Etgar Keret. Looking at only one side of the language misses out on its splendorous beauty. Plus, a solely negative view of the language bypasses the fact that Hebrew gestures toward the unknown, the things that are divine, beyond human comprehension, things that precede and follow our passing through this planet.

In this regard, Hebrew for Jews no doubt is linked to the act—and art—of dying, but not in a negative way, but rather in a positive, sustaining, affirming way. Hebrew is important at life's end, as a formula of acceptance, in *Baruch Dayan Haemet*, upon hearing news of a death; and comfort, *Hamakom Yenachem Etchem*, upon greeting a mourner, the one left after the death. It is also in the *Kaddish*, the mourner's prayer, repeated time and again on one's own and in religious services, often to say farewell to those we love. As such, it is featured in *Morirse está en hebreo*. The word "kaddish," it should be noted, is Aramaic for "holy," and, in fact, most of the prayer is in Aramaic too—a fact again indicating how Hebrew developed in contact with other languages. *Furthermore, Hebrew is the language tied in with the entire cycle of life. It is used* at the beginning of life: in *brit milahs*, in *bnei mitzvahs*, in the liturgy of Shabbat, at the outset of the year in Rosh Hashanah and as Jews atone at Yom Kippur and pray to have their names inscribed in the Book of Life *that, according to the Talmud, purportedly will be spoken when the Messiah comes. It holds the promise of redemption.*

In East Los Angeles, I once came across an endearing bumper sticker. It read: "Monolingualism is curable." Knowing only one language means living in a rather tight environment. By tight, I mean asphyxiating. Different languages represent different horizons. Opening oneself to them is developing a more capacious understanding of things. Wittgenstein is right: the limits of my language are the limits of my world. And George Orwell is also right: language corrupts thought, just as thought corrupts language. To go outside one's language, to see it from a distance, is to understand its limitations. At any rate, the condition of Jews is polyglotic. I rejoice in that quality. Jewish languages are used intra-ethnically, among Jews to distinguish themselves from others. But Jews have always spoken other languages too, often a plethora of them, to communicate with the environment. It is the American Jewish diaspora, bizarrely, that is, in comparison with all others, frighteningly monolingual. Is this the end of multilingualism? I hope not.

At any rate, I'm eager to go beyond the way outsiders see Hebrew as well as how insiders overromanticize it as a language of survival, of endurance, of sacrifice. It is all that, it's true, just as it violent, abusive, and inclement. Going beyond includes acknowledging these contradictory facets. In this regard, the story of the Tower of Babel (Genesis 11:1–9), with its tensions between one language and many, exerts enormous fascination for me. I have reread it compulsively over many years, like a riddle I'm trying to sort out. No sooner do I think I have come to understand it, to appreciate all its implications, than it comes back to me unencumbered. Just like the Hebrew language, as I explain further on, in my mind there is an up and a down to this Babel chapter of the Bible. The King James Version—still my favorite translation—begins with an emblematic statement: "And the whole earth was of one language, and of one speech." Then the people, called the children of men, decide to make brick and they build a city with a tower. Their purpose is clear: they want the top of the tower to reach to heaven so they can make themselves a name, "lest we be scattered abroad upon the face of the whole earth." So they go up. But then the narrative is about going down. First God comes down to see the city and the tower. And God says, "Behold, the people is one, and they have all one language; and this they begin to do: and now nothing will be restrained from them, which they have imagined to do." The statement is enigmatic. God, it seems to me, feels threatened. I might call this the threat of unity. God sees that the people are one, that is, that they are unified. Their unity is based on their having a single language. Through this single language they have now built a city and a tower. What will they do next, God ponders?

As in other cases in Genesis, God is referred to as plural. Line 7 reads: "Go to, let us go down, and there confound their language, that they may not understand one another's speech." The fact that God says "let us go down" shows that God, like the people building the city and the tower, is a plurality, one referred to by the pronoun "we." It is a truth universally accepted that the Hebrew God, the God of the Hebrew Bible, began in the Near East, in Mesopotamia, Phoenicia, and Egypt, as a sum. That is, Yahweh, the God in the chapter devoted to the Tower of Babel, isn't a one but a many; or better, a multiplicity on the road to become one. And that many is vulnerable by the people, also a many who, in their effort to reach the heavens, appear to this deity as a unified threat. The way to disband that threat is to smash that single, unified, universal language into a million little pieces. In other words, from the one language humankind had on the way up, there are many on the way down. And what was that universal language? Are we invited to infer that a universal language meant harmony among humankind? Or is the fact that the people building the city and the tower are ambitious, eager to reach the heavens, a testament to their disharmony? The way the narrative is presented, this desire to reach the divine throne, suggests that now, in the words of the Bible, "nothing will be restrained from them." What follows, in this quote, is emblematic: "which they have imagined to do." Human imagination, therefore, is limitless. That limitlessness must be understood as a form of theodicy. The next lines, 8-9, read in KJV: "So the LORD scattered them abroad from thence upon the face of all the earth: and they left off to build the city. Therefore is the name of it called Babel; because the LORD did there confound the language of all the earth: and from thence did the LORD scatter them abroad upon the face of all the earth." Appropriately, the word *babel* has come to mean "to confound."

Thereafter, the people stop the architectural effort: no more city, no more tower. On their way down, they are inflicted with a disease called polyglotism, with which they live forever on the planet. For me there is an irony in this—and I'm sure I'm not alone—because multilingualism is an asset: the more languages we speak, the ampler our perspective becomes. Yet the chapter on the Tower of Babel makes multilingualism a punishment: we shall speak countless languages in order for humankind not to understand itself. This up and down of the narrative to me is curious: to God's unhappiness, we are content with a universal language on the way up; on the way down, we are humbled by pride, our egotism, and haughtiness, but now God is satisfied. Linguists often don't like to think in geographic terms because there is nothing scientific in these coordinates then. Yet to me the coordinates point to a general hierarchy of languages that is, inevitably, about connections between humans and nature, humans and time, humans and death. What was the universal language spoken on the way up? Was it Hebrew, the language that the mystics say preceded creation? Or perhaps French? Voltaire, in an oft-quoted letter to Catherine the Great, wrote: "I am not like a lady at the court of Versailles, who said: 'What a great shame that the bother at the tower of Babel should have got language all mixed up; but for that, everyone would always have spoken French.'" Every language with global aspirations has the same attitude. Latin, during the Byzantine Empire, was thought to be the language of eternity. Along this line, an American superintendent once argued: 'If English is good enough for Jesus, is it not good enough for me?'"

Facetiously, I sometimes imagine myself as part of the generation that went up the Tower of Babel and then came down. We built the ziggurat in Mesopotamia. Its architecture looked like what Pieter Bruegel the Elder or Gustave Doré visualized: Roman arches swirling to the top. It is an emblem of the eternal city. But its collapse announces the vanity of human affairs. We all speak the same language—is it Hebrew?—as we build it up. And then, kaboom!, the curse falls on us. Nobody understands each other anymore. Things become transient. As everyone disperses, a plurality of languages spreads to the planet. Am I unhappy? Yes, I have lost my Hebrew. Am I pleased? Yes again, I have a gathering of other tongues. But—and herein the bonus—Hebrew is among them: the original tongue doesn't disappear; it simply makes room for others. This is because Hebrew isn't a pure, unsullied, sacred tongue, but a language that has changed over time, coming into contact and blending with other languages. And it is all the richer for it.

I come now to the home stretch of this attempt at reappraising my relationship—intimate, contradictory, feverish—with this language I wholeheartedly adore, just as I'm frequently dismayed by some of the troubling scenes in which it finds itself today. Ben Yehuda said that were he not a believer in the redemption of the Jewish people, he would have discarded Hebrew as a useless impediment. A useless impediment: I'm fifty-five years old now, and I don't believe in an afterlife: the end is the end is the end . . . I fell in love with utopian movements in my youth but have learned better with age. I have switched tongues a few times in my journey, shedding some, acquiring others. I have also spent a generous portion of my time thinking about words: what they mean, how they become current, and why they die. I love Hebrew profusely. I love its symbolism, its endurance. I love the fact that it isn't horizontal like other languages—that is, a tongue to use among mortals—but more so because it is vertical in that it connects us with the higher spheres, a door to the spiritual. I am dismayed by the fact that Hebrew, to its enemies, implies death. Actually, I hate that "it has enemies," as an activist told me in Gaza. How can a language have enemies? Hebrew is at once sacred and profane, pure and messy, peaceful and violent, the language of freedom and the language of occupation, the language of the Promised Land and the language of the diaspora: universal and particular, all-embracing and intolerant, prejudiced, and chauvinistic. It is a language that makes me see the world in 3-D.

I'm another visitor to this castle of memory. Baudelaire is right: to handle a language properly, one needs to be a magician. I'm not only referring to how deeply one knows it and how eloquently one is able to use it. I'm also thinking of the way one approaches it in more abstract terms, metaphysically even. To succeed in life is to leave the fortress a bit better, whether through education, writing a book, or helping others breathe easier somehow. When I die, Hebrew will accompany me in my departure. It has been an instrument of the redemption of the Jewish people, but that redemption still tarries. Dante, in *De vulgari eloquentia*, believed Hebrew was "the language which the lips of the first speaker formed." I trust it will be in the last speaker's lips too.

THE READING LIFE OF RICARDO PIGLIA

"Do not read, as children do, to amuse yourself;
or like the ambitious, for the purpose of instruction.
No, read in order to live."

—Gustave Flaubert

Ricardo Piglia was an assiduous reader, that most embattled of today's pastimes. (I was about to say "professions," but held my breath before the faux pas.) He published a book called *The Last Reader* (2005), in which he celebrated not speed in reading, as is often done in schools, but slowness. In the epilogue, he quoted a line from Wittgenstein: "In *philosophy* the *winner* of the *race* is *the one who* can *run* most *slowly*. Or: *the one who* gets there last." Piglia called sharp readers "private eyes," in honor of his obsession with detective fiction, the style in which he wrote most of his work. (He loved W. R. Burnett's *The Asphalt Jungle*, James M. Cain's *The Postman Always Rings Twice*, and Dashiell Hammett's *The Dain Curse*.) He often invoked a famous photograph of Borges, who became blind in his thirties, taken while he was director of Argentina's Biblioteca Nacional, holding a book a few inches from his nose. Borges said: "I am now a reader of pages my eyes cannot see." Piglia writes: "A reader is also one who misreads, distorts, perceives things confusingly." For him, it is important to do it idiosyncratically, against the current, at one's own range. In fact, what he cherished most was rereading, the drive to return to a book one already navigated through, in order "to be at its edge," that is, to find out that everything—every act, every thought, every dream—is part of a narrative.

A cornerstone of contemporary Latin American letters, he taught at Princeton until he moved back to Argentina after he was diagnosed with

---

Introduction to *The Diaries of Emilio Renzi*, vol. 1: *Formative Years*, by Ricardo Piglia (Brooklyn, NY: Restless Books, 2017).

amyotrophic lateral sclerosis, known as Lou Gehrig's disease, of which he ultimately died on January 6, 2017, at the age of seventy-five. He didn't only spend his entire life reading; he also invested a prodigious amount of time writing about it: his education; his relationship with his grandfather Emilio; the upheaval of Peronismo; his early attempts at writing, publishing, and teaching; as well as his responses to favorite books, especially Argentine classics (Macedonio Fernández, Roberto Arlt, Borges, Julio Cortázar, Manuel Puig, and Juan José Saer); his thrill at cautiously mapping various national traditions (American, Italian, Polish . . .); and his fascination with the *rezeptionsgeschichte* of certain authors (Joyce, Kafka, Faulkner, and Dostoyevsky).

Piglia identified himself as a critic who writes and as a writer who critiques. Actually, he believed that "criticism is a modern form of autobiography." He wrote stories, novels, operas, screenplays, and several volumes of essays (including *Criticism and Fiction* [1986], *Brief Forms* [2000], and *North American Authors* [2016]). Yet his most enduring effort, the one likely to get him a place in posterity, is the 327 notebooks he crafted, day in and day out between 1957 and 2015, in which he imagined himself not as Ricardo Piglia but, switching from the first to the third person and back, as his alter ego, Emilio Renzi. This generates a sense of alienation, wonderment, and displacement. The first volume starts: "'Ever since I was a boy, I've repeated what I don't understand,' laughed Emilio Renzi that afternoon, retrospective and radiant, in the bar on Arenales and Riobamba. 'We are amused by the unfamiliar; we enjoy the things we cannot explain.'"

In the *Symposium*, Aristophanes, who is Plato's mouthpiece, suggests that each human individual is made of two halves. At birth, these halves are divided, resulting in the vertigo and sense of incompletion that defines us as humans. This division is solved through love's quest of "finding the other half." In the case of Piglia, his solution came through fictionalization: the chronicling of his life as if it belonged to *el otro*, the other, that is, to Renzi. This strategy is often called "autofiction." *The Diaries of Emilio Renzi: Formative Years* is not a loyal distillation of what Piglia experienced, but a re-creation, maybe even a revision. He started the notebooks just as the pseudonym Emilio Renzi began to materialize. It isn't surprising that Piglia loved other people's diaries. There are reactions to a handful of them—by Goethe, Stendhal, Flaubert, Kafka, Woolf, Gadda, and Pavese—spread throughout the volumes. What attracts him in them, it seems, is that adulterated mode called "fictionalized autobiography." In that regard, *The Diaries of Emilio Renzi* is Latin America's response to Karl Ove Knausgaard's Scandinavian *My Struggle*. Yet Piglia's "autofiction" is different: the notebooks aren't a fait accompli but an experiment. In them the reader catches Renzi in an ongoing state of gestation, writing, as he himself puts it, "an imaginary version of myself." In the end, he catches himself as a palimpsest, made of evanescent stories that are "told over and over again, and through telling them and repeating them they improve, are refined like pebbles honed by water in the depths of rivers."

The name Emilio Renzi itself isn't arbitrary: Piglia's birth name was Ricardo Emilio Piglia Renzi. Emilio Renzi is the name he signed to his first publications. It is also the name of the detective in a number of his books, from *Artificial Respiration* (1980) to *Burnt Money* (1997) to *One-Way Road* (2013). These, however, are somehow tangential paths to appreciate Renzi's plight. The notebooks are his true habitat. In them his *argentinidad*, indeed his *latinoamericanidad*, come to full view. How can one write about Argentina?, Renzi wonders at some point. His answer is complex. It isn't the content of a book that makes it Argentine, because the Argentine writer is able to write about anything. So what is it? "We write our books, publish them," Renzi posits. "We are left to live, we have our circles, our audience . . . To say it another way, everything must be centered around the use of language. In this way, the content will have different effects. The subject does not matter so much as the particular type of structure and circulation of our works."

In a conversation with Roberto Bolaño in the Spanish newspaper *El País* in 2001, Piglia describes *Latin Americanism*, the identity of Latin Americans, as made of misbegotten dictators and clairvoyant prostitutes, "a kind of anti-intellectualism that tends toward simplifying everything, and which many of us resist." Bolaño responds that, "to our disgrace, we continue to be Latin Americans," and he argues that such condition is "the result of economic and political forces." Intriguingly, the two were disruptors, rather than endorsers, of this condition. Their fiction is a commentary on the merchandizing of stereotypes. Disruption for them meant laughing at how Latin America is exported abroad: a tropical, half-baked, exuberant landscape that is at once magical and anti-European. Like Bolaño, Piglia plotted that disruption meticulously. Aware of his end, he devoted his remaining years, from 2011 to the end, to adapting the 327 notebooks into three ample volumes and seeing them into publication. The first appeared in the Spanish-speaking world in 2015 and covers Renzi's "formative years," from 1957 to 1967. The second volume, going from 1968 to 1975, is called "the happy years" and was released in 2016. And the third, from 1975 to 2015, "one day in the life," was published in 2017. Every single aspect of him is explored in detail "as if through the veil," that is, though Renzi. He served as filter, intermediary, and perhaps also as demiurge.

Call them *Portrait of the Writer as Invention*. Rumors about the publication of the three volumes circulated for a while before they were released. In the Spanish-speaking world, they were greeted with enormous enthusiasm, a sign of Piglia's status as a canonical voice. In them Renzi isn't an empiricist like Hume. (He is closer to Spinoza.) His interest isn't in reality itself, but in the ways the brain imagines it. In *The Diaries of Emilio Renzi*, we witness Renzi's thinking process, his anxieties, his response to crucial actors in his life (for instance, his tyrannical father), even the way he constantly mucks his own seriousness—"I'm a trickster!," he enjoys saying. David Foster Wallace argued that fiction is where loneliness is not only confronted and relieved but also "countenanced, stared down, transfigured, and treated." In *The Diaries of Emilio Renzi*, Renzi articulates his principles as he faces his own boredom: his inaction at the platitudes he encounters, his restlessness with his own views. A descendent of Italian immigrants—and immigrants are forcibly aware of the division of selves—Piglia was born in Androgué, in the south of Buenos Aires. The family eventually moved to Mar del Plata, and in 1965, Piglia, by then already a passionate reader, returned to Buenos Aires on his own. "It is what you read when you don't have to," Oscar Wilde said, "that determines what you will be when you can't help it." Like many in his generation, he eventually found Borges, who in turn opened up Argentine letters in full. At one point, laughing in the afternoon in a bar on Arenales and Riobamba, Renzi says: "We lived in a quiet neighborhood, close to the railway station, and every half hour the passengers who had arrived on the train from the capital passed before us. And I was there, on the threshold, making myself look, when suddenly a long shadow leaned over me and said I was holding the book upside down. I think it must have been Borges . . . He used to spend the summers in Las Delicias Hotel back then, because who but old Borges would think of telling off a three-year-old boy like that?"

Renzi meets Borges during his student years. "He had an immediate and warm way of creating intimacy, Borges," he exclaims. "He was always that way with everyone he talked to: he was blind, he did not see them and always spoke to them as if they were near, and that closeness is in his texts, he is never patronizing and gives no air of superiority, he addresses everyone as if they were more intelligent than he, with so much common understatement that he has no need to explain what is already known. And it is that intimacy that his readers sense." If one doesn't know how to distill his work, Renzi argues, Borges's influence on others—and Cortázar's, too—becomes "a plague." Yet it is Borges who tells Renzi that "writing, he was telling me, changes the way of reading above all." Indeed, such was the allure of the author of "The Aleph" that much of Renzi's readings are built as a digression on Borges's ideas. He writes about him profusely. This fascination culminated in 2013, when *el otro*, Piglia, presented a cycle of four lectures on Borges in TV Pública, Argentina's public television. (Borges wrote a famous essay that starts: "Al otro, a Borges, es a quien le ocurren las cosas." The other one, Borges, is to whom things happen.)

One of the most emblematic images in literature connected with reading appears in *Hamlet*, Act II, Scene 2. It comes after the Danish prince meets the ghost of his father for the first time. It is in the form of a stage direction. Shakespeare states: "Enter HAMLET reading on a book." We aren't told what book Hamlet reads, only that he is reading one. This is symptomatic: having communicated with the dead, Hamlet is now in the world of signs. This universe of signs is at the core of the Hispanic world, which is itself populated with books about reading. At the core of that shelf is, of course, *Don Quixote*, where the brains of the protagonist dry up as a result of his insatiable thirst for chivalry novels. In the Second Part of the novel, the protagonists come across characters who have read the First Part. And in Chapter V, the priest and the barber enter Alonso Quijano's personal library and offer an array of comments on various books, including one by Cervantes. Likewise, in *One Hundred Years of Solitude*, in the concluding section, a Buendía descendant comes across the scrolls that tell the entire history of the family. And then there is Borges, who in an "Autobiographical Essay" published in *The New Yorker* in 1970 said that everyone imagines paradise in his own way and that for him, for Borges, it wasn't a garden but a library.

Piglia's oeuvre aims at that same insistence: living is reading and vice versa. In photos we have of him he is always caught looking at a book, his thick glasses at center stage, or else toying with a magnifying glass, or—and here's the trickster again!—giving the viewer (i.e., the reader) the middle finger. Clearly, reading isn't a metaphor for him. In fact, in *The Last Reader*, he argues that the history of Argentina isn't only the history of the struggle between civilization and barbarism, as Domingo Faustino Sarmiento posited in *Facundo*, but between looking at the world as sheer chaos or as decipherable order. He also contends that the task of the critic is to decode it as a constellation of symbols, which for him means that Argentines become citizens of their nation through the act of reading.

Piglia's apology of reading doesn't turn him into a hero whose mission it is to salvage an entire civilization, like Guy Montag and Clarisse McClellan in *Fahrenheit 451*. His quest is at once simpler and more complex: it is a defense of self-conscious.

ADIÓS, CHESPIRITO

I first came to grips with the true power of television when, in the late 1970s in my native Mexico, my father had a couple of guest appearances on the astoundingly popular TV variety show *Chespirito*. I was used to the fact that, as a soap opera actor in demand, my father would occasionally be stopped on the street for an autograph. If he played a principal character, people would even connect him personally to whatever traits that character had. If a villain, people would harass him; if a hero, he would suddenly hear applause as he walked by.

But, as I remember it, at no time was my father more besieged than when he played an amusement park owner in *Chespirito*. He would be seated in a restaurant without delay. Groups of people would ask him to take a picture with them. And at the bank where he did his business, the manager told him never to wait in line. I even remember an old lady coming up to him at a grocery store in tears, telling him he had been saved by Jesus Christ because of the amusement park owner's connection to one character in the program, El Chavo.

Chespirito featured rotating sketches, some of whose characters were later spun off into separate shows; El Chavo was the protagonist of *El Chavo del Ocho* (The Boy From No. 8); another sketch revolved around a character named Chespirito. All the leads were played by the show's creator, Roberto Gómez Bolaños, who died on November 28, 2014, in Cancún, at the age of eighty-five, and who was nicknamed Chespirito—"Little Shakespeare"—in real life.

The names of all these lead characters started with "Ch": El Doctor Chapatín (Doctor Chapatín) and El Chapulín Colorado (The Crimson Grasshopper). At a time when American TV shows, dubbed into Spanish, were already the talk of the town, *Chespirito* was fully—and truly—Mexican,

---

First published in the *New York Times*, December 5, 2014.

albeit in bizarre, unexplored ways. It was about being a homeless kid with a limited vocabulary in a poor neighborhood, or about becoming a humble superhero in an age when Batman and Superman were quintessential icons.

Chespirito aired from 1971 to 1992. To this day, it is watched by millions in syndication (from which I get no income). Not only was it a fixture of my upbringing, but it also shaped that of scores of my students. There have been all sorts of spinoffs of the show, including a weekly comic strip and an animated TV version. The faces of Chespirito, La Chilindrina, El Profesor Jirafales, La Mococha Pechocha, and its other characters still appear on T-shirts, sandals, and lunchboxes. For years I had an action figure of El Chavo on my office desk. Sentences in the show have become fixtures of speech. There are online encyclopedias devoted to it.

Interestingly, the content of the show is utterly apolitical. That, it strikes me, is probably why Televisa, the Mexican media conglomerate often seen as a mouthpiece of the Institutional Revolutionary Party (PRI), Mexico's ruling party from 1929 to 2000, endorsed it without reservations. It never directly addressed issues like violence. Nor did it talk about drugs, abortion, or homosexuality. Its repertoire overflowed with stereotypes like the crying girl, the fat real estate developer, and the goofy teacher. In short, its content was docile, even anodyne in the milieu of its time. And although it might have been lowbrow, it was never of low taste. It humanized its characters with a sense of humor that was accessible to all social classes. No wonder my father felt immortalized by it.

It is fitting that right now, when Mexico seems to have become one of the antechambers of Dante's hell—pushed to the brink of chaos by the presumed murders of forty-three innocent students who disappeared on September 26 in the town of Iguala—a comedian who entertained audiences by ignoring the obvious was bid farewell with unreserved devotion. Indeed, instead of placing Roberto Gómez Bolaños's body at the Palacio de Bellas Artes, as President Enrique Peña Nieto ordered when Gabriel García Márquez died, the actor's body was displayed in the legendary Estadio Azteca, the country's most important soccer stadium. There thousands of followers, dressed up as El Chavo and El Chapulín, danced around him. A champion of the masses had returned to his origins.

The nickname "Chespirito" was a nod to Mr. Gómez Bolaños's apparently inexhaustible capacity to create stories. But it also points to his universality, which I came to understand only after I left Mexico in 1985 and immigrated to the United States. My point of entry was New York City. Upon my arrival, I sought a place among other Spanish speakers. Soon I realized there was no such thing as a "Latino," at least not yet. We were all still Mexicans, Dominicans, Puerto Ricans, Cubans, and so on—members of different countries who ate different food, danced to different rhythms, and used the Spanish language in subtly different ways.

With time, I came to understand that what united us all was neither geography nor history but popular culture. A number of undisputed kings of our imagination transcended national backgrounds, among them the freedom fighter Che Guevara, the poet Pablo Neruda, the comedian Cantinflas, and, yes, the TV star Chespirito. Whenever a Spanish speaker found out I was Mexican, he would manage to insert in the conversation the sentence "¡Síganme los buenos!"—"Follow me, good guys!"—uttered by El Chapulín as he readies himself for another adventure. And if by chance I responded by confessing that my father had been part of the Chespirito cadre, the love I would immediately receive would be palpable.

In truth, Chespirito is no longer only Mexican. He has become a symbol of the Hispanic middle class, no matter where it is.

PART IV

ON *FÚTBOL*

"SUDDEN DEATH"

I love the expression "sudden death." It refers to a FIFA tiebreaking rule last used in 2002, when South Korea and Japan hosted the World Cup, but most of the matches in this year's El Mundial, as the games are known to Spanish-language viewers of Univision, all felt like sudden death, at least in the round of sixteen, which concluded Tuesday. (By the way, Univision's newscast has been far superior to ESPN's, at least at the level of wordplay.) The Netherlands-Mexico match was a nail-biter (I'm Mexican!), as was Costa Rica versus Greece. Watching these games is like reading a superb thriller: tension is high, and time seems to stand still.

Like much of the rest of humanity (according to various sources, half of the globe's population is tuning in), I wait—patiently!—four years for this fiesta. This one in Brazil is among the best I've seen, and I'm watching every minute of it. This is the life for an academic: finding ideas even in leisure. To study what? The way Brazilians throw a party? Whether countries' uniform styles, or their varied goal celebrations, reflect ethnic and nationalistic identities?

Seriously, the World Cup provides a range of topics for scholars to consider: Governance. Economics. Justice and morality. Theater. Masculinity. Not to mention the layers of meaning in carnival, *carnaval do futebol* in Portuguese. Let me ponder them one by one:

Governance. There may be twenty-two players on the field, but only one person matters in a game, and it isn't one of the players. It is the referee. He is the judge, the pardoner, the decider. Teams compete to score the most goals, but they also work on the ref. He might be objective. But you know—everyone does—that there is no such thing as objectivity.

The ref's authority is bestowed on him by FIFA, world football's governing body. To participate, all parties must adhere to its rules. It is a true international body, like the UN, the EU, or the Group of Eight. Unlike

---

First published in *The Chronicle of Higher Education*, July 2, 2014.

in those entities, however, no single country exerts more power, or more influence, than another over FIFA. That makes the World Cup illustrious. This is a stage in which small nations like Chile (population 17.5 million) are as important as France (65.7 million), Russia (143.5 million), and the United States (313.9 million). They all abide by the same rules. They dress the same way. They play the same number of games. Is this a model for global equality, or what? Obviously, finding a champion, whose reign lasts for four years, is the purpose. But what does being the winner mean? *Nada*, really. It is about reputation, not control.

FIFA is often criticized for being corrupt. And it is. The controversy over the Qatar games in 2022 is proof. Governance is never pure. Yet the World Cup is the best example I know of authentic, peaceful coexistence at the global level. Plus, as I wrote recently in *the New Republic*, the World Cup is God's way of teaching people geography, getting us out of our cocoons—making us realize, as E.T. suggested, that, yep, we aren't alone.

Economics. We might think the World Cup is all grand spectacle, but it is also a marketplace of ability. Established players already play in La Liga, the Premier League, and on other important stages. Younger talent makes a splash, hoping to command top dollar, while high-end scouts appreciate—and, when needed, depreciate—those players' value.

"Value" is the crucial word. What we see is worth money. Not only on the field. The host nation capitalizes on its investment by bringing tourists from everywhere. Billions are spent on broadcasting. The Brazilian smiles on the TV screen are lessons in joie de vivre. But value is also measured in spiritual power. Are the spirits favoring one team or the other? What voodoo practices must be performed to motivate a higher force to bring down an opponent? The value of certain religious practices thus is critical, showcasing how the material and spiritual realms are intertwined.

Justice and morality. Some games are Shakespearean. Like when Zinedine Zidane of France head butted the Italian player Marco Materazzi in the 2006 final for insulting his sister—clearly, there is one thing more important than winning a World Cup, and that is honor. Or in the Uruguay-Ghana match of 2010, when Luis Suárez of Uruguay stopped a strike by Ghana with his hand. The goal would have eliminated Uruguay. Suárez was expelled, and Ghana got a penalty kick. But the striker missed, making Suárez a hero.

Real life isn't fair. Neither is soccer. Moral decisions make each game a battle between good and evil. How do players reach a decision? Is it possible to balance reason and impulse?

Suárez was suspended before for biting an Italian player. That is the third time he has engaged in such unsportsmanlike behavior, and he was punished the previous two times. He now has been banned from four months of play in FIFA matches. Suárez, in my view, suffers from mental illness. The biting wasn't designed to push the game in a particular direction. He simply lost control. On the surface, his action doesn't have much to do with morality. If he does warrant a psychiatric diagnosis, perhaps FIFA should use the incident to alert fans about the mental anguish players face during a match. Óscar Tabárez, the Uruguayan coach, bitterly complained after the incident, saying "this is about football, not about morality." Most of the world did see it as immoral, or at least uncivilized. Yet Uruguayan fans agreed with Tabárez, saying—in a paranoid mode—that FIFA was after them.

The World Cup is like a Dostoyevsky novel. When is a sinner an actual sinner? Is defending one's honor as justified as Raskolnikov's killing of Alyona Ivanovna, an abusive old moneylender?

Theater. A graduate student could write a dissertation on the dramatic talents of World Cup players. Most must have taken a course, not only in pantomime but also in melodrama. I haven't seen any statistics, but the number of histrionic dives in the tournament seems considerably higher than in previous World Cups.

The king of them all—a veritable master of the art of pretending to suffer—is the Netherlands striker Arjen Robben. In the Netherlands-Mexico match, he worked the ref, Pedro Proença of Portugal, to exhaustion—until he finally got what he wanted: a penalty kick at a crucial point. Lo and behold, Holland converted it into a 2–1 win.

Americans dislike the theatrics, and, believe me, Mexicans were unhappy with Robben's action. But life, like I said, is a spectacle, and *fútbol*, as Hamlet said of poetry, "holds the mirror up to nature, to show virtue her own feature."

Masculinity. Where else does one see twenty-five vigorous males on the field (counting the three referees) for an hour and a half, all in short pants, running, kicking, jumping, touching each other, doing all sorts of pirouettes, and competing to see who puts the ball in the net more often? None of these men is accused of being gay—not even Ronaldo, the Portuguese superstar, who loves taking his shirt off after scoring a goal and flexing his muscles. Are gender boundaries more flexible during the World Cup?

Subversion. Stereotypes are a dime a dozen in El Mundial. To start with, nationalism is pushed to its limit. Just look at the stands. Fans, scores of them, dress in their country's flags, their faces plastered with the colors. They scream and shout patriotic slogans, cursing other nations. I cannot think of another forum where nationalism is as excessive. It is all in the spirit of partying, of course. And, in that context, becoming a stereotype is useful. Colombians show up as coffee makers, Mexicans as mariachis and Frida Kahlos; the Greeks come in togas, Italians as Luciano Pavarottis; Americans dress like Uncle Sam. Everything you ever hated about your own background is now beyond criticism. What does this say about respect and intellectual freedom? A lot. For the World Cup—and the one in Brazil for sure—is, as I mentioned, a *carnaval*, meaning it embraces subversion, turning it into a commodity. You can say whatever you want during those five weeks, you can pretend to be who you're not, you can cry in public, as long as it is done in an atmosphere of camaraderie.

The role of social media is more important than in the past. Every match prompts endless tweets. The email conversations I have with friends around the globe are inspiring. Every major incident on the TV screen is accompanied by images Photoshopped in a matter of seconds, as when Memo Ochoa, the Mexican goalie, stopped an onslaught of attacks from Brazil and Holland. I received his image superimposed on the Corcovado, atop which stands the legendary statue of Christ the Redeemer in Rio de Janeiro. Or superimposed on a portrait of Neo in *The Matrix*.

Frankly, we academics are boring in comparison! We aren't used to this much excitement, to the "sudden death"–like drama. El Mundial is fertile ground for academic, not to mention classroom, reflection. Let us wake up from our stupor and turn to this raw material.

VAN PERSIE'S GOAL

I am sure there will be a few memorable goals during the rest of the World Cup—we're only on day three—but the one scored by Robin van Persie of Holland against Spain to tie the game justifies the entire tournament. Those of us who wait four years for this *fiesta de fútbol* so that moments such as these might nourish us know full well they are few and far between. This one came early and might not be surpassed.

I searched the web for the best words to describe the goal—in any language—but came away empty-handed. That might be because beauty, when encountered in pure, unadulterated form, is inexpressible. At first I thought van Persie's movements were those of a ballet dancer at the height of his form. Yet his actions looked less human than birdlike. He looked like a seagull floating over ocean waves, patiently reaching for its catch. Daley Blind made the forty-yard pass in the forty-third minute. The ball was suspended in midair for what seemed like an eternity. When it finally reached him, van Persie's body acquired enviable plasticity. It undulated and, with a soft touch of the head, he made the ball jump over Iker Casillas and go into the net, which reacted by shaking as stylishly as the player had a second before. The Spanish goalie seemed stunned—like the rest of us—by the ease of the entire performance.

The fact that Casillas was about to beat the record of the most minutes without conceding a goal in international games (Walter Zenga held it for 517 minutes; Casillas had 433) makes the episode all the more spectacular. Of course, Holland went on to score four more times, utterly humiliating Spain. Maybe it is finally scheduled to become the champion it has so often come close to being. For now, though, it is van Persie's sublime execution that is already a triumph beyond compare. Edna St. Vincent Millay was right: beauty is whatever gives joy.

First published in the *New Republic*, June 14, 2014.

BOX OF RESONANCE

Each of the matches at the World Cup is an exercise in baroque self-reflection. One gets the feeling of being trapped in a house of mirrors. Or maybe inside an image by M. C. Escher. On the surface, the twenty-two players, plus their coaches, the subs, and the three refs, have the leading roles in the spectacle. They are the reason we tune in. This, after all, is the biggest stage in the world. It has an audience of billions. Not even the pope reaches that many followers. These actors know that everything they do—every gesture, every noise—is theatrical. The key to a successful act is to be natural. Nature itself, of course, has little to do here, for we are in the realm of artifice, of pretense. When the TV camera focuses on them, the players are trained to ignore it because their task is to look like they are just themselves: casual.

The fans, on the other hand, don't need to be casual; they don't need to pretend. For them, the theatrical aspect of the whole thing isn't about selflessness; on the contrary, they themselves are the epitome of self-awareness, their personalities in performative drive. They know they are watching while being watched. They are eager to see their own images immortalized on the stadium's big screen. This shot automatically makes them famous, albeit for only a few seconds. Not the fifteen minutes Andy Warhol predicted we all would get in the future. Still, a few seconds on this stage is a lifetime of memories.

As for the rest of us, we are remote onlookers, maybe even sheer props. But are we truly that detached? Does our existence matter that little? Beyond the screen, where our mundane existence unravels, soccer fever is explosive. At home, in bars and restaurants, on iPhones, passion is on vibrating mode. We have come to understand that the spectacle isn't exclusive to the stadium, but that, in this reflection inside a reflection, we

---

First published in the *New Republic*, July 1, 2014.

are but characters in a self-referential dream. Maybe this is what Diego Velázquez's *Las Meninas* is about: a painting eternally unfolding onto itself.

"*Futebol* is beautiful!" we proudly say, in unison (in five thousand different languages), as the World Cup gives meaning to the word *simultaneity*.

PART V

LANGUAGE AND POLITICS

TRUMP AND THE WALL

In an emblematic essay called "The Wall and the Books," Borges wrote about Shih Huang Ti (also known as Qin Shi Huang), the Chinese emperor who in 220–206 B.C. built the original Great Wall of China. In his essay Borges points out that the same emperor who implemented the project also banned all books from the kingdom. His intention was clear: the wall was meant to defend his people against enemy incursions; and the burning of all literature announced that all memory of the past needed to be erased. History for Shih Huang Ti started with him.

President Trump is looking more and more like an emperor these days. The decision by his administration to bring down the Spanish-language side of the White House website is an egregious attack against an essential aspect of today's America. And next comes the wall he has ordered along the United States–Mexican border.

Ours, after all, is a multilingual culture. And in the last few decades, the Spanish language unquestionably has become one of the most significant in that plurality. It is the second most used tongue in the land, with about 38 million speakers. In the context of the Hispanic world, Spanish speakers in the United States are the fifth-largest community after Mexico, Colombia, Spain, and Argentina. Such is its ubiquity that calling it foreign no longer seems logical.

The president is nefariously monolingual. At the beginning of the Republican primary, Trump admonished Jeb Bush for speaking in the native tongue of his wife, Columba, a Mexican American. "This is a country where we speak English, not Spanish," he said.

Barack Obama speaks some Indonesian, and George W. Bush is conversational in Spanish. Bill Clinton understands German. The farther back we go in time, the more polyglot our leaders become: Franklin D. Roosevelt spoke French and German, as did his uncle Teddy. The list of United States

---

First published in the *New York Times*, January 30, 2017.

presidents with knowledge of Greek and Latin is substantial. And then there's Thomas Jefferson, who was fluent in Greek and Latin as well as Italian, French, and Spanish. A role model. Or perhaps an endangered species.

Trump is not only among the most limited of this bunch. He also appears to be allergic to foreign languages, especially Spanish. The list of his misuses during the presidential campaign is, in and of itself, infamous, including expressions like "bad hombres."

Sean Spicer, Trump's former press secretary and a man also not known for his subtleties, announced recently that the disappearance of all Spanish is temporary and said technicians are working on updating the content. "It will take awhile longer," he added.

While this is to be hoped, the sheer decision to vanish what was on display during the Obama administration sends a clear signal. This is the same strategy that may be used against Obamacare: first repeal, then . . . we'll see! In other words, discard what's in use in order to start from scratch, on your own terms, as if the past were of little importance.

Under Obama, the White House kept a Spanish-language blog, too. In fact, President Obama himself tweeted en español on January 13: "*Gracias por todo. Mi último pedido es el mismo que el primero. Que creas, no en mi capacidad de crear cambio, sino en la tuya.*" ("Thanks for everything. My last wish is the same as the first. That you believe not in my capacity for change, but in yours.")

Of course, language can thrive in adverse circumstances. Spanish is already a magisterial economic force in the United States. It is the most frequently taught foreign language on college campuses. Likewise, Latinos are the only minority ever to have two full-fledged TV networks in their own immigrant tongue, Univision and Telemundo. Spanish radio is enormously influential in political terms. And I'm referring here only to culture. At the corporate level, investment in the Spanish-language market is among the most vigorous in the nation.

Trump ought to know all this. Yet he feigns ignorance, such is his disdain for Latinos. His team doesn't have a single prominent Latino. He seldom talks of Latin America in his geopolitical plans, except when he talks about Mexico, which he sees as a nest of criminals.

My feeling is that the efforts to suppress Spanish have the opposite effect. It will increasingly be seen as a language of resistance, which will only help its cause. Trump won the election in a crusade against globalization. Now that he is in power, the rationale against isolationism needs to be made even sharper. The Spanish language is the perfect place to start.

From Florida to the Southwest, it is in the substratum of America. A large portion of our land started in Spanish, just as a substantial portion of our population lives in it. Spanish is also a bridge to our southern neighbors. Globalization starts in the kitchen, the classroom, the street—it starts by recognizing our multifaceted heritage in the mirror.

Actually, there is a lesson in the resistance Latin Americans engaged in as they navigated dictatorships in the darkest moments of the twentieth century: it was often through language—in protest songs, storytelling, and poetry—that they kept freedom alive. Thanks to Trump, the Spanish language in the United States has suddenly become a tool of defiance.

Obliterating history and building walls is a common task of emperors.

WHY DOESN'T ENGLISH HAVE AN ACADEMY?

The question routinely becomes a subject of debate. Does English need an institution to safeguard it, or at least to regulate its health? Spanish has the Real Academia Española; French, L'Académie française; Arabic, the Academy of the Arabic Language; Mandarin Chinese, the National Languages Committee; Dutch, the Nederlandse Taalunie; German, the Rat für deutsche Rechtschreibung; Hebrew, the Academy of the Hebrew Language; Irish, the Foras na Gaeilge; Italian, the Accademia della Crusca; and so on. So why doesn't English have its equivalent?

There have been repeated attempts to create an Academy of English, first in England, then in the United States. Intellectuals in England, such as Daniel Defoe and Jonathan Swift, passionately debated the issue, and politicians on this side of the Atlantic, such as John Adams and his son John Quincy Adams, suggested its function ought to be "to collect, interchange, and diffuse literary intelligence; to promote the purity and uniformity of the English language; to invite a correspondence with distinguished scholars in other countries speaking this language in connection with ourselves; to cultivate throughout our extensive territory a friendly intercourse among those who feel an interest in the progress of American literature, and, as far as may depend on well meant endeavors, to aid the general course of learning in the United States."

In an age such as ours, in which immigrants get blamed for not "becoming" Americans as fast, and as consistently, as their predecessors did, the impression prevails that immigrants are the ones not speaking the language as much as howling it. In England, Canada, Australia, and other Anglophone habitats, a similar if less vociferous complaint is heard today:

First published in *The Chronicle of Higher Education*, December 16, 2013.

immigrants ought to be blamed for the general decline of civilization and along with it—of course—the standard of our beloved language. Yet it is immigrants who in the end often uphold the language with more pride. For they came from the outside and thus need to prove their true worth. The effect is similar to the convert to a new religion, who through the conversion process becomes a more knowledgeable, more devout believer than those who were born into the religion. Ironically, it is immigrants like Mary Antin, Vladimir Nabokov, Isaac Bashevis Singer, Frank McCourt, Jhumpa Lahiri, and Junot Diaz, to name only a few in the United States, who at once protect and expand the parameters of the language, making it more elastic, less constrained. A student of mine from Quito, Ecuador, often repeats to me that he prefers English, his adopted tongue, because "it chose me, Profe. So I must honor it."

One might say that in the English-speaking world we have the *Oxford English Dictionary*, *Merriam-Webster*, and other such lexicological organizations. Don't they serve the same role? Not quite, for these entities aren't in the business of decreeing a constitution that establishes the parameters of what is permissible and what isn't. The *OED*, for example, doesn't prescribe what words we use; instead, it describes the way those words change across time and space.

Do we need one, then? Linguistic academies are intimately linked to nationalist ideologies. The Academy of the Hebrew Language came about as the State of Israel consolidated its status as a free country. Centuries earlier, the L'Académie française was established in 1635 by Cardinal Richelieu. The Real Academia Española in Spain opened its doors in 1713 to compete with its neighbor, L'Académie française. It would be preposterous to suggest that we aren't nationalistic because we don't have one. On the contrary, English is vitalized all the time because it is an imperial language: in reaching out, it absorbs influences from various environments. It is said that for every native English speaker today there are between three and four non-natives. This equation signals the pressure felt by those who were born into speaking English. It also points to the buoyancy nurturing it everywhere on the globe.

My own response to the question is *fuhgettaboutit*. For better or worse, the English language is an expression of the democratic values we uphold. In other words, ours is a language of the people, by the people, for the people. We are the only ones capable of defending it. And, needless to say, we can also mess up with it. But that mess-up, in my opinion, is precisely what keeps it on its toes. When I immigrated to the United States, in the mid-eighties, bad in English was the antonym of good. Today bad and good are often synonyms. Is that bad? No, it's good.

SHAKESPEARE IN PRISON

"Why, then, 'tis none to you; for there is nothing either good or bad, but thinking makes it so: to me it is a prison." Try this line—*Hamlet*, Act II, Scene 2—not in a regular classroom, but inside the prison system itself. You'll be stunned by its unforeseen resonances.

I currently have about thirty students in a course I'm teaching on Shakespeare at the Hampshire County Jail in Northampton. Half of them are inmates, all men between the ages of twenty-two and forty-five, black, white, and Latino. The other half are mainly from Amherst College, with a few Five College students in the mix. The combination of these two populations is conducive to deep knowledge.

At the outset, the inmates, who average a high school diploma or its equivalent and whom I refer to, in the classroom, as "inside students," at first looked intimidated by their counterparts from the outside, all clearly well equipped for academic research. And vice versa: the outside students felt like novices in contrast to the inmates' experience in the art of living. Happily, it took no time for anxiety to give place to conviviality. Soon this brought levelheadedness. The way the two student bodies complement each other feels magical.

Teaching in state and federal penal institutions these days is largely oriented toward earning a high school equivalency diploma. College courses have faced immense hurdles since 1994, when Congress passed the Violent Crime Control and Law Enforcement Act, which overturned a section of the Higher Education Act of 1965, thus taking away basic higher education grants to prisoners. The solution has been to fund these efforts independently. Mine is paid for by Amherst.

All of those enrolled, without exception, get college credit. Several of my Amherst colleagues—Barry O'Connell, Martha Saxton, and Kristin

---

First published in *Amherst Magazine*, Spring 2016.

Bumiller—have taught before me at the Hampshire County Jail, among the nation's most progressive prisons of its kind when it comes to curriculum. They were trained through the Inside-Out Prison Exchange Program. They, in turned, have taught me.

As a literary scholar, I am usually interested as much in textual analysis as I am in the ethical, cultural, and ideological implications of text. My syllabus focuses on Shakespeare's later plays (*Hamlet, King Lear,* and *The Tempest*) as well on as his sonnets. We also take a tour of the Elizabethan and Jacobean eras, the King's Men and Europe at the dawn of the seventeenth century. In addition, I invoke responses to Shakespeare by commentators such as Samuel Johnson, Samuel Taylor Coleridge, Frank Kermode, and Helen Vendler, as well as by non-Europeans like Jorge Luis Borges and Ismail Kadare. Students watch Kenneth Branagh as Hamlet and Helen Mirren as Prospero on-screen, scrutinizing their every move. They survey Renaissance London in various ways, including through the eyes of British playwright Tom Stoppard, who cowrote the screenplay of *Shakespeare in Love*.

Assignments include performing memorized segments of one of the dramas and writing in the creative mode: plays, stories, and essays. There are cameras in the room recording at all times. The class meets on Wednesdays for two hours. I have three Amherst students who serve as TAs; they transport the outside students to and from the jail and have tutorial sessions with the inside students twice a week, in which they help with the reading and writing.

Along the way, I keep asking myself: Does the Bard teach us how to live?

Not surprisingly, among the constellation of characters (Lear, Prospero, Ophelia, Gloucester, Miranda, Ariel, and Caliban), the Danish prince is the indisputable favorite. The play, written a few years after Shakespeare lost his only son, Hamnet, and around the time his own father also died, is about fathers and sons, a theme about which everyone in my class has something to say. Other themes are electrifying too: succession, ghosts, and especially revenge. But it is the question of Hamlet's madness—or the way he pretends to be mad—that incites the most heated reactions. Can criminals understand his mind-set better than the rest of us?

I asked this question after everyone listened to episode 218 of NPR's *This American Life*. It describes an effort to stage Act V of *Hamlet* with inmates (several of them rotating the role of the prince) at the high-security Missouri Eastern Correctional Center. One of the interviewees in the show asserts, in a nutshell, that it indeed takes a felon to know a felon.

Fittingly, my students, inside and out, were of two minds about this statement. They empathized deeply with the prince's dilemma—one of them, an inmate, even argued in favor of vengeance ("Eye-for-an-eye is law in the hood"). Others thought acting is acting: in make-believe, you don't have to kill to act like a killer. "Before and after the crime, we are always actors," said an inmate to me.

Hamlet's statement that nature is empty of morality and that it's the mind's eye that makes things good and evil is equally fruitful. All of us converge in the same classroom having made decisions that led us there. What we get from the classroom may help us better understand those decisions.

Among the most memorable aspect of teaching at the Hampshire County Jail is the writing. An Amherst student wrote a splendid essay on her father's betrayal of trust when he had an affair that broke the family apart. Another reflected on the fact that she seeks distance from her mother even as she perceives her as a role model. A third compared Hamlet's histrionics to Don Quixote's.

In turn, an inmate rewrote *Hamlet*, relocating the action among rappers. Another crafted a masterful story about a homeless man, who, after being repeatedly beaten by the police, desperately looks for a bathroom in which to shower, to cleanse himself from the pain. A third chronicled his life of heroin addiction and the degree to which the drug is the only freedom he truly cherishes. I am dumbfounded by the high quality of some of the writing.

A couple of inmates are now in the process of turning their writing into novels. Another one is writing a memoir. The facilities at the Hampshire County Jail don't allow for Internet access. And the time they are allowed to use a computer is limited. Still, they take turns. And they share their drafts with one another.

All this is to say that literature palpitates uniquely in this setting. It feels alive, full of possibilities. Inmates read passionately: they exercise their freedom by delving into a text with gusto. This is a medium that allows them to study human behavior scrupulously.

The common, mistaken, perception is that penal institutions are where felons go to rot. Somewhere in the future there is a promise of redemption, but it is just a promise. In my experience, inmates, for the most part, recognize themselves as at fault for their present condition. That isn't the issue. The issue is how not to rot, how to mature while in confinement.

Literature, I'm convinced, holds a key. The inmates' minds need to grow. They have all the time in the world. And at least those I have in the classroom are eager to become critical thinkers. They want to recalibrate themselves. We all know that as soon as they leave the jail, some will relapse immediately. Others, a minority perhaps, will position themselves anew. Either way, the life of the mind behind bars needs to be more fertile. It doesn't matter what comes next: in and of themselves, the years in prison might be precious. If just one felon is able to achieve a single, lasting epiphany from reading Shakespeare, and if from that epiphany a single outside student considers how humans who lost their liberty learn from its absence, the effort is worth it.

In any given ecosystem, each individual learns differently. Teaching, in my view, is less about lessons than about creating an atmosphere where heterogeneous minds inspire each other, about showing people how to ask questions, how to turn information into knowledge—and knowledge into wisdom. Inside the jail, those tasks have a distinct urgency.

Interacting with Amherst students shows inmates, in tangible ways, an existential path closed to them before. And the other way around. Not long ago, I asked the entire class if they believed the interaction between inside and outside was helpful. Outside students said that at the Hampshire County Jail they fashioned a side of themselves different from who they are on campus. Similarly, inmates stated they got permission in the course to be brainy, less rough. "These two hours a week make me intelligent," one said.

The Talmud says the best way to learn is through example. It is foolish—nah, stupid!—to think of the incarcerated as ignorant and of the rest of us as intelligent. To fully explore the intricacies of our world, it is crucial to appreciate the magic of one's own intellect. Shakespeare is a superb conduit for such an endeavor. It is true: "Why, then, 'tis none to you; for there is nothing either good or bad, but thinking makes it so."

THE SPANISH LANGUAGE IN LATIN AMERICA SINCE INDEPENDENCE

CASTELLANO, ESPAÑOL, OR ESPAÑOLES?

Spanish is spoken today as a native language by almost half a billion people. The vast majority of them are in Latin America, including the Spanish-speaking Caribbean. The foundation for the formidable presence of Spanish in the region is traceable to the period of colonization, a time in which the language, having been brought in from the Iberian Peninsula by soldiers, conquistadors, missionaries, and entrepreneurs representing the Spanish Crown, took hold across all elements of society within a relatively short period of time. Indigenous tongues struggled to survive under the implacable presence of an imperial mandate intent on making all subjects part of the empire. As colonization came to a close and during the age of independence (1810–1910), a succession of republics in the Americas declared their autonomy by pushing for a nationalist agenda. Spanish was an essential agglutinating force in the shaping of these national identities.

Before proceeding with an exploration of the linguistic development of Spanish in the Americas, it is crucial to fine-tune an issue of nomenclature. In the vernacular, Spanish is often called by two names: *castellano* and *español*. The Harvard scholar Amado Alonso pondered the theme in his book *Castellano, español, idioma nacional* (1938). The former recognizes its origin, around the year 1000, as a regional language in Castile, in central Spain. The latter refers to the transition the language made from the regional to the national around 1492, as the project of the Reconquista

---

First published in *Oxford Research Encyclopedia on Latin American History*, April 2017.

was in full gear and Antonio de Nebrija, a philologist at the University of Salamanca, published *Gramática sobre la lengua castellana*, a grammar of the language in which, in a dedication to Queen Isabella, he referred to it as *"la compañera del imperio,"* the companion of empire, portraying it as a tool Spain needed to use in its trans-Atlantic forays. In Latin America, people don't distinguish between *castellano* and *español*. Although these terms are seen as synonymous nowadays, it is historically appropriate to choose the latter when discussing the vicissitudes of the language in the Spanish colonies across the Atlantic.

The spirit of freedom gave place to insurrections in Latin America starting at the end of the eighteenth century. The first country to achieve independence was Mexico. As such, it serves as a useful case study. Among the creoles, the decision to secede was inspired by two foreign models: the American Revolution of 1776 and the French Revolution of 1789. Leaders such as Father Miguel Hidalgo y Costilla and José María Morelos y Pavón, in what was then known as Nueva España, mimicked the ideals of freedom, equality, and republicanism. Democracy, as a concept, was less developed. Their entire ideological rhetoric was conveyed in Spanish, which by then was the lingua franca of all social classes. The spirit of liberation spread quickly mostly across urban centers, primarily in the capital, originally built in what was known during the pre-Columbian era as Tenochtitlán, the heart of Aztec civilization, which used Nahuatl as its lingua franca. The name chosen for the new nation was "Méjico," but a switch to spelling it with an x came about when the letter was perceived to be symbolically connected with Nahuatl. An effort by lexicographers, philologists, and educators involved legitimizing indigenous words, such as *hamaca* (hammock), *cacahuate* (peanut), *escuincle* (child), and *aguacate* (avocado).

Independence was followed in Mexico by an extended period of political instability. Among the first political projects was a monarchy ruled by Joaquín de Iturbide that undermined the drive toward democracy and pluralism. It encompassed what is described as Mesoamerica, stretching northward from present-day El Salvador, Nicaragua, Costa Rica, Guatemala, Belize, and Honduras in the south to what was once the American Southwest, including California, Texas, Utah, Arizona, New Mexico, and Colorado. It isn't surprising, then, that the varieties of Spanish in these regions coincide with the standard Mexican variety. Given the broad territory, that variety was never homogenous. It has been noticed by linguists of diverse theoretical persuasions that Mexican Spanish, particularly in the center of the country, loses strength in the pronunciation of vowels, whereas consonants are pronounced strongly. There are several varieties of Mexican Spanish: Norteño, both eastern and western; Bajacaliforniano; Western; Bajío (lowlands); Altiplano (central); Sureño (southern); Costeño (coastal), Chiapaneco (southeastern), and Yucateco (eastern peninsular).

Next in line in the fight for independence was Brazil, which is part of Latin America, although culturally and linguistically its roots are quite different. (Pedro Henríquez Ureña, an influential twentieth-century philologist from the Dominican Republic, who in the mid-1940s delivered the Charles Eliot Norton Lectures at Harvard under the title of *Literary Currents in Hispanic America* [1945], preferred to refer to the region as two: Hispanic America and Luso [Portuguese] America.) In 1823, Brazil finally pushed the Portuguese out, followed by the liberation of various regions of South America, from Argentina to Peru and from Venezuela and Colombia. Figures like Simón Bolívar, Francisco de Miranda, and José de San Martín fought an extended series of insurrections that spread over decades.

The Spanish spoken in Argentina, also known as *español rioplatense*, uses the pronoun *vos* instead of the informal *tú* and the formal *usted*. This feature is known as *voseo* (from *vosotros*) in contrast with *tuteo* (from *tú*) where the form *tú* is used flexibly. It is obvious in oral communication. The conjugation of verbs with *vos* employs the second-person singular (*vos estás*), and *usted* uses the third-person singular (*usted está*). In Central America, the phenomenon of *voseo* affects verbal conjugations in the present, present subjunctive, and imperative. For instance, instead of saying *piensas* they say *tú pensás*, instead of *pienses* it is *tú pensés*, and instead of *piensa* it is *tú pensá*. There are other linguistic patterns distinguishing it from Iberian Spanish (*loísmo* instead of *leísmo*, *seseo*, etc.).

Argentine Spanish, again studied by Amado Alonso as well as by Américo Castro (*La peculiaridad lingüística rioplatense y su sentido histórico* [The linguistic peculiarity of the River Plate and its historical meaning, 1961]), is essentially colored by the infusion of immigrants to the region, at first from Italy, Eastern Europe, and the Iberian Peninsula and subsequently from Asia and elsewhere. Unlike Mexico and Central America, where the aboriginal population played a crucial role, in Argentina and Uruguay the role of indigenous tribes was rather small in comparison. Intriguingly, there developed in the region a rural type, called Gaucho, that in complex ways is the equivalent of the cowboy in the American West and, in the national imagination, is seen as a kind of aboriginal type. The question of what role the gaucho ought to play was explored, notably, by Domingo Faustino Sarmiento, an important nineteenth-century intellectual during the Rosas dictatorship and eventually the country's president. In *Civilización y barbarie* (*Facundo: Civilization and Barbarism*, 1845), he looks at the Gaucho as an obstacle—awkward, primitive—to Argentina becoming a modern nation. The antidote, he proposes, is European immigration.

Indeed, Argentina opened its doors in the 1870s to an influx of immigrants. People with diverse origins arrived: Spanish, Basque, Galician, Portuguese, and northern Italian. There were also new arrivals from France, Germany, and other European countries. Between 1910 and 1945, immigration came from Southern Italy. (Approximately 40 percent of all Argentines have Italian ancestry.) In turn, they were followed by Jews from Russia, Poland, and elsewhere in Eastern Europe, whose influx lasted until the Second World War. Additionally, Argentina always had a population of English speakers, particularly from Britain and Ireland. As a result of this influx, the slang of the lower class, Lunfardo, which ended up defining Argentine Spanish, originated among Italian immigrants. It was at first the parlance of prostitutes and criminals. Jorge Luis Borges, always fascinated with linguistic changes, explored it in parts of his oeuvre.

ANDRÉS BELLO: THE PHILOLOGIST'S TASK

From the philological perspectives, arguably the most important figure in the development of Spanish in Latin America at the time of independence is the Venezuelan essayist, linguist, and diplomat Andrés Bello, who established an agenda that helped define the cultural parameters of the young republics in terms of grammar, syntax, lexicography, and morphology. It is difficult to overestimate Bello's impact. Keeping in mind fundamental cultural differences, he is a figure of the type of Samuel Johnson, the eighteenth-century English lexicographer and man of letters, author of a magisterial dictionary of the English language. Bello's task was straightforward: in the quest to identify a culture that was authentically American, he wanted to make Spanish suitable for Americans, simplifying its grammar and recognizing its lexicographic variants.

Born in Caracas, Venezuela, he was a man of diverse talents who entered the diplomatic service early on in his life, living in London, where he befriended Simón Bolívar, known as El Libertador, the leader in the fight to create a republic in South America (one that included portions of what are today Panama, Colombia, Venezuela, Chile, Peru, and Argentina) that matched, in scope and strength, the United States. Bello caught the bug, hoping to translate the political dreams into the cultural realm through essays, articles, and philological investigations about what made the region unique. In the realm of linguistics, he published an assortment of in-depth studies that include *Principios de la ortografía y métrica de la lengua castellana* (Principles of Castilian orthography and prosody 1835), *Análisis ideológica de los tiempos de la conjugación castellana* (Ideological analysis of Castilian conjugation, 1841), and his monumental *Gramática de la lengua castellana destinada para el uso de los americanos* (Grammar of the Castilian language destined for American usage, 1847).

This last work is an attempt to adapt the language to regional usage. His target audience was "mis hermanos, los habitantes de Hispanoamérica" (my siblings, the inhabitants of Hispanic America). Organized in a methodical way that looks at the syntactical structure of the Spanish language, his book seeks to offer a way for speakers in the Americas to use the language according to their own needs and not in deference to Iberian attitudes. He wants his readers to adapt *"los significados y usos de cada forma como si no hubiese en el mundo otra lengua que la castellana"* (the meanings and uses to each form as if the world didn't know any other language than Castilian). Convinced that what would give coherence and stability to the new republics would be their culture and, consequently, their language, Bello looked for ways to standardize the written form. He wanted the language of the Americas to be unified: *"Juzgo importante la conservación de la lengua de nuestros padres en su posible . . . como un medio providencial de comunicación y un vínculo de fraternidad entre las varias naciones de origen español derramadas sobre los dos continentes"* (I deem important the conservation of our ancestors' language as much as possible, as a providential means of communication and a fraternal tie among the various nations of Spanish origin spread out across the two continents). Bello stressed, time and again, that the Spanish used in Spain is a different form than the one in the Americas, and that this difference should be embraced. He believed that Iberian grammarians were too conservative, rejecting as malapropisms anything that came from the New World.

At the same time, Bello admonished his fellow Americans to use the language properly and according to basic rules. He was appalled by the way Chileans (the *Gramática* was written in Santiago) deformed the language and were disdainful of formal structures. He proposed simplifying spelling, adapting regional use, and in general recognizing the creativity on this side of the Atlantic. His effort, then, is a balancing act between giving the newly independent republics a sense of worth by recognizing varieties within the language and the drive to keep Spanish across countries as a unified entity. Yet by the end of the independence period, it was obvious that Spanish in the vast geography of the Americas had evolved in peculiar ways, fostering varieties dependent on regional factors. The result is that rather than a single, homogenized language, each national sphere developed its own characteristics. These differences are most tangible in terms of accent—that is, at the oral level. And within those theaters, there are multiple subdivisions. Colombian Spanish tends to be fuller in terms of pronunciation, whereas Caribbean varieties (in Cuba, Puerto Rico, and the Dominican Republic) abbreviate the last syllable of words. Vocabulary tends to be shaped by local needs and acquires unique characteristics in connection with food, flora and fauna, and sexual references. There are myriad comparative dictionaries where the varieties of Latin American Spanish are represented.

One of the philologists in Latin America influenced by Bello was Colombian Rufino José Cuervo. An avid reader of Bello, he sought to improve on an aspect he found lacking in his predecessor: the historical content. For Cuervo, language is an organism in constant mutation. He studied closely the parlance of Bogotá, producing an insightful compendium of linguistic behavior called *Apuntaciones críticas sobre el lenguaje bogotano* (Critical notes on Bogotá's language, 1872). His magnum opus is the unfinished two-volume *Diccionario de construcción y régimen de la lengua castellana* (Dictionary of structure of the Spanish language, 1893), in which he attempted to produce a historical lexicon in the scope of *The Oxford English Dictionary*, with a focus on Latin America, accounting for variants.

TOWARD A MODERN TONGUE

At the end of the nineteenth century, as the wars of independence were bearing fruit, the Spanish Empire faced its collapse. This became evident during the Spanish-American War of 1898, when Spain faced the loss of some of its last remaining territories, including Cuba, Puerto Rico, and the Philippines, and the United States, a nascent global force, become the conquering force in the Caribbean Basin, the Pacific, and beyond. A referendum of Spanish culture in the Americas took place. The former mother country was perceived as intrusive, imperialistic. The citizens of the new republics were eager to look elsewhere for inspiration, especially to France.

It is during this period that an aesthetic movement, involving music, painting, and architecture but especially writing, known as *modernismo*, swept through the Americas (spanning roughly from 1885 to 1915). Its general objective was to encourage the region to embrace modernity in order to become a partner with the rest of the industrial world. At the level of language and literature, it imitated French symbolism, Parnassianism, and other trends, and it looked to Paris as the capital of culture. Its promoters were Nicaraguan Rubén Darío and Cuban José Martí, considered the two major leaders, followed by figures like José Asunción Silva of Colombia, Amado Nervo and Enrique González Martínez of Mexico, Leopoldo Lugones of Argentina, and Delmira Agustini and José Enrique Rodó of Uruguay, among others. It was the first time that intellectuals from various parts of Latin America were seen as belonging to the same artistic movement.

Darío and Martí fashioned a verbal style that was free, as much as possible, of Iberian mannerisms. Their dream was to make American Spanish fluid, harmonious, and transnational. Whenever they included localisms in their poems, stories, essays, and reportage, it was to emphasize the particular in the context of the universal. Yet the majority of them generally avoided sounding too regional. Their quest was to show that the Spanish they used, four hundred years after the conquest, was free, autonomous, and democratic. Such was their impact, first in Spain and decades later in other parts of Europe, that their work began to be regularly translated to French, German, Italian, and Portuguese.

Indeed, translation for the *modernistas* was an essential component to success. Just as they read broadly in the spirit of cosmopolitanism, they wanted their needs to be understood beyond their immediate circumstances. Modernity, for them, was a type of urban angst felt wherever culture mattered in the world, regardless of language. This prompted them to look attentively at their own language, Spanish, as a ticket to humanism. Thus, Darío, Martí, and other members of the generation often include references to idiosyncratic elements in their tongue, or write about exotic terms, immigrant modalities, and philological trends.

Distribution of books was difficult, though. Volumes released in Managua or Caracas seldom traveled beyond the immediate region. The capitals of publishing at the time were Buenos Aires, Mexico City, and Havana. Whatever appeared there was noticed by newspapers. Yet it was through word of mouth, to a large extent, that the *modernista* fever jumped national borders. There was another component that also helped. The members of this generation understood travel differently from their predecessors. Modernity, in and of itself, implied constant motion, whether within one's own urban milieu or across cultural landscapes. To be educated was to travel, and to travel was to be exposed to different kinds of stimulation. The extent to which the *modernistas* were frequent collaborators in international periodicals, then, makes sense.

That cross-fertilization, again, was an invaluable resource not only in the spread of a modern sensibility but also in the effort to standardize Spanish as a language that spoke to millions across nations. In that sense, it is important to stress the role the *modernistas* had as public intellectuals in exploring the worth of Spanish throughout Latin America. While they didn't conceive of themselves as teachers per se, their active—indeed, almost frantic—didactic tone enabled audiences from Colombia to Argentina, from Cuba to Chile, to feel like contemporaries.

One of the most liberating manifestos to emerge from the *modernista* generation was José Enrique Rodó's *Ariel* (1900). Using the characters of Ariel and Caliban from Shakespeare's *The Tempest* as metaphors, Rodó succinctly argues that Spain's influence on Latin America is all but eclipsed. The new paradigm is the United States, which at the dawn of the twentieth century was still establishing itself as a global empire. Latin Americans, in Rodó's opinion, must choose between a spirituality connected with the indigenous civilizations of the pre-Columbian past as well as with a genuine desire for freedom on the one hand and the brutish materialism of the United States on the other. In his view, the language of spirituality is Spanish.

THE EMBATTLED REAL ACADEMIA ESPAÑOLA: THE QUESTION OF REGIONALISMS

Perhaps the best way to understand the new, emerging consciousness is through the consolidation of the Real Academia Española de la Lengua (Spanish Royal Academy; RAE). The institution was founded in 1713. Its role from the outset was to vigorously safeguard the language as it changes internally and reacts to outside influences—the Academia's motto is *"Limpia, fija y da splendor"* (Clean, define, and give splendor). The institution remained captive to its Iberian origins for some 150 years, its activities generating only marginal interest in the Americas. One must remember that Spain in the eighteenth century was in a period of political, military, economic, and cultural decline. This climate led to a self-imposed ostracism. In truth, it might be better described as collective depression, a syndrome often acknowledged by diplomats and artists. At any rate, what was happening in the colonies, now that they were increasingly independent, seemed in Spanish eyes like a punch in the face. Those colonies, their language and culture, were perceived as awkward, primitive, unworthy of legitimate interest.

The *modernistas* changed that attitude, pushing for openness. With time that spilled into the RAE activities. The academy progressively added branches in countries across the Atlantic, with a total of twenty-two, starting with Colombia (1871), Ecuador (1874), and Mexico (1875), and ending with Honduras (1949), Puerto Rico (1955), and the United States (1973). The inauguration of each of them was a carefully orchestrated event in which Spain was careful not to be perceived as imposing its own linguistic mandate, although avoiding such ideological effort was seldom successful. In the end, the structure was centralized, with the Madrid matrix functioning as headquarters. Among the most important projects of the institution, if not the central one, is the ongoing publication of the *Diccionario de la Lengua Española* (*DLE*), a prescriptive lexicon encompassing the breadth and complexity of the language in Hispanic civilization. Inevitably, the making of the *DLE* was always seen as an endeavor concerned with the surge, development, and health of Iberian Spanish. The connection to the Americas was tenuous at first. As the twentieth century approached, an invitation was sent to those academies already established to contribute with *"regionalismos."* With bureaucratic disarray reigning in their realm, a few of them—the Colombian and Mexican ones, for instance—proceeded to submit their contribution. It often took them longer than anticipated. Only after submitting it did they realize that the *DLE* was selective in what it was ready to include in the *Diccionario*. The negotiations of what to include and what to exclude were often lengthy. They allowed for the various branches to come to terms with their own condition as colonial entities and to gather resources to create their own lexicons, rejecting the concept of "regionalism" as paternalistic. Thus started an age of linguistic self-confidence that within decades led to the publication of dictionaries of various Spanish varieties in their respective countries of origin.

In 1951, an added institution came to the fore: Asociación de Academias de la Lengua Española, known as ASALE (Association of Spanish Language Academies), is in charge of regulating the Spanish language. Both the academy and its dictionary, and to a much lesser extent the ASALE, regularly come under attack for their outmoded understanding of the language and their colonial attitude toward the Americas. Yet even that attack is seldom representative, because the population at large in Latin America appears unaffected by its activities. The disassociation between these institutions and the people is an example of the limitations of linguistic legislation. The Spanish language is a living organism, built as a series of interrelated structures. No single power is capable of controlling its development. In that sense, scholarship, including lexicography, is by definition descriptive rather than prescriptive. Its duty is to account for the changes, not to tinker with them.

THE POWER OF VARIETY

A look at the growth of Spanish in the twentieth century is uncontestable proof of the plentiful nature of the language. After the Spanish-American War of 1898 deflated Spain's dreams across the Atlantic, and Cuba, Puerto Rico, and the Philippines severed their ties with the former empire, each of these countries proceeded to cultivate its national identity according to internal needs and conditions. With the exception of the Philippines after 1902, Spanish became one of the tools. Such were the dictates of nationalism that as the local verbal traits were recognized and studied, they became paradigmatic of what made Cubans, for instance, a distinctly singular people.

Consequently, there is an abundance of books, published from the 1920s onward, on what makes Cuban parlance unique. Ethnographers, anthropologists, and sociolinguists set out to research the local flavor, including linguistic idiosyncrasies. Two examples are Fernando Ortíz's *Catauro de cubanismos* (*Corpus of Cubanisms*, 1923), in which the language of former slaves is scrutinized, then catalogued, and *Contrapunteo cubano del tabaco y el azúcar* (*Cuban Counterpoint: Tobacco and Sugar*, 1940), a study of the place of tobacco and sugar in the Cuban psyche and language. To a considerable extent, although keeping individual objectives in mind, this has been the mandate of philologists such as Venezuelan Ángel Rosenblat and Henríquez-Ureña. Indeed, just as tourism was starting to become a source of national pride as well as income, the relationship between the Spanish language and regional and national folklore became a way to showcase difference.

Each nation established an educational program that subscribed to some linguistic patterns recognized as linked to an approved norm. In Mexico, for instance, José Vasconcelos, a philosopher, author of *The Cosmic Race* (1925), minister of education, and rector of the national university, UNAM, articulated in the 1930s a series of principles whereby Mexican children in schools would become acquainted with their collective heritage, which he related to *mestizaje*, ethnic cross-breeding, starting with the

Spanish conquest that defined Mexico as a nation. *Mestizaje* quickly became more than a buzzword: it was turned into an ideology. Mexican Spanish, as well as some Central American Spanish, is characterized by a distinctive use of affricates and fricatives that were inherited from Nahuatl and other pre-Columbian languages (Tlanepantla and Xochimilco, for instance), the reduction of unstressed vowels, the abundance of suffixes (*amiguito, casucha*), and a distinct lexicon. What made Mexicans distinct, according to Vasconcelos and his followers, was their hybrid character: part European, part aboriginal. Similar endeavors were accomplished in Argentina, Colombia, Venezuela, Cuba, and Peru.

Another crucial facet of the growth of nationalism in Latin America in the twentieth century is the surge of a media (print, radio, and TV) that responds to the particular needs of each of the Latin American countries. It is well known that media is a force that simultaneously incorporates a plethora of voices that are part of the national conversation and standardizes the language in which that conversation takes. The study of particular cases is beyond the scope of this chapter. Suffice it to say that in each nation, Spanish in the media is articulated in different ways. Depending on the circumstances (e.g., who is in control of power, what the ideological agenda is), those ways incorporate, to various degrees, age, class, gender, and racial differences, as well as the parlance of specific groups like indigenous tribes, tourists, and ethnic minorities.

The result of these programmatic strategies suggests a tension, in terms of linguistic expansion, between the universal and the particular. That tension is visible in the literary movement known as "el Boom," which came about in the 1960s, represented by writers including Argentina's Julio Cortázar, Mexico's Carlos Fuentes, Peru's Mario Vargas Llosa, Chile's José Donoso, and Colombia's Gabriel García Márquez. Like the *modernistas* less than a century before them, these authors came to be recognized as a force in world literature. Their novels, infused with magical realism (a mix of dreamlike images and politically charged plots), were turned, though translation, into desirable global artifacts. The images they offered together were of a continent suspended in time, deeply rooted in its ancestral legacy, and struggling to incorporate influences from a variety of sources. Perhaps the most notable example is García Márquez's genealogical narrative *One Hundred Years of Solitude* (1967), about a fictional coastal town, Macondo, and its rowdy, multilayered family, the Buendías. Such is the influence the book still exerts that an entire creed, known as *Macondismo* (from McOndo, an amalgam of "Macondo" and "McDonald's"), has evolved out of it. The premise behind it is simple: Latin America never became fully modern.

Significantly, the language that the writers of "el Boom," including García Márquez, employed in their work is perhaps their most lasting contribution. International readers approach it with reverence. Each author stresses national elements (Peruvianisms, Colombianisms, and so on) while finding a neutral vehicle of communication understood beyond borders. Here, in a nutshell, is what the diversity of the Spanish language in Latin America is capable of accomplishing.

AGAINST "DIVERSITY"

I have become allergic to the word *diversity*. It feels empty or, worse, like a chore. Words lose capital when they are overused or when the cultural climate that fostered their meaning changes. *Diversity* is a good example.

I am a Latino. I have strongly benefited from the drive toward diversity. I like to think of myself as fostering that drive as well. But the fervor behind it belongs to past decades. Our cultural moment is an altogether different one. America is already deeply, irrevocably diverse. Where do we go from here?

Life in the United States today is unlike what I encountered when I emigrated from Mexico in the mid-1980s. Faces have changed in overt as well as subtle ways. The changes were well under way when I arrived, thanks to the civil rights movement and feminism; that is, they began with race and gender.

Colleges at the forefront of these changes have encountered substantial challenges. Today the transformation also includes class and gender stereotypes, although the impact of those shifts hasn't been as dramatic as it could be nationwide. The rich are fewer than before, with extravagant amounts of wealth, and the poor are poorer. Lesbian, gay, bisexual, and transgender students have begun to be recognized on a few campuses; elsewhere, not at all. These movements are growing.

Institutions of higher learning have realized that it isn't enough to open the door to previously excluded groups; the real effort is in following suit with programs that help newcomers experience themselves not as aliens in these habitats but as integral to their institutions' overall missions. And colleges must adapt their missions to these new demographic configurations.

Not long ago, I delivered a lecture to five hundred students at a small liberal arts college in the Northeast that uses the phrase "people

---

First published in *The Chronicle of Higher Education*, July 10, 2016.

of color" in its brochures, even though its student body is more than 95 percent white. (Believe me, it takes only seconds for visitors to a campus to recognize a collective lie). I talked about "fake diversity." My comments received enthusiastic applause from the young audience, while administrators in the back looked embarrassed. Not that they were the guilty ones. In my experience, obstacles to diversity often come from a higher level, like an institution's Board of Trustees, where outdated ideas may simmer.

Universities are a microcosm of society, where anxiety over race, gender, and class is writ large. It is the stuff of constant jokes that the Washington elite is mostly white, whereas the electorate—the rest of us—is increasingly heterogeneous. The Supreme Court may be increasingly diverse; the first Latina justice, Sonia Sotomayor, has now been on the bench for four years. But whenever the Court prepares to ponder an issue with lasting social consequences, I can't help but wonder who will win: those who prefer the America of the past or those who understand the future.

So we are all aware of the implications of our seismic moment, the rapid pace with which the status quo is reconfigured. The question is how to describe—or better, what name to give to that plurality—the components of that reconfiguration. Maybe it isn't about finding a replacement word for *diversity* that will also lose currency in time. *Diversity* came about to diagnose a deficit. The diagnosis has been established, and stratagems have been sought. Now we as a culture have moved on.

Merriam-Webster defines *diversity* as "the quality or state of having many different forms, types, ideas, etc.," and also as "the state of having people who are different races or who have different cultures in a group or organization." It goes without saying that any environment, made of parts, is a composite, a sum of elements. In 2015, to describe the United States as racially or culturally diverse was to state the obvious. What happens in that environment, to what extent its dissimilar components are able to find a common ground, and whether that common ground has the capacity to become a feature of the collective body, is what the present-day United States is truly about.

At the macro level, we have a black president—with a legacy as uneven as that of his precursors. Women, non-whites, and gay people are leaders at all levels across the country, including on campuses. We even have a pope from Argentina, which in Latin America is often described as the edge of the world. There is still a lot to achieve, and that task pertains to us all. But the glass ceiling has been broken.

This is not to say that say that diversity in leadership and other realms will solve our problems. It simply allows for equal opportunity to succeed as well as to fail.

It seems to me that when college administrators open a diversity center or appoint a chief diversity officer these days, they are showcasing an outmoded mentality. That center is likely to become a ghetto, reserved for those who aren't like everyone else. The objective of diversity is no longer to make groups or projects more heterogeneous; instead, it is to find a new normal for a diverse ecosystem.

In short, *diversity* feels jingoistic, its message old-fashioned. It has lost cachet. Americans no longer strive to be pluralistic; we already are. Our present objective is to find out what kind of balance our pluralism can sustain, and whether such political, social, and cultural transformations will ever truly lead to *e pluribus unum*, "of the many, one."

ROLLING ONE'S *R*'S

Rather than simply delivering the news, Vanessa Ruiz, an anchor for *12 News* in Arizona, recently became news herself when her pronunciation of Spanish words drew complaints. The feeling was that, in an English-language TV newscast, she ought to be pronouncing these words the way a majority of English speakers do—not as Spanish speakers would.

Exhibit A in this controversy is that when certain Spanish words crop up in the course of speaking English, she rolls her *R*'s.

She also pronounces a Spanish name like "Mesa" as "Mess-ah" and not as "May-suh," as English speakers do. In online comments, some viewers criticized these pronunciations as annoying, stupid, or wrong.

The controversy over Ms. Ruiz's rolled *R*'s can easily be framed in the context of a troubling strain of anti-immigrant sentiment, rooted in Arizona in this case, but much in evidence elsewhere. At issue is the contested coexistence not only of two languages, but also of two cultures. In a public statement, Ms. Ruiz politely pointed out that her pronunciation honors Arizona's original settlers, who were all Iberian.

But there is an even larger picture that deserves our attention: the miraculous malleability of language.

Ms. Ruiz, who was born in Miami and grew up in Colombia, is bilingual, as are about 20 percent of Americans. She started her career at Telemundo, one of the two largest Spanish-language TV networks, then moved to English-language newscasting positions in Florida and California. In other words, she moves between cultures, registering along the way many varieties of speech.

On the air, she speaks English with a standard American accent, in the tradition of Walter Cronkite. And in Spanish, she speaks with a neutral, pan-Latino accent, without any Colombian "localisms."

First published in *The New York Times*, September 16, 2016.

It is wrong to think that polyglots inhabit several alternative universes, each defined by a different tongue. In truth, they live only one life, just like everyone else—except that they have the advantage of looking at it through different linguistic lenses.

Languages rarely exist in isolation from one another. English and Spanish, for example, are so intertwined that it sometimes feels as though they're dancing a tango together. At times, this encounter looks like a fight; at others, a romantic affair.

To me, the most creative manifestation of this phenomenon is code switching: the spontaneous, even joyful, combining of elements of two or more tongues in a single sentence. Hybrid dialects like Yinglish, Spanglish, and Chinglish are examples of this cross-fertilization.

But there are more discreet, less showy ways. One is to sprinkle one's speech in one language with occasional words from another. This is done with an insider's knowledge, pronouncing syllables with a natural cadence.

To be sure, there are always those who wish to police language and protect it from such promiscuous mixing. Yet all languages are mutable over time. The original explorers, missionaries and colonists who migrated from Spain to the American Southwest, spoke quite differently than Spanish speakers today. They themselves came from different provinces, with different phonological, grammatical, and lexical variations, so who even knows how any of them would have pronounced "Mesa."

Each linguistic epoch has its own standardizing forces. History is made by cumulative additions.

Down to the present: there are approximately 450 million Spanish speakers with native competence in the world today, and perhaps an additional 100 million non-native Spanish speakers. The United States alone has more Spanish-language speakers than Spain itself, where the language came to life, in the region of Castile, more than a millennium back. Four hundred years ago this year, Miguel de Cervantes came out with the second volume of his masterpiece, *Don Quixote*, and gave the language its gravitas.

The region encompassing Phoenix, Mesa, and Glendale in Arizona has almost 775,000 Spanish speakers, which amounts to 19.8 percent of the local population (a proportion quite close to the percentage of Latinos in the country overall). While Mexicans make up the largest group, they speak varieties of Spanish depending on their ancestry north of the border, some going back to before the Treaty of Guadalupe Hidalgo was signed, ending the Mexican-American War in 1848. The "neutral" Spanish heard on Arizona's media coexists with the multiple ways the language is used on the street.

Even that mainstream usage is never static. Words are continuously being remodeled—both in meaning and in pronunciation.

Think of the word "Mexico." One hears emphatically different pronunciations in the United States: "MEH-hee-co" among Mexicans (an original spelling was "Méjico"). Non-native Spanish speakers at times say "MAY-hee-co," whereas for English speakers it is "MEX-i-co."

When a Telemundo anchor says "Mexico" on the air, laughter ensues because he appears to be mocking the Anglos. Yet whenever I hear English-language Latinos on National Public Radio saying "MEH-hee-co," there is no fuss. This, arguably, is because, with the American population undergoing a seismic shift of demography and culture, the standard pronunciation of the word is changing.

Ms. Ruiz's use of Spanish words in English newscasts, and her choice of pronunciation, would have been unthinkable fifty years ago. Today they are polemical; tomorrow, it will seem inexplicable that there was ever a fuss.

English, perhaps more than any other imperial language, is extraordinarily flexible. For centuries, its vitality has been the result of conquests and colonization. It lends and borrows words with astonishing ease. Unlike Spanish, which has the Real Academia Española, an institution devoted to safeguarding it, English is of, by, and for the people—meaning that the only ones capable of legislating over it are its users.

The contempt expressed by some viewers of *12 News* in Arizona might be seen as exactly that: an attempt at legislating language. But Ms. Ruiz's desire to use Spanish pronunciations also reflects the new social reality to which Shakespeare's tongue must adapt.

PART VI

CONVERSATIONS

THE POET'S ALCHEMY

(with Richard Wilbur)

Ilan Stavans: What is the difference between the way students talk today and how they talked when you were an undergraduate?

Richard Wilbur: Students nowadays strike me as brighter than we were, but many of them choose to speak in a blurting, confused manner, as if clarity would be pretentious.

IS: Is it because they are less connected with the written word? Are they impatient with the art of talking? Is it because reading as an activity is in decline?

RW: Although they often write well, in speech they are in no danger of talking like a book. Perhaps the answer must be sought historically, in the '60s, when the influence of the Beat Generation was strongly felt by students in America. They began to start every sentence with "like" as a way of saying "so to speak." They botched their thoughts in hopes of seeming spontaneous and natural.

IS: Is there something positive about the way people are more relaxed today in the way they speak? Or is it all loss?

RW: I'm mostly aware of a kind of incoherence that doesn't do justice to the students' intelligence. I'm not sure that there is any gain in this collapse of eloquence and formality of speech.

First published in *Amherst Magazine*, Summer 2009.

IS: Language isn't a measure of intelligence, but it is intelligence manifested. Are you suggesting that intelligence has gone down? I gather that what you're saying is that the way intelligence manifests itself, language as the expression of thought, has crumbled.

RW: That's my feeling . . .

IS: It was Proust who said that all poets, even those who are monolingual, write in a foreign language. I'd like to get your view of what a foreign language is to a poet like you.

RW: There are people like yourself who are fully competent in a number of languages. For such people, translating is a different experience from anything to which I as a translator could lay claim. I remember talking with Richard Howard a few years ago. He's an awfully good translator from the French and a good poet in English. Howard said to me that for him, possessing French amounted to possessing a second self, another person whom he can be when he's tired of the one that he was given in the first place. When he said that, I was aware of how utterly unlike him I was in that regard. I can rather awkwardly converse in French, I can speak kitchen Italian, and I can beg someone's pardon in Russian. I can enjoy the sounds and savors of those languages and a certain amount of strained intercourse in them. But I am myself all the time. I am hopelessly an eleventh-generation American.

IS: Yet should one say that the relationship toward one's own language is defined by foreignness?

RW: I, like most Americans, speak sometimes in the easygoing language of an ordinary citizen and at other times in a language that is specialized. I can't count the possible ways of talking English that there are, but I'm sure that unconsciously I switch gears between one kind of English discourse and another all the time.

IS: You're obviously talking about your oral communication. What about as a poet? How many different Englishes do you have at your disposal?

RW: As a poet there is a basic vocabulary which I use, and I try to make it adequate to the delicacy and complexity of the subject. I also depart from conversational English at need, and reach for the word that's rare but exact; sometimes I echo the language of prior poets in English and in other tongues as well. Poets have always done that. Offhand, I think of the Latinity of John Milton, since an echoing Latin was something he could switch into while still writing in English. In a lesser sense that sort of thing is true of me. I can converse in poetry with John Keats, for example, letting my language be touched by him in a way which the reader can divine and understand.

IS: A poet is always in conversation with the past.

RW: Yes.

IS: And with the future too?

RW: I'm not sure. The future is a mystery to me. I suppose when I do think of the relationship of present poetry to the future, I simply hope that our poetry at its most vital will be enhanced of life in times to come. Even for poets who are not bookish, poetry is a conversation with one's neighbors, of course, but also with all of the poets who have ever written. At least with all of the poets who matter to us. We address the future with less confidence, but with hope.

IS: I want to draw a parallel here. If poetry is a conversation with time, isn't conversation—I'm again talking about oral communication—the same thing? For when speaking to one another, we're using many of the same words, if not always the same syntactical structures, our ancestors employed.

RW: That's true. Even when trying to be desperately modern, many words we use have a historic flavor to them, and no one can use them without making a gesture toward what has been said by other people in the past.

IS: I read recently, and was puzzled by it, that French has a total of 125,000 different words, German has 180,000, and English—and this is according to the *Oxford English Dictionary*—has around a quarter million just in over 400,000 words. How to explain these different sizes in linguistic banks? If these numbers are true, the French, a language from which you've translated extensively, has little over 12 percent of the number of words that English has.

RW: We're well acquainted with the purism of the French, their desire to preserve their language as of a certain date in a pure condition. I don't know if the same spirit is important in German. As for English, we have been unashamedly acquisitive of other words, other ways of putting things, other names for things. It's one of the great glories of our highly manipulable language. I remember discovering two years ago that when we speak the simple sentence "Please pass the ketchup," we're using a word, *ketchup*, which originated on an island between Japan and China. I forget the island's name, but I wouldn't be without the word. We have rendered it our own, and it seems as American as any other word.

IS: Is an English poet today able to do much more because there are more words in the language? Are there simply more tools at his disposal? Is the world different when one has almost a million words to describe it? Numerically, I don't know the scope of Spanish, but my guess is that it compares to French.

RW: I don't know how much any of us is in possession of this great treasury of American English, but one has a sense that if there's anything that needs naming, any concept that needs expressing, one can, with the help of a dictionary, find that it exists in our language. There isn't anything one has to attack by a painful circumlocution. There's almost always a word at our disposal. Whether it's part of the working vocabulary of any poet or speaker is another matter. I don't know how eloquent we may be considered to be, compared to a good speaker of French, Spanish, or German. Certainly we are less formulaic.

IS: By way of talking about translation, let me ask you a question about travel. Do you believe travel is important in the art of translation? I'm imagining a man like Kaspar Hauser, a bastard born and raised in Germany in total isolation in a dungeon, who is able to reach beyond his limited universe through intellectual curiosity, and through passion ends up becoming enlightened, in the nineteenth-century sense of the term. This Kaspar Hauser, considered by some a half-wild human (Werner Herzog made a film about him in 1974), learns to speak more than one language and has books at his disposal. Does one need to leave the dungeon in order to become a good translator? Is natural talent and access to information enough?

RW: I'm not sure that travel is important for the purposes of successful translation. For some people, immersion in the language of the text they will translate is part of the drill. For Richard Howard it was. Transformation of the self, broadening of the self, came of long and real association with French culture. I suppose one has to judge the likelihood of one's conversion to another language and nationality in order to see how practical it is for one's purposes. I have translated chiefly from seventeenth-century French, and I don't know that travel would have helped me.

IS: In order to be a fine translator of poetry, does one need to be a poet?

RW: Yes, to produce the sort of translation which brings a foreign poem over into a language once and for all, one probably needs a poet's developed ability. Yet wonderful things have been done, can be done, in translation by people who are equipped simply with good intelligence and taste.

IS: Can you think of examples of poems written in another language that traveled to English successfully in the hands of translators who were not themselves poets?

RW: There are people who know infinitely more about some literature than poets do, and have a profounder sense of its language. Such scholars produce translations that are useful keys to what's in the original, but which rarely reincarnate it. Let me hasten to say, however, that though Edward FitzGerald's own poetry was unremarkable, his *Rubáiyát* is one of the great translations of all time.

IS: Indeed, FitzGerald's *Rubáiyát* is superb, although the majority of us are ignorant of Omar Khayyám's Persian. For all we know, FitzGerald arranged the quatrains at will, manipulating the original. In any case, I was born in Mexico and immigrated to the United States. Learning English for me was a way of reinventing who I was. It took years to find some degree of comfort, however limited, in English. The truth is that no matter how much I make my home in the language, I still feel as an outsider. You've done something I find adventurous, not to say dangerous: you've translated into English from languages you don't know—Russian, Bulgarian, and Spanish. Joseph Brodsky also did it. He translated into Russian the poetry of Juan Ramón Jiménez. Once I asked Brodsky how is it possible to achieve the task when he didn't even have enough knowledge of Spanish to make his way around a kitchen. He told me that one doesn't need to know the original language in order to be able to bring the poem into one's own language (in his case, two own languages: Russian and English), because there is something mathematical about translation. Once you have the basic cultural information about what the words mean and the poet's intention, once you understand the poetic structure being handled, it's a rather easy equation.

RW: Successful translation can be done against such odds. For example, I translated a number of poems by Andrei Voznesensky with the help of Max Hayward, the translator of *Dr. Zhivago*. He, along with Patricia Blake, was editing a book of contemporary Russian poetry in translation, and he came to see me at our house in Connecticut. He took his place at one end of the couch. From time to time I brought him whiskey. He stayed for three days talking poems to me. He was careful not to do the job of translation, not to say anything final. He kept giving me first the gist, and then the answers to all of my questions. He instructed me—and this is most important—in the tone of the original poems. So I'm credited with a number of translations from Voznesensky and some other Russian poets.

IS: Would you describe Max Hayward as your co-translator? Shouldn't the translation be credited to both? Is he just a facilitator? A cultural commentator?

RW: A cultural commentator. He was careful not to say anything in iambic pentameter, to suggest what seemed to him a brilliant word to solve a problem in a certain line.

IS: As a poet, you need a surveyor to map out the original for you. You depend on his interpretation to get the tone. This means that there are two layers here: not only is the translator interpreting but there's a cultural commentator interpreting for the translator to be an interpreter. Might too much be getting lost in the affair?

RW: One factor in this relationship between facilitator and poet is that it matters greatly whether the facilitator has been accurate in thinking that you would be the person to translate this poem.

IS: The other way around matters too: you have to trust that facilitator as the bridge, since he is your connection with that thing called the poem.

RW: You do have to trust him. You get as close as you can to the original through and in spite of the facilitator. You ask him to read it out loud in the original language.

IS: How about visualizing an experiment like this: Two close friends of yours who are Russian, each quite different from the other, invite you to translate the same poem. They read it out loud to you, they comment on its cultural meaning, they feed you the tone and make you feel it. You spend three days and whiskey with one, and, allowing some time to elapse, three days and whiskey with the other. Would you produce two very different translations?

RW: Undoubtedly, since the flavor of any translation arrived at in that way has something to do with the personality of the helper. The results would be different, though not "very different."

IS: Are you predisposed, as a poet, toward certain languages? Do you go to French, Russian, Spanish, and Italian because those languages mean something to you but you don't toward others, like Hindi? I guess what I'm suggesting is that even if you had cultural commentators in Hindi, you couldn't do a translation from any language into English, only from those you are inclined to.

RW: Yes, because one has a kind of romance with some languages and cultures and is ignorant of others, or cold to them.

IS: What's the difference, in terms of romance, in your relationship with French, Russian, and Spanish? What do these languages mean to you?

RW: I suppose it mostly has to do with my experience of reading in them. I have a cumulative pleasure in French, which comes from having had a lot of individual pleasant experiences of the language. I'm also drawn to French because I spent a lot of time in France during World War II. Likewise, I have some experience as a soldier and as a resident in Italy. I have a favorable feeling for Italian culture, and I share the opinion of the person who told me, after crossing over into northern Italy, "Ah, now we're among the human race. . . ."

IS: So the question of travel does matter.

RW: Everyone has different notions of what it means to be human. And experiential knowledge is indeed important.

IS: Did your experience as a soldier during World War II, while connecting you to French, draw you away from German?

RW: I'm sure it did. Later, I had to study German when I was preparing for a PhD, which I never got. While doing it, I managed to overcome a little political repugnance. I still feel that repugnance. It troubles me that there's a great deal I can't fully enjoy because of that political blockage. However, there are grateful echoes of Hölderlin in my poems.

IS: There are two approaches to translation. First is the one endorsed by the latter Nabokov: a translation needs to remind the reader that it is an artifice, that the poem wasn't written originally in the language into which it has traveled. The second approach is linked in my mind with Flaubert, who wasn't a translator himself but who believed that in a work of literature the author should disappear, be erased without a trace. A translation of this kind then seeks not only to compete but to supplant the original. That is, a translation should free itself from its enabler, the translator.

RW: I remember enjoying Nabokov's early translations, partly because they were my only access to some Russian writers, but also because they were rather nicely executed. I have found no pleasure in looking at Nabokov's latter operations in that theater. Like most translators, what I'm interested in are miracles. By patience and good fortune, I want to bring something over to English that is faithful to the thought of the original, and does something which corresponds to its form, and has a tone as exact as possible.

IS: Since you've rendered Molière in English, I want to consider another component. When translating a historical piece, the translator must decide whether to re-create in his own language the parlance of the time in which the original was written or is supposedly conveying, or to opt for a modern approach. In Molière, you seem to want your translation to be reminiscent of the past yet utterly contemporary.

RW: That is my hope. Molière requires little mediation. The attitudes of his characters, the playwright's judgments on them, are quite intelligible to us today. I'm always combative about the efforts of some stage directors to update him, because he's already modern. Everything in his plays is quite familiar. I'm opposed to a conspicuous modernization of what doesn't need it. I detest the sort of director who has Tartuffe, while approaching an audience with Elmire, hum "I'm in the mood for love."

IS: I wonder what your experience as a translated writer is. In my own case, I make myself available to the translators who have rendered my work into another language, yet I want to be as nonintrusive as possible.

RW: Me too. I try to be useful and don't wish to hog-tie anybody. One Frenchman who has translated my poems has been entirely faithful to the metrical and rhyming patterns. Another translator into French felt that the tone perished if he strove for an excessive faithfulness to the forms. He's accomplished a felicitous but loose approximation of the formal patterns in the interest of keeping the tone.

IS: Do you have a preference?

RW: Sometimes one works and sometimes the other. Yet both of these translators have had their happy moments.

IS: What would you make of a poet in Romania with no access to the English language other than a limited dictionary and who, in order to translate a poem by Richard Wilbur, needs to find a cultural commentator? Would you be unhappy to go through the same grinder?

RW: I wouldn't object to having been used in that way. I would simply hope he was an able poet and had a good enabler.

IS: Have you chosen the translations that you've done or have they chosen you? For instance, the Spanish translation you've done of Borges?

RW: Most of my translations from Spanish, Russian, or Bulgarian were done at the suggestion of others whom I trusted. In the Jorge Guillén poems I attempted, I had Willis Barnstone check me out. Norman Thomas di

Giovanni got in touch with me about translating several of Borges's sonnets. I responded to those sonnets by an author whom I had already enjoyed in prose. I translated Borges's poem "Compass," and the happiest thing that can happen to a translator happened to me: Borges sent word to me by way of di Giovanni that one line, which I had translated as "Homes to the utmost of the sea its love," surpassed the original. A very generous thing to say!

IS: This prompts me to ask: Can a translation be better than the original? It is often said—and the Italians have a saying about it: traduttore traditore—that translation is a form of betrayal. If a translation improved on the original, can the original be the betrayer?

RW: I don't understand. The original always comes first. . . .

IS: Not really. As a composition, it does comes first in chronological time. But for the reader the translation might come first, followed by a curiosity to find what the original actually says.

RW: In the case of a superb translation, I could imagine the original, for the reader, being a letdown. But I don't think it is at all the function of translation to improve upon the original, to go it one better. I wouldn't wish to fancy that I was doing better than Molière. The challenge is to be adequate.

IS: Since translations aren't sacred—that is, we can revamp them as often as we want—do you find, upon rereading them, that they are an expression of who you were when you translated them but that they could now be improved?

RW: I'm so slavish as a translator, I work so long and hard on everything I do, that I'm not tempted to go back and retouch anything. I might see in an old translation I did years back that I struck the wrong note here or there, but—rightly or wrongly—I would not be tempted to tinker with it.

IS: What would Richard Wilbur's poetry be today had you not done any translations?

RW: I can't guess. I don't think of my poems as artificial or multivoiced. My poems speak with my whole self, and whatever my self is, it has been modified by my experience with other poets and other languages. On the other hand, I don't sense any "translationese" in my own poetry.

IS: I now want to go back to where I began. Do you think people today, young and old, speak faster than when you were an undergraduate?

RW: Yes, although my impression might have to do with the fact that I'm sometimes wearing hearing aids.

IS: Is it a truism that the American language is spoken today in a speedier way?

RW: Faster and with less forethought. Some sentences of my bright young students have six or seven "likes" in them.

IS: A cancer. I tell my students that if we eliminated the "likes" in their conversation, the class would shrink from eighty to sixty minutes. Anyway, given the state of the English language today, the impact of the Beat Generation, the use—and abuse—of the Internet, what is your recommendation to an aspiring translator and maybe to those who simply want to toy with what I would call "language travel"? I, for one, believe we don't pay enough attention to translation in small liberal arts colleges, although we surely are mindful of it. Even for those who don't dream of a life as a translator, attempting to bring a text from one language to another is a revelation, don't you think?

RW: My advice to the interested student is to first make sure you know how to write in English meter and rhyme. A fair part of what one might wish to do honor to is going to require not only an equivalent form but a well-chosen equivalent form. In translating from French alexandrines, for instance, it would be horrible to render them in English six-footers. One has to equal them in some way. Happily, the English pentameter will house almost everything that can exist in an alexandrine. It is crucial to develop corresponding forms for what one may encounter in the languages from which one wants to translate.

IS: And then what—patience? Patience is very hard to teach.

RW: Patience is the translator's chief virtue. What gives my translations such merit as they have is that I will really spend a whole day trying to solve a couplet. To many people, that is unimaginably dull, not to say confining. But until that couplet is properly done, I won't go on to the next.

ON SILENCE

(with Charles Hatfield)

Charles Hatfield: I want to talk about Octavio Paz and Jorge Luis Borges as translators. Let's start with one of the translations in *Versiones y diversiones* (1973/1978/1995), the volume that brought together Paz's translations of poets ranging from William Carlos Williams and Hart Crane to Pierre Reverdy and Guillaume Apollinaire. One of Paz's richest translations is of Elizabeth Bishop's "A Summer's Dream" (1948), and maybe we should begin by reflecting on what Paz wrote about Bishop in an essay from the late 1970s: "Poetry is not in what words say," he wrote, "but in what is said between them, that which appears fleetingly in pauses and silences." Of course, we know that the idea of silence was *huge* for Paz. You once characterized Paz's translations of poets like Bishop and others as "personal versions" and "appropriations." Is there something we can say about Paz's translation of "A Summer's Dream" in particular that might help us understand the nature of Paz's appropriations better? Or should we begin by talking about Paz's theories of poetic translation (you'll recall that in his 1973 prologue to *Versiones y diversiones*, Paz wrote that his essay "Literatura y literalidad" contained his "teoría de la traducción poética," or theory of translating poetry)?

Ilan Stavans: The relationship between the two is fascinating: he translated her, she translated him. In *The FSG Book of Twentieth-Century Latin American Poetry* (2011), I included some of her versions of his poetry (as well as numerous poems by Brazilian authors she translated). To what extent is the relationship between them symmetrical? Who is more respectful?

Ezra Pound believed that no one who isn't a poet should dare to translate poetry. He is right and he is wrong. Right because only a poet is

---

First published in *The Buenos Aires Review*, July 15, 2015.

able to understand another poet. By *understand* I mean to know what the trade means, what concocting universes through bricks of words amounts to. And wrong because a poet might know too much, might be too close to "the real thing" to engage in the effort objectively. In the comparison, Bishop strikes me as a more respectful translator of Paz's Spanish than Paz is of Bishop's English. Take the penultimate stanza:

> He was morose,
> but she was cheerful.
> The bedroom was cold,
> the feather bed close.
> Él siempre malhumorado,
> aleluyas ella siempre.
> Recámara congelada,
> mullido lecho de plumas.

Paz eliminates almost all the verbs and articles. He introduces a staccato quality to the stanza. But do they say the same thing? My answer is a rotund no: "He was morose" doesn't mean, by any stretch of the imagination, "*Él siempre malhumorado.*" And so on. As an exercise, let me retranslate—rather plainly—Paz's translation back to English (without looking at her English):

> He always in a bad mood,
> she always in halleluiahs.
> Frozen bedroom,
> fluffy feather bed.

Paz's silences are thefts. Or else, I could gently say that he doesn't translate as much as he rewrites. The latter is a polite statement. But his rendition—let me not sugarcoat it—at its heart, verges on disrespect.

That's why I'm always in favor of releasing poetry in translation with the original serving as companion.

CH: Bishop's poem must have interested Paz in part because of its treatment of silence. The poem, of course, isn't actually silent, but the people and things in it are: the "gentle storekeeper" is "asleep"; the "shrunken seamstress" doesn't speak and only "smiled"; the "boarding house" is "streaked / as though it had been crying" (its streaks are silent residues of a sound from the past). The speaker declares that "we listened / for a horned owl," but they don't hear it. When we do get sound in the poem, it's not really language—the "stammer" and "grumbling" of the "giant"; and when we get language, it's not really sound—it comes in the form of the "old grammar" that the "giant" is poring over. In the last stanza, the speakers are awakened by the brook "dreaming audibly," which Paz translates as "soñaba hablando en voz alta." Paz's translation seems to diminish the paradox of "dreaming audibly" by having the brook actually speak out loud *while* dreaming ("*hablando en voz alta*").

What I'm getting at is this: what must have interested Paz about this poem in particular is its treatment of both silence and the paradoxes involved in representing it (in his poem "On Reading John Cage," Paz wrote that "Music is not silence: / It is not saying / What silence says, / It is saying / What it doesn't say"). But in his translation of Bishop's "A Summer's Dream," Paz actually *adds* sound to the poem where there was none. For example, Bishop writes that "Every night we listened / for a horned owl," and so the horned owl is expressed as a kind of silence in the poem—the speakers listen for it, but it is not heard. Yet in Paz's translation, the speakers "*escuchábamos gritar al búho cornudo*," meaning they actually "heard" (*escuchábamos*) the owl "shout" or "cry" (*gritar*). Whereas the owl is silent and absent in Bishop's poem, it is screeching and audible in Paz's. Another instance of this (not to belabor the point) is Paz's choice of the verb "*rezongar*" to express Bishop's "grumbling" of the giant, in which what is clearly not language in Bishop's poem approaches language in Paz's—"*rezongar*" can mean "grumbling," but it can also mean "complaining."

I love what you did with Paz's translation of "she was cheerful" as "aleluyas ella siempre." I was struck by your idea that Paz's omissions of fundamental linguistic components of the sentence—the verbs—constitute both a silence and theft. He literally takes words, verbs no less, out of his Spanish version. Yet it's also interesting to note that Paz actually *adds* sound. Being "cheerful" doesn't imply any kind of sound at all: it's just a state of being that can be expressed without any sounds. But even though the idea of the landlady as "always in halleluiahs" gets us the image of a pretty cheerful lady, the literal meaning is of someone who expresses her state of being *through sound*. So we end up with a perplexing situation in which Paz translates a poem that masterfully renders (and depends on) silence in a markedly not-silent way. In fact, Paz seems to convert silence into sound at virtually every turn. What can we make of this? I have to wonder if it gets us to the problems involved in thinking of silence as meaningful. As Paz put it in "On Reading John Cage," "Silence has no sense, / sense has no silence," which is one way of saying that as soon we see silences as meaningful, it's hard to think of them as silences, or at least as what Paz calls "the nothing in between."

IS: Paz at times is right on target. And his talents as a translator—or, at least, as a poet—are obvious and consistent. Let's consider another Bishop poem translated by Paz: the gorgeous "Visits to St. Elizabeths," which dates to 1950 and is loosely connected with her friend Robert Lowell's life. In this case, Paz does an admirable job. Yes, there are liberties, maybe even abuses. But in the end he lands on solid ground.

For starters, notice the double plural in the original. Paz translates the title as "Visitas a St. Elizabeth," the hospital name now in singular. Bishop, of course, is invoking her own name. But it isn't easy to translate. Anyway, the poem begins:

> This is the house of Bedlam.
> This is the man
> that lies in the house of Bedlam.
> This is the time
> of the tragic man
> that lies in the house of Bedlam.
> This is a wristwatch
> telling the time
> of the talkative man
> that lies in the house of Bedlam.
> This is a sailor
> wearing the watch
> that tells the time
> of the honored man
> that lies in the house of Bedlam.

The poem falsely mimics a children's song built around repetition. Paz's delivery of these first five stanzas goes:

> Esta es la casa de los locos.
> Este es el hombre
> que está en la casa de los locos.
> Este es el tiempo

> del hombre trágico
> que está en la casa de los locos.
> Este es el reloj-pulsera
> que da la hora
> del hombre locuaz
> que está en la casa de los locos.
> Este es el marinero
> que usa el reloj
> que da la hora
> del hombre tan celebrado
> que está en la casa de los locos.

Bishop plays with an archaism: *bedlam* is used for lunatic. The route she takes is intriguing: Bethlem is a mental hospital, Bethlem Royal Hospital in London, from which the word *bedlam* came to mean madness. She turns it into a name: the house of Bedlam, that is, the house of madness. There are strange word choices ("tan celebrado" for "honored," and so on). But the soar, the biggest challenge, is Bishop's "house of Bedlam," where she uses an uppercase *B* to refer to the place. Is Paz creative? In this case, I believe he is, for I see no other way out.
In the last stanza, Bishop writes:

> This is the soldier home from the war.
> These are the years and the walls and the door
> that shut on a boy that pats the floor
> to see if the world is round or flat.
> This is a Jew in a newspaper hat
> that dances carefully down the ward,
> walking the plank of a coffin board
> with the crazy sailor
> that shows his watch
> that tells the time
> of the wretched man
> that lies in the house of Bedlam.

In Paz's rendition:

> Este es el soldado que vuelve de la guerra.
> Estos son los años y los muros y la puerta

que se cierra sobre un muchacho que golpea el piso
para saber si el mundo es plano o redondo.
Este es el judío con un gorro de papel periódico
que baila con cuidado por el dormitorio
caminando sobre la tabla de un ataúd
con el marinero chiflado
que muestra el reloj
que da la hora
del desdichado
que está en la casa de los locos.

Frankly, the rendition is admirable: one needs the liberties Paz takes in order to make the poem tick in Spanish.

CH: Let's now turn to Borges. Elsewhere we have discussed in depth some of his strategies as a translator. Now I want to focus on some of the mysteries and polemics surrounding his translation of William Faulkner's *The Wild Palms*. Douglas Day wrote a great essay called "Borges, Faulkner, and *The Wild Palms*," which I will always be grateful to if only for having brought to my attention Alan Tate's description of Faulkner as a "Dixie Gongorist." Day's essay settles an important point: it's often said that Borges sanitized Faulkner's text, when in fact, as Day points out, Borges was merely basing his translation on an already sanitized British edition of the novel published by Chatto and Windus in London.

We don't need to get into all the intricacies in Day's argument beyond the following: Borges, Day points out, wrote reviews of *Absalom! Absalom!*, *The Unvanquished*, and *The Wild Palms* in the journal *El Hogar* during the late 1930s, and while he had high praise for *Absalom* and *The Unvanquished*, he wrote that in *The Wild Palms*, Faulkner's "technical novelties" seemed "less attractive than bothersome, less justifiable than exasperating." In the end, Borges concluded that the novel wouldn't be a good introduction to Faulkner's writing. So why did he translate it? The reasons, Day suggests, are banal, having to do more with rights and contracts than with Borges's own tastes and values. But the more interesting question has to do with why, years later, Borges seemed to attribute the translation to his mother. Day's answer is that he did so because his translation of *The Wild Palms* came at a time in Borges's career when he was turning away "from the psychological experimentalism and brutal (one is tempted to say 'messy') content of a William Faulkner and turned to a form which for him rendered the novel redundant and irrelevant: *Ficciones*."

As to the translation itself, Day called it "very good." There's been a good deal of debate surrounding Borges's translation of *The Wild Palms*. Whereas, for example, Day argues that *The Wild* Palms represented just the kind of fiction writing Borges was getting away from in *Ficciones*, Earl and Ezra Fitz argue just the opposite: *Las palmeras salvajes*, they say, "should be read in conjunction with "Pierre Menard, Author of the *Quixote*" as a crucial part of Borges's narrative revolution, one that depends on the reader's role in the creative process and on the innumerable ways the act of translation makes manifest this then audacious theory." I recently came across a useful account of different assessments of Borges's translation in Gareth Wood's book on Javier Marías and translation. One is by Marías himself, who wrote that Borges translated Faulkner *"bastante mal,"* adding that it was not *"por sus argentinismos, sino por su conocimiento imperfecto del inglés"* and also, more interestingly, because of his "falta de aliento novelístico." Then there's Piglia's claim that "lo que uno encuentra en esa traducción es una lucha entre el estilo de Borges y el estilo de Faulkner."

Wood looks carefully at Borges's translation and uncovers interesting renderings, such as, for example, when Borges translates "You're mad because he used a scalpel without having a diploma" as *"Te has enloquecido porque ha usado un bisturí sin tener diploma,"* mistaking *mad* meaning "angry" for *mad* meaning "crazy." The other assessment of Borges's translation that Wood discusses is by Juan Benet, who wrote in reference to Borges's edition that *"me veo obligado a transcribir las citas del texto traducido por Borges, por carecer de otra edición."* Wood himself calls parts of the translation—and the dialogue in particular—"flat and staid, attempting none of the verbal idiosyncrasies of popular speech."

I recently had the pleasure of reading your essay "Beyond Translation: Borges and Faulkner" (included in *Borges, The Jew*, 2016), which ends with a detailed analysis of Borges's translation of *The Wild Palms*. You suggest that Borges's *ars poetica* of translation comes in four parts—his story "Pierre Menard, Author of the *Quixote*"; his essays "On *Vathek*, by William Beckford" and "The Translators of the *1001 Nights*"; and finally his own translation of Faulkner's *The Wild Palms*. You note that "the resemblance—in syntax, in spirit—is startling" between the two texts, and you go on to argue that if it can be said there are two approaches to translation (one in which the translator "disappears," and another in which "the translator endlessly stresses the artificiality of his endeavor"), Borges comes down on the side of the former. In his translation of *The Wild Palms*, Borges is "*behind* Faulkner, not in front or at his side." Maybe we can continue our discussion of Borges's translation of Faulkner, which raises a lot of questions and promises to be a long discussion, by asking you to revisit some of your claims.

IS: I'm glad you've found the essay provocative. Translation is a cornerstone in his oeuvre. Menardismo, as you know, has even become an ideology, just as Quixotismo is. Borges translated lots of texts throughout his career. He started quite young, with Oscar Wilde. The translation was for a time mistakenly credited to his father. He also translated Virginia Woolf, for whom he had little patience. In Buenos Aires magazines, he translated ghost stories, essays by G. K. Chesterton and Poe, and other stuff. As for Faulkner, he loved him, as did Onetti and García Márquez: because his Deep South was much like Latin America, a region scarred by history. Except that Borges didn't seek to rewrite Yoknapatawpha County; he simply savors it as a reader.

Reading and translating are one and the same thing, for Borges and for myself. In his essay on Beckford, he says that the original can be untruthful to the translation. And in his meditation on *1001 Nights*, he argues that translators have taken liberties that have gone beyond the semantic level, sometimes introducing entirely new characters, as in the case of Sinbad.

Nabokov, in rendering Pushkin's *Eugene Onegin* into English, makes his version baroque, artificial. He abuses the footnote. His onetime friend Edmund Wilson attacked this Pushkin version rather viciously in the pages of the newly created *New York Review of Books*. Borges cannot escape his own semantics; he translates using adjectives the way only Borges would use them. (Remember the opening of "The Circular Ruins": "*Nadie lo vio desembarcar en la unánime noche.*") But he has no intention of upstaging Faulkner, at least not overtly.

CH: What fascinates me most in the end is the attention that Borges's translation of *The Wild Palms* has generated. It sounds like a weird question, but why do we care so much about Borges's *Las palmeras salvajes*? It can't only be because the text was largely responsible for introducing generations of Latin American writers to Faulkner, nor can it only be because we all love Borges and thus we naturally are fascinated by his translations. In other words, I wonder if there's some anxiety getting worked out through all of this—an old anxiety about the "originality" of the Latin American novel, or about what it would mean if *el gran* Borges just did the translation (as Day sort of implies) for the cash, or about *translation* as an activity writ large. It might not be an entirely useful question, but I do wonder what we're all really trying to work out when we argue that Borges *did it well* or *did it badly* or *made it his own* or *didn't make it his own* or *theorized through doing it*, etc. What do you think?

IS: Thank you for the intriguing context you've provided, which offers a more complete picture than the one I had when I wrote my essay on Borges and Faulkner. First, let me endorse the serendipitous argument. Biography is always written in hindsight, through the rearview mirror. Yet life is never lived that way: it's always unpredictable, arbitrary, even chaotic. Borges was a master in the art of curating his own career. When we look at it, it seems consistent, coherent, straightforward to a degree that, frankly, is suspicious. We all take detours, don't we? We all get lost. We embark on projects that become dead ends. Of course, a convincing career is always measured by the thread uniting the successful projects. Yet what happens with those that ended up in the dumpster? That Borges probably did the job for money seems too pedestrian, like when I was hired to write a how-to book for the Smithsonian: I needed money to pay for my first child's diapers, plain and simple.

Generally speaking, I'm not a fan of Piglia; but I like Piglia's description of Borges's translation of *Las palmeras salvajes* as a boxing ring. Borges's false starts are fascinating. His incapacity to let Faulkner's style breathe is symptomatic of his own overwhelming *barroquismo*. Why is this rendition so controversial? You may have hit the nail on the head. Faulkner will end up becoming the patron saint for Rulfo, Onetti, García Márquez, and others, the father of the fractured, experimental novel. Yet Borges, at this point, is already dissing the novel as a literary genre. He finds it exhausting, too malleable. He ridicules Dostoyevsky's *Crime and Punishment* for convincing the reader that a heinous crime is worth committing for moral reasons. Plus, this comes at a time when translation is increasingly taken seriously in Latin America. Many intellectuals embrace it as a worthy endeavor. And finally: almost every translation by Borges has generated rivers of ink; therein his role as the Moses of literary translation in the Spanish-language Americas. The Faulkner case is emblematic, but so is his fragmentary version of *Leaves of Grass*, for instance.

TRANSLATING CERVANTES

(with Diana de Armas Wilson)

Ilan Stavans: Not too long ago, I participated in the controversy surrounding Andrés Trapiello's intralinguistic translation of *El Quijote* (2015). His quest was to modernize the early seventeenth-century Spanish, making it accessible to contemporary readers.

Diana de Armas Wilson: The year 2015 also saw the Oregon Shakespeare Festival's decision to commission thirty-six playwrights to "translate" all of Shakespeare's plays into contemporary English. Unlike Trapiello's modernization of Cervantes's prose, the prospect of modernizing Shakespeare's poetry—of losing the rhythm and music of his iambic pentameter—disturbs me.

A staged performance of a poetic play seems a far cry from a private reading of a prose novel. I'm therefore of two minds about the recent moves to modernize Shakespeare and Cervantes, both hypercanonical figures. Although Trapiello's adaptation of *Don Quijote* has angered numerous Spaniards—one Madrid academic called it a "crime against literature"—I celebrate his achievement.

Trapiello's edition aims to reach Spanish readers and students dismayed by excessive erudition, by having to chase an endnote to discover that *"menear las negras"* meant swordplay in antiquated Castilian. The original *Don Quijote* is still available to those of us who enjoy the chase. Noble Laureate Mario Vargas Llosa claims that Trapiello "rejuvenates" *Don Quijote*. Cornell professor María Antonia Garcés honors Trapiello's daring, his *"atrevimiento."* The impulse to modernize venerated prose works may occasionally lead purists to press criminal charges.

It may even lead, as in the shocking case of your own Spanglish version of *Don Quijote*, to death threats. Are we returning to the world of books-as-heretics, to the world parodied in the famous "inquisition" of Don Quijote's library?

IS: I discussed a number of aspects of Trapiello's endeavor in *The Guardian* and *El País*, but not Vargas Llosa's perplexing prologue. This conversation feels like a suitable place for it. In it, Vargas Llosa reminisces of his time as a young artist in Paris in the sixties, recalling how André Malraux, Minister of Cultural Affairs under De Gaulle, after announcing he would clean up the façade of grand classic buildings throughout France, provoked an outcry "from erudite scholars and academics according to whom it was a true heresy to deprive the great historical monuments of the reverential patina centuries had covered them with." Nevertheless, sometime later, when the dirt and dust they were enwrapped in disappeared and "the architectural marvels of Notre Dame, the Louvre, the Tour Saint-Jacques, and the bridges over the Seine appeared with their clean face and everyone was able to admire in its primordial splendor the delicacy of their details, the achievements and beauties of these atemporal jewels, a kind of unanimity prevailed" in regards to Malraux's wise decision "to actualize the cultural past, turning it to the present."

Vargas Llosa uses a false image here, it's clear to me. The implication is that *El Quijote*, covered with dirt after centuries of reading, is being cleansed by Trapiello. But there's nothing dirty in Cervantes's language. Successive generations of readers haven't obscured its message. Yes, language has aged, although one doesn't clean a classic like Jane Austen's *Pride and Prejudice* or Goethe's *Faust* from archaisms. Cleaning a building is a cosmetic undertaking. It doesn't undermine the original architecture; it simply makes visible the invisible in its surface. Is that what translation does in general? Yes, but it isn't a cosmetic exercise. There is something far deeper, reaching for the essence of a literary work. In any case, "actualizing" a literary classic, as Trapiello does, replaces the time-framed language of the original (its colors, to use a visual reference) with its contemporary counterpart: the same language, Spanish, yet different.

By invoking a metaphor of cleanliness, Vargas Llosa—once again—tangentially invokes purity as a necessary effort in connection with language and, in this case, the classics. Like you, I admire Trapiello's venture. But, like all translation, it is doomed to be replaced by subsequent ones, while the original remains intact. As you know, a similar debate is taking place in the Shakespeare world after the Oregon Shakespeare Festival invited the project as a way to clean the dust surrounding The Bard.

DW: Centuries of dirt or reverential patina? Scrubbing a building or a text? Trapiello did not set out to give Cervantes's masterpiece a "clean face," as

Vargas Llosa implies in his prologue. But his comparative cleanup act brings to mind similar rituals during Cervantes's day. Cleaning up one's ancestry, for instance. Who could forget the Purity of Blood statutes legislated in Toledo in 1547—the same year Cervantes was born? For his ideas of blood purity, we need only turn to the interlude of *El retablo de las maravillas*, where the concept is wittily satirized. A version of "The Emperor's New Clothes" staged by a picaresque couple, this farce of a play-within-a play can only be seen by spectators of "pure" Christian blood who are not illegitimate. Although there is nothing to see, everyone in this small Spanish town, fearful of being considered tainted, pretends to see it.

IS: What is there to do when a Nobel Prize winner delivers a prologue to one of your books and you realize its message is misconstrued? I don't know if it was Trapiello who asked Vargas Llosa for it, or if it was his publisher. If the purpose of a prologue (always more succinct than an introduction) is to spark interest, the objective was achieved handsomely. Even the idea of turning the past to present is misguided: Trapiello, in my view, doesn't have such an aim.

The past is always the past . . . Classics, in that sense, are visitors to the present, where they are read in multiple, sometimes disconcerting ways, as Pierre Menard amply proves. Intriguingly, Borges's blindness—his myopia, in particular—forced him, after the age of thirty, to bring books closer to his eyes. There is a photograph of him in Buenos Aires's Biblioteca Nacional holding one only a few inches away. Classics ask to be read closely; also, in terms of speed they require a slower, more meticulous pace. This is because their language and much more in them aren't current. In the face of that antiquity, readers become decoders. Trapiello does more than decode *El Quijote*: he rereads it.

As for the cleanup act, for me the opening lines of Cervantes's novel are precisely about concealment and not about revelation. Who is this hidalgo we are about to spend a hundred and twenty-five chapters with? As in Kafka's *The Metamorphosis* (the Czech, it is universally known, was a Quixote devotee), we have no information whatsoever about Kafka's bug-hero's ancestry.

Fortunately, Trapiello doesn't add any extemporaneous material in that regard. Actually, he is quite knowledgeable, even reverential when it comes to the original. After all, he is also a novelist . . . It is scholars, not writers, who have done as much as possible—even against Cervantes's intentions—to fill in the blanks.

Incidentally, I find it intriguing, as I stated in my book *Quixote: The Novel and the World*, that, in historiographic terms, we know more about Cervantes than we know about Shakespeare. They lived concurrent lives, of course. Did one know of the other? An intertwined double biography awaits to be written. *Hamlet* was written sometime between 1599 and 1602. The prince's intellectual paralysis, his philosophical inquisitiveness, and Don Quixote's critique of reason play on each other. Plus, the two works have texts-within-texts. Clearly, in the second half of the sixteenth century there was something in the air in England and Spain (and in Montaigne's France, I might add)—call it the "Age of Introspection," fostered by Erasmism—that allowed for the modernity of these authors to coalesce.

In regard to the link between Shakespeare and Cervantes, in recent years, *Cardenio*, the collaborative play by Shakespeare and John Fletcher, has regained traction and, along the way, our attention.

DW: Yes, critics are talking about a twenty-first-century "Cardenio boom," with Anglo-Americans suddenly curious about the distraught lover-turned-madman in Part One of *Don Quijote*. Why the centuries-long delay? We know that a play called *Cardenna* or *Cardenno* was performed in 1613 at court in Greenwich by the King's Men, a London theater company. The play was later attributed to Shakespeare and his collaborator John Fletcher in a 1653 Stationers' Register entry. And then in 1727 the Shakespearean editor Lewis Theobald produced a play called *Double Falsehood*, which he claimed to be "built upon a Novel in *Don Quixot*."

While the plot of the 1613 *Cardenno* remains a mystery, re-creations of the lost play now abound. The director of the Royal Shakespeare Company, Gregory Doran, "reimagined" Cardenio in 2011 by turning to *Don Quijote* to fill in the blanks in Theobald's *Double Falshood*. Or, as Doran himself puts it, "to put the Iberian 'cojones' back into it." Although the staged production of his grafting has received sterling reviews, Barbara Fuchs questions some of its colorful Iberian addenda. For a lively commentary on the twenty-first-century returns of Cardenio, see *The Poetics of Piracy* (2013), where Fuchs stresses England's cultural indebtedness—its "willed blindness"—to the Spanish origins of the lost play. She rightly claims that the Anglo-American academy, thanks to a combination of the Black Legend and anti-Spanish prejudice, has not recognized those early debts.

A wider recognition is now occurring, with playwrights across the globe resuscitating Cervantes's character, largely in response to Stephen

Greenblatt's Cardenio Project, funded by the Mellon Foundation. The Project's website, which asks theater companies to produce their very own cultural versions of Cardenio, includes plays written in Brazil, Poland, Croatia, Turkey, Egypt, India, Japan, and Spain. The Spanish version, a metatheatrical piece about an author commissioned to write his own version of Cardenio, contains such deathless lines as "Shit, I really don't know about this. It's good money. I can't say no. It's Harvard. Greenblatt, Stephen Greenblatt or Greenbalt?" All the plays in the Cardenio Project are supposed to be transmutations, experiments in "cultural mobility." Greenblatt's own 2003 recycling of Cardenio, together with the playwright Charles Mee, serves as a model. "Inspired by a lost play of Shakepeare's," their version is set in Tuscany, its main plot oddly based on another of Cervantes's interpolated tales, *El curioso impertinente*.

IS: "Inspired by a lost play . . ." It reminds me of the fact that the narrator of *El Quijote* presents the story to us as a palimpsest based on a folktale often retold in La Mancha, and the version we are given is a rendition by an improvised translator of a manuscript in Arabic sold by a young man in Toledo ("*llegó un muchacho a vender unos cartapacios y papeles viejos a un sedero*"), written by an Arab historian. This is an exquisite device. Arabs, including Arab historians, are liars who can't be trusted, we are repeatedly told. In other words, the story of Alonso Quijano, a dreamer who does nothing but ridicule himself, is all a game.

Still, to me Greenblatt's Cardenio Project isn't only unfortunate but infantile: an abuse in relativism. More compelling is your question, why the long delay in appreciating *Cardenio*? The answer, I trust, has to do with a telluric shift in Shakespeare scholarship. The Bard used to be appraised as a lone genius, above the rest of humanity. However, in recent decades the interest is on collaboration: How much of his plays did Shakespeare actually write? What were the strategies in regards to composition among playwrights in Elizabethan England? In other words, how should authorship be understood when actors and directors, let alone editors and publishers, were responsible for adapting the Bard's lines? And, with collaborators like Fletcher, Shakespeare probably compartmentalized sections of the play, some of which he was responsible for, and others he didn't even read before the play was staged.

Theobald's play *Double Falshood* comes with a long and complicated history. And the version by Doran is also disappointing. In sum, the play itself, in its various current versions, is rather tedious. Its magnetism derives from the fact that Shakespeare was involved in it, albeit marginally. The same is true with *Henry the Eighth, King John*, and *The Two Noble Kinsmen*, for instance. The material from the novella "The Ill-Conceived Curiosity" in *El Quijote* is used—or rather, abused—so loosely (names are changed, the plot is reconfigured) as to become almost indistinguishable. What attracts me, however, is the fact that it shows the degree to which Thomas Shelton's English translation of the First Part of *El Quijote*, called *The History of the Valorous and Wittie Knight-Errant Don Quixote of the Mancha*, was popular in London in the early half of the seventeenth century. Almost nothing is known about Shelton other than that he was born in Dublin to a Roman Catholic family and that his brother John was hanged for his participation in the taking of Dublin Castle. This was the first full rendition ever (a small portion of the book had appeared in French earlier) and was done in 1607, shortly after the Spanish appeared in 1605, apparently "in the space of forty daies: being thereunto more then halfe enforced, through the importunitie of a very deere friend, that was desirous to understand the subject." It was dedicated "To the Right Honourable His Verie Good Lord, The Lord of Walden, &c.," Theophilus Howard, son of Thomas Howard, first Earl of Suffolk. The translation didn't reach the printing firm of Edward Blount and William Barret until 1612.

DW: It's curious that the first English translator of *Don Quijote* was an Irish Catholic, that he dedicated his work to an English nobleman, and that his translation took a mere forty days. This would make a gripping novel, including chapters on the hanged brother.

IS: In 1620, the translation of the Second Part of *El Quijote*, which had appeared in Spanish in 1615, was released. This time the printer was only Edward Blount. Although it is often credited to Shelton too, there is considerable controversy as to who did the job, since Shelton's name doesn't appear in the publication, and the dedication is signed by the publisher. Be that as it may, we know almost nothing about Shelton. Is it possible that he traveled to Spain, as it has been speculated, and that he read *El Quijote* there? Could he have met Cervantes himself? These are questions without answers.

At any rate, it was an auspicious introduction to a Spanish book and its author, for, within a relatively short period of time, the two would become favorites of English readers: not only was Shelton's version, as it is known (that is, the two parts together), frequently abridged, illustrated, and revised by anonymous hands—it was republished in 1652, 1672, and 1675—but also it has the honor of having been read by, among others, Ben Jonson, John Milton, and John Dryden; and Cervantes's assortment of smaller works (short plays, poems, his *Exemplary Novels*, and other works like *The Travails of Persiles and Sigismunda*) would be rendered into English, at regular intervals, throughout the seventeenth century.

On the London stage, Jonson refers to *El Quijote* in *The Alchemist*. Fletcher himself, in collaboration with Philip Massinger, wrote another play, *The Double Marriage*, also based on Cervantes's canonical novel. It focuses on a portion of the Second Part, in which Sancho Panza, about to become governor of the island of Barataria, is tormented during dinner by a physician.

Other plays by Fletcher and Massinger, alone and in collaboration, most of them lost, such as *The Prophetess*, *The Picture*, and *The Renegado: or, The Gentleman of Venice*, were also probably inspired by the novel. Finally, *The Custom of the Country*, based on Cervantes's *Persiles y Sigismunda*, is not lost—although it should be.

DW: Shelton's *History of the Valorous and Wittie Knight-Errant Don Quixote of the Mancha* seems to have also inspired English readers across the Ocean. We find Don Quixote tilting at windmills as early as the 1630s in the New England colonies. When the Mayflower passenger and Pilgrim Miles Standish attacked Thomas Morton for his sinful lifestyle—for erecting a maypole and singing drinking songs in Merrymount—the Pilgrims chopped down the maypole, had Morton arrested, carried back to England, and imprisoned. Morton compared the blows dealt him and other Puritan "worthies" as akin to "Don Kwik-sot against the Windmill." Apart from his merry pranks, Morton was clearly a reader. Cotton Mather also appropriated the same metaphoric windmills to vilify Roger Williams, whom he portrayed as "not only the first rebel against the divine-church order in the wilderness," but also a man with such a furious "windmill" whirling in his head that "a whole country in America" was likely "to be set on fire" for it. The imitation of Don Quijote here is of a crazed and dangerous rebel against "the divine-church order," which tells us more about Cotton Mather than about Cervantes.

IS: Last night I had dinner with an Emily Dickinson scholar, who reflected on the references by the "belle of Amherst" to *El Quijote* in her correspondence. She had in her personal library a copy of the translation published in Philadelphia. In one letter, she compares the knight with a local obsessed with "fighting the anti-Christ." The fight against the Catholic Church—it's the same Manichean opposition one finds in the Broadway musical *Man of La Mancha* and countless other adaptations. Personally, I find it ironic that Cervantes has been turned into a universal symbol against the Holy Inquisition. There are more suitable seventeenth-century candidates, a number of them martyrs, for that job. Sor Juana Inés de La Cruz, for instance, whose intellectual quest ended abruptly when she was forced to take a vow of silence. Anyway, the stratagem is proof, yet again, that the Cervantes who died in 1616 wasn't the Cervantes of today, just as the Shakespeare who also died that year didn't imagine for a second he would become the most important figure ever to write in the English language. Proof of it is the fact that, while Ben Jonson was carefully overseeing the publication of his plays, The Bard appears not to have had any interest whatsoever in doing the same. He only cared to publish his poetry, *The Sonnets*, *Venus and Adonis*, and *The Rape of Lucrece*.

DW: Your mention of *Man of La Mancha* makes me wonder about the strange attachment of our countrymen to that longtime staple of American dinner theater. And not only our countrymen: the 1964 musical has enjoyed productions in many languages, including Uzbek, Gujarati, and Swahili. *Man of La Mancha* stages Cervantes in prison, awaiting trial by the Spanish Inquisition.

Besides funding that Manichean opposition you mention, this is a fiction. Cervantes spent five years in an Algerian prison as a captive of the Muslims, and another stint in a Seville prison for a tax shortfall. Unlike those "more suitable seventeenth-century candidates" you mention, Cervantes was never tried by the Holy Inquisition. I gather that Dale Wasserman, who wrote the original teleplay, complained about the musical. Much of its popularity may stem from the song "The Impossible Dream." Sad that this tired and sentimental musical has not only trumped Cervantes's novel but also rescripted his life.

IS: A while back, William P. Childers and I toyed with the idea of an anthology called *Don Quixote in America*, featuring pieces like part of Book II, Chapter 15 of Thomas Morton's *New English Canaan* (1637), quotes from Washington Irving's correspondence, a scene from María Amparo Ruíz de Burton's *Don Quixote de la Mancha: A Comedy in Five Acts* (published in 1876 but performed earlier), a segment from Chapter 3 of Mark Twain's

Adventures of Huckleberry Finn (1884), a portion of the screenplay *Bananas* (1971) by Woody Allen and Mickey Rose, and other stuff by John Dos Passos, William Faulkner, John Steinbeck, and so on. The idea was to restrict our attention to the United States in order to see how *El Quijote* has been put to use.

DW: And let's not forget Tennessee Williams, who claimed that Don Quijote was "the true American." According to this playwright, "you do not have to look into many American eyes to suddenly meet somewhere the beautiful grave lunacy of his gaze."

IS: To me *El Quijote* is as enthralling for what readers find in it as for what they concoct, the misreadings they've produced. In that sense, there are two *Quijotes*: one with everything Cervantes put in and an altogether different one with everything that isn't by Cervantes himself. One of the original librettists of *Man of La Mancha* was W. H. Auden. There are remnants of his version, which, not surprisingly, ended up in the dustbin of history. Translators are also to blame for creating all sorts of alternative narratives. For instance, in 1677 François Filleau de Saint-Martin translated *El Quijote* into French as *Histoire de l'admirable Don Quichotte de la Manche*, leaving out the last chapter of the Second Part because he wanted to write a sequel of his own and having Don Quixote die in his bed was an avoidable block. Then there is Tobias Smollett's English translation in 1755, still mired in controversy. Needless to say, these liberties are nothing new. The translators of the *Arabian Nights* often included stories of their own, another night in Scheherazade's struggle to save herself from the cruel Sultan, including, most prominently, Sinbad's adventure.

Only recently has the discipline of translation become professionalized. For a long time, it was also the refuge of auspicious careerists, con artists, and plagiarists.

DW: In *Quixote: The Novel and the World*, you note that Smollett's 1755 version has been judged as a hoax, notably by Carmine R. Linsalata (*Smollett's Hoax*, 1956). Yet you also wonder why the successful author of *Roderick Random* (1748) would have taken on yet another translation, given the series of extant English versions—by Shelton, Phillips, Motteux, and Jarvis. I'm with the late A. A. Parker, who judged Linsalata's attack as "unconvincing." My objection to Smollett, however, is not to his use of parallel passages from earlier translators of the *Quijote*, but to his abuse of their better versions. Consider Smollett's scolding of Shelton as an "ingenious annotator" in this coarse and crazed footnote on *"duelos y quebrantos"*: "Having considered this momentous affair with all the deliberation it deserves, we in our turn present the reader, with cucumbers, greens and pease-porridge, as the fruit of our industrious researches, being thereunto determined, by the literal signification of the text, which is not 'grumblings and groanings,' as the last mentioned ingenious annotator seems to think; but rather pains and breakings; and evidently points at such eatables as generate and expel wind; qualities (as everyone knows) eminently inherent in those vegetables we have mentioned as our hero's Saturday repast."

IS: I'm riveted by cases of translators, and there's an abundance of them, who don't know the language they work from. Joseph Brodsky translated Juan Ramón Jiménez into Russian without knowing Spanish. Richard Wilbur did the same with Anna Akhmatova into English. Notice I'm not listing amateurs but esteemed luminaries. Actually, I spoke to both of them about their efforts, which, by the way, were lauded by natives and foreigners alike, and they explained, in detail, the method they used. They translated poetry, not prose, as Smollett did, in my mind a more arduous—perhaps impossible—task. I read A. A. Parker's rebuttal but remain persuaded by Linsalata. I don't see the Smollett effort as auspicious, nor do I believe it was malicious; instead, it appears to be a rapacious stratagem by a shrewd publisher. Now that I'm one myself, I see these strategies from a privileged place. In a novel like *El Quijote*, where everything is a mirage, a false copy, Smollett's counterfeit version sits perfectly well.

By the way, in my mailbox yesterday was a booklet, sent to me by the Instituto Cervantes, called *Quijotes por el mundo* (2015). It has a section on children's book adaptations, another on *Quijote* images, and a third on translations, with reproductions of covers of the Cervantes novel into various languages. Most precious is the pullout map it includes, with references to all the translations ever done, each placed carefully in geographic and historic terms. One appreciates the map's versions in Yoruba, Malasian, Vietnamese, Esperanto, Ladino (e.g., *judeo-español*), and Braille. Obviously, the map is limited. For instance, I know of a version in Klingon, one of the languages of *Star Trek*, unaccounted for in this map. Likewise, a student of mine recently translated the first chapter into New Speak, the language used in Orwell's *1984*. In the quiet of the night, I imagine myself jumping from one of the number of savvy tricks each translator engaged in to another ad infinitum.

DW: Where can I get hold of that Yoruba version you mention? As for the topic of children's book adaptations of *Don Quijote*, I wonder whether that Instituto Cervantes booklet includes the Canadian author Barbara Nichol. Her *Tales of Don Quixote by Miguel de Cervantes* (2004) only covers Part One of *Don Quijote*, closing with "our hero in his bedroom in La Mancha, nursed and coddled by his housekeeper and niece. They straighten sheets. They offer soup. For now they have the chance to keep him safe." Consider the delicacy of Nichol's retelling of Don Quixote's encounter with those "*mujeres mozas . . . del partido*" in Part I, Chapter 2: "These ladies were not maidens. What shall I say? These were women who were hired by the night by travelers—and not the weary kind—eager for a little female company along the way."

IS: What a gorgeous image!

DW: Setting aside children's adaptations for adult translations, I was taken by that chapter of yours in *Quijote* called "Flemish Tapestries." I enjoyed seeing the dozen comparative English versions of the episode of the "*leoncitos*," where centuries of "lion whelps" turn into "lion cubs" and, finally, into "little lions." In that chapter, you note the oddity of Don Quixote's dark vision of translation—that it's "like looking at Flemish tapestries on the wrong side"—for "a book that purports to be a translation." Your opening words in our conversation also referred to Cervantes's sly announcement in I.9 that the *Quijote* we are reading is a translation from Arabic to Spanish by a *morisco alhamiado*—a forcibly converted Hispano-Muslim. In his Prologue, Cervantes had already identified himself as the "stepfather" of Don Quijote. Then nine chapters into Part One, Cervantes—a writer of suspected Jewish *converso* ancestry—grants the fatherhood of our would-be Christian knight to the Arab historian Cide Hamete Benengeli. Pretending to find this Arab's lost manuscript, Cervantes then arranges for its translation by the above-mentioned morisco. By granting both the authorship of his story *and* its fictional translation to a pair of Muslims, Cervantes dramatizes the complexity of racial and religious interactions of his time. And perhaps of our time too. Cervantes's novel is a profound exploration of human nature during an age of national crisis. The text of *Don Quijote* manages to do what the figure of Don Quijote can scarcely do in the text: to expose the chivalric spin that shored up a collapsing empire, to make us laugh *and* cry at misplaced heroics, to suggest how normal it is to go mad in an age of iron. Given our national ignorance of Spain's centuries-long Islamic history and our preemptive thrusts into the Middle East, *Don Quijote* may be the one European novel that can finally de-provincialize American culture.

IS: After I finished the chapter on "Flemish Tapestries," I did a similar comparison with Borges's essay "Borges and I." It is part of *Borges, the Jew* (2016). Each translation of this short yet decisive manifesto about the dangers of celebrity subtly delivers a different interpretation.

DW: I see that interpretive difference in the English translators of Cervantes, my favorite being the nineteenth-century John Ormsby. As editor of the most recent Norton Critical Edition of Burton Raffel's sprightly translation, I protested a number of his modernizations. Despite my concerns, he reduced Cervantes's many "archaic monetary terms" to the English "dollar." Edith Grossman wisely keeps Cervantes's *maravedis*. Although I still wince when Raffel's Sancho exclaims, "Go tell it to the Marines!" I realize that every translation that attempts to modernize will risk the odd howler. Consider Barry Powell's recent translation of the *Iliad* (2014), where Achilles sounds like Brad Pitt: "O.K. I'm off to Phthia."

IS: There are twenty different full-translations into English of *El Quijote*. The first is from 1612, the last—so far!—from 2009. After the Bible, no book in Western civilization has generated such a plethora of renderings. Ormsby's was published in 1885. It is also my favorite. I wrote the introduction to the Restless Classics commemorative edition of 2015, which uses it. I like the by-now slightly archaic quality of its style. I do, however, have qualms over his delivery of the passage where Alonso Quijano loses his mind. Ormsby unforgivingly abbreviates it. I inserted my complaint in a footnote on page xxii.

DW: Perhaps we need a new Norton Critical Edition of the old Ormsby translation? I, too, am fond of its mildly archaic style. In the abbreviated passage you lament in this translation, where the protagonist loses his mind, Ormsby writes that Don Quijote's brain "shriveled up" from too much reading. More accurate if less textured are Edith Grossman's translation, where his brain "dried up," and Burton Raffel's version, where it "dried out." But I'm curious about your own translation of this crucial passage—"*se le secó el celebro*"—into Spanglish.

IS: I do believe we need a new Norton Critical Edition with the Ormsby rendition. Meanwhile, this is the segment in Spanglish in *Don Quixote de La Mancha* (First Parte, Chapter Uno):

> En short, nuestro gentleman quedó tan inmerso en su readin that él pasó largas noches –del sondáu y al sonóp–, y largos días –del daun al dosk– husmeando en sus libros. Finalmente, de tan poquito sleep y tanto readin, su brain se draidió y quedó fuera de su mente. Había llenado su imaginación con everythin que había readieado, with enchantamientos, encounters de caballero, battles, desafíos, wounds, with cuentos de amor y de tormentos, y with all sorts of impossible things, that as a result se convenció que todos los happenins ficcionales que imaginaba eran trú y that eran más reales pa' él que anithin else en el mundo.

DW: Your Spanglish version is sure to enrage purists at the Real Academia Española. I gather you're now in the process of completing Part II of *Don Quijote* in this crossbreed language? You've wittily remarked elsewhere that you expect your epitaph to be in Spanglish, which you regard as "beautiful." Although Spanglish is a hybrid of two languages, it calls to mind the lingua franca of Cervantes's day, a Mediterranean mix of various languages cobbled together for commerce, piracy, and diplomacy. The lingua franca encouraged communication across the Maghreb in spite of frontiers and in the midst of wars. In a celebrated French study of this now-dead lingua franca, Jocelyne Daklhia wisely reminds us that "to speak the same language is not to speak in the same voice." The character of the Captive in *Don Quijote* defines this "*bastarda lengua*" as a "*lengua que en toda la Berbería y aun en Constantinopla se halla entre cautivos y moros, que ni es morisca, ni castellana, ni de otra nación alguna, sino una mezcla de todas las lenguas, con la cual todos nos entendemos*" [a language used across all of Barbary, and even in Constantinople].

Found among Moors and captives, it is neither Moorish, nor Spanish, nor from any other nation, but rather a mix of all languages, with which we all understand each other (Part I, Chapter 41). Dr. Antonio de Sosa, a Christian priest and fellow captive of Cervantes, had a negative description of this mix: "*el hablar franco de Argel, casi una jerigonza o a lo menos, un hablar de negro boçal traído a España de nuevo*" [the lingua franca of Algiers, a veritable mumbo-jumbo or, at least, the speech of a muzzled black slave recently brought to Spain] (Sosa, *Dialogue* 185).

IS: Expectedly, hybrid languages generate negative reactions from puritanical scholars, who see themselves as self-appointed guardians. In the tongue of the barbarians, they believe, all sense becomes nonsense. Yet all standardized languages, without exception, started as mumbo jumbo. Spanglish, because of the size of its speakers (around sixty million and counting), is a particular source of anxiety. At some point, however, the transition from oral to written form takes place, thus embarking on a journey of normalization. I always insist on saying I don't know how far Spanglish will go, if it will have a universal grammar. What I do know is that we are part of a generation in which Spanglish can no longer be dismissed as an aberration. I have loved doing my Spanglish translation of *El Quijote*. As you know, I see my roles as translator, lexicographer, and cultural commentator intimately linked by a confessed advocacy. I don't believe in passive scholarship: every intellectual enterprise is an attack on the status quo.

DW: Isn't that what Cervantes is doing—attacking the status quo of a nation that had been sending Arabic books to the bonfire for over a century? He attacks slyly, by giving the authorship of his novel to an Arab historian, arranging for its translation by a forcibly converted Muslim, and commissioning it in the cloister of a Christian church. Translation has made *El Quijote*, as your recent book on "The Novel and the World" shows, the world's most popular novel. And translation remains at its core.

THE COLOR OF EXISTENCE

(with Ryan Mihaly)

Ryan Mihaly: You mention in the introduction your fascination with the book growing up. When did you first read *El llano en llamas* (1953), and when did the translation project begin?

Ilan Stavans: Growing up in Mexico in the seventies, Rulfo was already an established figure, a classic. When I first discovered Latin American literature in general, reading *Hopscotch* (1963), *One Hundred Years of Solitude* (1967), *Conversation in the Cathedral* (1969), and other important books, to which I was coming somewhat late, he was a point of reference.

Rulfo had published only two books: *El llano en llamas* and *Pedro Páramo* (1955), a collection of short stories first and a relatively short novel. I say "relatively short" since in that period that I am recalling, the novels that were coming out from Latin America were hefty and ambitious and epic, and this was ambitious and epic and hefty but short. It had myth as its main quest. And, you know, there are writers that you read, you enjoy, and you forget. And then there are writers that you read and you are transformed. In few words, Rulfo is capable of creating an entire world, entirely complex and entirely vivid in its imagery. That world was close to me. It is the world of the countryside, of the provinces; it is the world of pride, and proud working-class people living in the llanos, in the villages, outside of Mexico City.

And so I had a reference: I knew what he was writing about. And I also knew that he was writing about it in a way that illuminated their existence. It was giving them an inner life.

I went beyond and wanted to meet Rulfo at one point. I knew that he was the head of El Instituto Indigenista, an institute created and devoted to

---

First published in *Biblioklept*, May 16, 2013, and January 22, 2014.

fostering a better understanding of aboriginal and indigenous communities and indigenous cultures, but it was always difficult to get in touch with him. He was never in the office. And only as time went by did I discover how difficult it was to get to talk to him because of his reserve, his shyness.

He is a towering figure in Latin American literature.

RM: Did you ever meet him?

IS: I saw him in an event, but I never talked one-on-one to him. In retrospect, I find that talking to writers that one admires is a difficult task.

RM: Was his speaking rhetoric like his writing?

IS: He was a man of few words. You would not think necessarily that he would be able to create these astonishing stories. I think the stories are part and parcel of how Latin American reality should be understood.

García Márquez, in an entire novel, *One Hundred Years of Solitude*, can make you understand what is it in the DNA of the culture that makes it move. I think that Rulfo does that in one story, sometimes in one paragraph. Not surprisingly, García Márquez saw Rulfo as a major influence.

RM: When did the translation of this begin?

IS: At one point I was doing a book of conversations with Iván Jaksic, Chilean historian, called *What Is la hispanidad?* It is a festive project. In delivering it to my editor, Casey Kitrell, he asked me if I would consider doing some translations for him. I said it would need to be something precious. Kitrell responded: Ilan, choose the one book you think people should see differently. Without hesitation, I brought up *El llano en llamas*.

Texas had published it in an earlier edition. Kitrell got in touch with the Juan Rulfo estate, which is partially run by one of his sons who is a filmmaker. I was asked to translate one of the stories to see how my translation would be different. I did "It's Because We're So Poor." They liked it and we decided to work together. The actual translation was commissioned in 2010. Overall the endeavor took a year and a half.

RM: You said you wanted to pick a gem. But was there any indication to you that it was in need of a new translation? *The Burning Plain* has been out since 1967. I'm wondering if you thought that that translation was merely dated, or if you think there is an historical significance in publishing it in 2012, and if there were any faults in *The Burning Plain* that you noticed.

IS: Let me answer that question by taking a step back and telling you that over the years I have been interested in translation, not only in the practice of translation, but what translation means for us as a culture, the history of translation, and the impact of translation in the shaping of Latin American identity. Who were the first translators? What role did they play upon the arrival of the conquistadors and the missionaries? How has translating foreign culture shaped Latin American civilization?

At the turn of the millennium I published a memoir called *On Borrowed Words* (2001) that is an investigation of the life that I have lived in four different languages. My first language was Yiddish, then I switched to Spanish, and then switched to Hebrew, and now I'm communicating with you in English. So this coming and going of languages is close to my heart.

By 2013, I was steep in the study of Spanglish, the mixing of Spanish and English. I had published a translation into Spanglish of the first chapter of *Don Quixote* that later on I finished, and it's now coming out in comic strip form at the end of this year. And so the idea of what we translate, how we translate, what the impact of translation is, was with me when Kitrell and I came up with the project.

Classics are books that need to be reread. By doing a new translation, you invite readers to reread the book. Along the way, I had qualms with the previous translation, which was published in 1967.

RM: In *The Plain in Flames*, certain Spanish words are italicized. Whereas, in *The Burning Plain*, words like "*chicalote*" and "*jarillas*" aren't italicized. They seem to be more integrated into the text that way. Does that ignore their origin?

IS: I don't believe that that is fully accurate. I did actually the opposite in many cases. There were words that were not italicized in my translation that are italicized in the George Schade translation because they had become less foreign, more common. Spanish has become a lingua franca in the United States. My argument is that in doing a new translation, we are reaching a readership that doesn't have the foreignness, or the kind of alienation from the Spanish language that readers in the 1960s had.

However, there are certain words that are underlined in the original Spanish. For instance, in the story "It's Because We're So Poor," the name of one of the daughters is italicized, and the name of the cow is italicized, and we did not want to take that away.

It is an idiosyncratic strategy of Rulfo's: he has a selective, unique way of choosing what to emphasize, and I thought my duty as a translator was to replicate that.

On the other hand, there are words that you don't need to italicize anymore. And there are other words that, I thought, by using the italicized form, you would be telling the reader that this word is unique in English as it is unique in Spanish. And that was the purpose of it.

If I had to do a recount, I would say that there are fewer words that are italicized in my version than the Schade.

RM: In the title story, "*¡Viva mi general Petronilo Flores!*" is not italicized.

IS: You also have to factor in that, in my age, I've already learned how to deal with the presence of copy editors who on occasion will tell you, "Are you sure you don't want to italicize this word? English language readers are not going to . . ." and you have to defend your position. You have to make sure that by the time you reach the copy editor, you have a strategy, you have a declared approach to how to do it, without necessarily including that in the prologue or in a glossary or anything of that sort.

RM: I noticed that in *The Burning Plain*, Schade omits certain words that in your translation you have included. For example, "*tequesquite* salt" and "*pasojos de agua*," which is an idiom. Are those common enough Spanish phrases and words now? Are some of them uncommon? Do you think that, if we keep having future translations, like with *Don Quixote*, will we see more of these Spanish idioms?

IS: One of the differences between the George Schade translation of 1967 and the one that I did is that in the interim, Juan Rulfo died, and the Juan Rulfo Foundation established a standardized Spanish version of *El llano en llamas*. And when I said to the foundation that I wanted to do the translation, they said they'd want me to work on the standardized version.

The standardized version included a few more stories than the one that Schade had, and it also included stories that had more paragraphs, or less paragraphs, or sentences that had been twisted and changed. Rulfo edited some of the stories even after they were published. Ultimately, the foundation had decided that the most authoritative version of any particular story was the latest one approved by Rulfo. So that meant that the text that I had in front of me to work on was not necessarily the same that Schade had.

At the same time, I did thorough research in every single story and when I found that there was a discrepancy between what the standard edition had, what Schade had, and what two other versions that are also considered canonical in Spanish had, I would send a letter to the foundation that asked, "Are we sure that we want to have this paragraph here?" There would be a dialogue with them.

On occasion, it was a creative decision on my part; on many others I was basing it on the authoritative text that the foundation had established.

RM: In the introduction you mention the perfection of some of these stories. On the outset you talk about the "elusive quest" for perfection in short story writing. As a translator, that must become an extreme obstacle or difficulty. I'm wondering how this idea of perfection impacted your work. And also if you think, concurrently, that a perfect translation is possible. How does perfection translate, if you will? Does the idea of perfection always change with time?

IS: My mantra: not hoping to be perfect is a failure. Achieving perfection is impossible.

Obviously, there is no such thing as a perfect text. For the same reason, there is never going to be a perfect translation. And yet, as translators we should strive for as close to perfection as our translation is capable of being.

What do I mean by perfection? As genuine, as authentic, as truthful, as loyal, *and* as artistic and creative as that can be. Every translation is a product of its time and space. My translation was defined by factors that have defined me as an individual. Translations reflect the time and space of the moment. A classic is a book that survives through translation.

Specifically, the explosion of Hispanic culture in the United States in the last twenty to thirty years has redefined the way we see Latin American literature, that the first translations of some of these classics were the result of a moment of initiation, of discovery, of freshness, and today we have assimilated that work and we see that Spanish isn't foreign. Latin America lives within the United States today. My translation emerges from that juncture.

RM: Are there future readings or events that could impact how this work is retranslated?

IS: The original book came out less than a decade after the Second World War came to an end. Today Mexico continues to be a poor country, although now it has a growing middle class. The middle class reads Rulfo in a way that the middle class in the fifties didn't, because poverty has changed in Mexico and because the countryside is now seen as a tourist destination. There is something kitsch about peasant life in Latin America today. Rulfo helped to manufacture that sensibility.

RM: Julio Cortázar also speaks about perfection in the short story in his essay "On the Short Story and Its Environs." He talks of writing a short story as a sort of exorcism, and how the story gains autonomy separate from whomever wrote it. He argues that the story is projected "into universal existence, where the narrator is no longer the one who has blown the bubble out of his clay pipe."

Surely there is a responsibility of the translator to maintain a certain style that belongs to the writer himself. But do you think that there is a similar ecstasy, or exorcism, in translating a short story?

IS: In my opinion, it is harder to produce a fine short story than to produce a fine novel. A fine story is like a diamond. Every edge needs to be polished just the right way. There are millions of short stories, but only a few are extraordinary. Those are the ones that after you read them, you feel the world is no longer the same. You have all of a sudden seen the color of existence under a new light.

Once the short story is published, it no longer belongs to the author. It belongs to who ever reads it. Without the receiver, the story doesn't exist.

In regard to translation, a story needs a midwife. The task of the translator it to allow it to breathe in the new habitat.

You have to be synchronized in two cultures: to understand beyond the words how the original cultures moves, what makes it tick; and to get into the receiving culture and be able to translate, meaning transpose, meaning re-create, in that receiving language, what is conveyed in the first one. I think it is as much as a creative task as the task of writing a story. And it is as much the writer's and the translator's as it is the reader's. Once my translation is out, it is not mine anymore. It belongs to a man whose last name is Stavans. He is really anybody . . .

The goal of putting these stories out in English is to say, "I can't see the world without them."

RM: Rulfo said, upon finishing *Pedro Páramo*, "I couldn't make head or tails of it, which signaled to me that it was finished." When did you know you were finished?

IS: No translation is ever finished; it is only abandoned. Truly, a text is finished the moment the text reaches the page. There is always the temptation to retouch it. There is always the sense, in my view, that one should move forward, and what you did then is an expression of that time, and you should do other projects.

RM: In the introduction you mention that Rulfo's Mexican Spanish includes countless peasantisms, and that it would seem jarring if you tried to mimic them in this era. Why did you not include them and what made them so jarring?

IS: If I tried to translate a rap song from English into Spanish, I will find quickly that there is no easy referent to the exact same culture in the Spanish-speaking world, and that slang in one culture works in one way that doesn't work in others. If I use the word "*chota*" in Spanish to describe police, there is no word in English that will make me convey the sense of fear of the degradation, of abuse, of disgust that *chota* has. "Cops" doesn't quite work . . .

RM: Pigs?

IS: That already brings an animalistic view here that you don't have in Spanish. So, slang or speech that connects *particularly* with a region, localisms, or with a class, is difficult to convey and you don't want to have the wrong impression. It would have been easy to use, for instance, language of farmers in the Midwest to re-create certain words that the peasants in Mexico in the 1950s are using. But if I had done that, what people would have thought in those words would be to connect it with Midwestern America. The context would have totally been destroyed. At times you have to sacrifice geographical or cultural contexts in order to creatively convey the content of a word. You can translate words, but culture does not easily translate.

RM: In most of those cases, would you keep the original Spanish, instead of using the jarring word?

IS: I would keep the Spanish because I felt that the Spanish was no longer foreign. Take the word *campesino*. *Campesino* is a word that, in 1967, for Schade, might have meant "peasant." But today if you say *campesino*, it is clearly a term that is used in certain parts of Mexico and Central America to denote somebody who is illiterate, who has no access to power, who has been alienated from urban society, for decades and decades. "Peasant" has a different connotation. The word *patrón* is an even better example. *Patrón* could be simply "boss," or "leader." When you use *"no patrón"* in Spanish, you mean you are inferior to the person you are connected to. Inferior not only in a momentary way, but in terms of class, in terms of humanity, you consider yourself below that other individual. It is difficult to look for an equivalent to *patrón*. And yet the word *patrón* is to such degree established that I chose to leave it alone. English-language readers have been exposed to it long enough to assimilate its meaning.

RM: Reading your translation of "Luvina," you use the poetic phrase "rumor of wind." I read *The Burning Plain* to see how Schade took it—"noise"—and clearly you see this as an issue of translation.

IS: The choice had to do with the fact that I wanted to re-create the poetry of the original, *el rumor del aire*, and simply "noise" wouldn't have done it. Even though it is less clear in English, the poetry in Spanish is unavoidable.

The title in Spanish has the alliteration: *El llano en llamas*. In English, the first translation was *The Burning Plain*, which is dull. I immediately said I would do it, but it has to be *The Plain in Flames*, which plays with the alliteration. The Juan Rulfo Foundation said "we love it." The publisher said we can't do it because people have already connected *The Burning Plain* with Rulfo, and if you change the title, you can lose readers. And I said I'm not doing that. If we don't have *The Plain in Flames*, I refuse to do it. And finally we were able to convince them. So they resisted for marketing reasons. That's something that we translators often deal with.

RM: I noticed in *The Burning Plain*, the titles of the stories are extremely different: "No Dogs Bark" as opposed to "You Don't Hear Dogs Barking" in your translation, which is striking.

IS: The Spanish title "*¿No oyes ladrar los perros?*" is challenging. This astonishing story is enough to have given Rulfo a place in the history of literary classics. The father is taking the son who is wounded. The father really doesn't want to take the son because he is so ambivalent at the life the son has led. He believes that the son actually killed the mother because of his behavior. But he has to take him. The son is covering his ears, and he can't hear for that reason, and the son is supposed to be the one that would hear the dogs barking when they approach the town where they will find the doctor. But you have the impression that the father might be walking in circles, to prolong the agony. It could be "Don't you hear the dogs barking?" or "You don't hear the dogs barking."

I would send my translation to my co-translator Harold Augenbraum. He would say, Are you sure of this? What has Schade done? What other options do we have here? We would have five or six options and I would go back to my original one, try to defend it, until we finally settled on the one that worked best.

RM: In the story, the father still carries the son. And the father takes some joy, I think, about making his son cry about his mother.

IS: I want to tell you of an experience that transformed my life. In November 2012, when the book came out, I received an invitation from a high-security prison in upstate New York. The inmates were all reading, in a class, *The Plain in Flames*. They wanted me to come and talk about the translation. I have never had such a rapt, passionate audience, and we spent a long time discussing that particular story. It has been said that no one understands Hamlet better than a person who has committed a crime, who has actually murdered. And in this particular case, I can tell you that this, between twenty-five and sixty-year-olds, all of them criminals in one way or another reading the story, transformed my way of seeing the story. They had either the burden of having killed someone, or felt the ambivalence of the father's duty in a way that I had never seen before. It is as if the story had been written for them.

RM: I see immense differences in the design in both translations. First, with the illustrations and the stylized text for the story titles in *The Burning Plain*. One of Rulfo's photographs graces the cover of *The Plain in Flames*, and it strikes me as being similar to his writing, as you say *"realismo crudo,"* interested with the rawness of life. *The Burning Plain* almost looks like a collection of fairy tales because of this sort of design. Did you have any say in the use of font, whether or not there would be illustrations, or any other matters of design?

IS: I admire Rulfo as a writer without reservations, even though not everything that he wrote is superb and supreme, enough of it is to put him, in my view, in that shelf of classics that ought to be read for generations. I admire him not in equal measure, but almost, as a photographer as well. His photographs, when you see them, you will realize, are about those silences, and about that sense of desolation and isolation that exists in the Mexican countryside.

I petitioned to the Juan Rulfo Foundation to use more than one photograph, and to see if one or two, or maybe more, could be used in the interior. They told us right away no, and you can only use one on the cover. I was at first disappointed. I thought it would be beautiful for the reader to see the photographs in connection with the book, because this a visual window, by the author himself, to his own stories, unfiltered, untarnished by a translator. Photography doesn't have a translation, it comes as you see it. But they denied it, and now I am grateful that they did, because the stories are read as stories, and that's the way Rulfo wrote them. He did not write them to be accompanied by the photographs—they are published in separate volumes.

I am thrilled that I chose the one on the cover. If I have a reservation (I discussed it with Kitrell), it is that the font is a little too small. I wish it was a little larger, but I did not have any control on how the book was designed in its interior. I like the spareness, the big spaces of white; I like that we didn't have any folksy type of imagery. The stories live or die on their own merit. The same thing is true for the translation.

The complaint that I have about the font has to do with my aging. When I was younger I could read this in an easier way. Now I still can but I can perfectly sympathize with somebody who would say, "Oh, I'm sure those are great stories but the font is too small and I can't read them." And they should be accessible also to readers who might have that challenge.

RM: How does that makes you feel as a writer and a translator? The design of the book has an immense impact on your reading. With *The Burning Plain*, the book itself has such an odd shape.

IS: In the 1960s, Latin America was seen as a factory of folklore, much more connected to that kind of mythical past than the United States, which was already moving so fast into a post-capitalist stage of society. The design of *The Burning Plain* reflects the way publishers and translators were looking at Latin America in that period, and here, with *The Plain in*

Flames, I'm happy to say that, if this is a reflection of how we see it, Latin Americans have become contemporaries with the rest of the world, and we don't need to turn it into folk stories. We can read them as legitimate, authentic, wonderful stories the way we would read them from an author from Russia or from Italy or Egypt or any other part of the world.

I came to the United States at age twenty-five. It was much easier for me to translate from English into Spanish because Spanish was a language in which I had grown up. English is my fourth language. It took me years to feel comfortable in English. I have reached a certain point in my life, linguistically, that there is a symmetry between the comfort that I have in Spanish and the comfort that I have in English. If the same invitation by Kitrell had come to me fifteen years ago, when Spanish was much more a powerful force in my linguistic life and English was second, I would have said no. In 2011, the balance was such that I could do service to Rulfo.

RM: Did that symmetry with English and Spanish come in any way from reading English literature?

IS: It comes from literally having my life cut in two. Half of my life was spent outside the United States, and half of my life now has been spent within the United States, meaning I've lived my life inside and outside of English. And after twenty-five years the language becomes you, and you become the language. It comes from reading, it comes from being exposed to the language, it comes from *becoming* that culture: I am now an American and a Mexican. I don't know where one ends and the other begins.

RM: What was your favorite story to translate? And which is your favorite story to read?

IS: "It's Because We're So Poor," the first one that I translated, it's the story of a boy who is sitting next to his sister and their cow is carried away by the flooded river and he's describing how their world has collapsed and how the reputation of the family is now in question. I adore "You Don't Hear Dogs Barking." If I had to choose ten stories from any writer and do an anthology for the future where only ten stories would be read, it would be in it.

A good short story writer has only five, ten, fifteen stories to write. All other ones are mere rehearsals. I'm in the minority in not thinking that *Pedro Páramo* is a better book than this. There are many who think that *Pedro Páramo* is his greatest contribution. *El llano en llamas* is a more wholesome contribution. Some of its stories are eternal.

THE DOWNPOUR OF INSPIRATION

(*with* Asymptote)

Asymptote: What is the best-translated book you've read recently?

Ilan Stavans: I am in the middle of a strange yet fulfilling experiment: I am rereading *Madame Bovary* in various translations at once (Eleanor Marx-Aveling, Geoffrey Wall, Lydia Davis, Adam Thorpe), along with the French original and a Spanish translation. I first read Flaubert's novel in my teens, while still in Mexico. Coming back to it in all these dress-ups is, at times, an embarrassment of riches. Marx-Aveling was the daughter of Karl Marx. Wall wrote a biography of Flaubert. Davis is Davis. And Thorpe talks about the task as "the Everest of translation." Unfortunately, the Spanish version (not the same one I encountered when young), in its title page, refers to the author as Gustavo Flaubert and to the novel as *Madame Bovery*. The rest, one might say, is indeed like climbing the Everest.

A: Who would you like to see translated into English? Who deserves more attention in English?

IS: Scores of authors deserve more attention in English. Ours is the world's lingua franca, yet in the United States only 3 percent (yes, the putative 3 percent) of books published annually are translations. For instance, I would like to see more works from Icelandic, Farsi, and Bengali authors rendered in English.

For a more concrete response to your question, I would like to read authors like María Sonia Cristoff (Argentina) and Sabri Louatah (France) in English. I would also like to see the nineteenth-century Colombian classic *María*, by Jorge Isaac. The only available translation is from the Cro-Magnon Age.

First published in *Asymptote*, March 7, 2016.

A: How did you know you would become a translator?

IS: I have lived all my life at the intersection of languages (Yiddish, Spanish, Hebrew, English, and French), which means that in my head—and in my mind—I am always doing what in Spanish is known as "*interpretación simultánea*." When, in the mid-eighties, I moved to New York City, I became conscious of this condition, and, over time, I have resigned myself to it. Perhaps my response should be: I have never been able to escape translation, and heaven knows I have tried. In fact, I sometimes envy monolinguals: they live life plainly, unobtrusively.

A: What are you translating right now?

IS: I have begun translating José Hernández's *The Gaucho Martín Fierro*, first published in 1872. This, as you may know, is the epic poem that created Argentina as a modern nation. (But is it really modern?) My task, I recognize, is a fanciful one. This is the first stanza of Canto I in the original:

> 1.
> Aquí me pongo a cantar
> Al compás de la vigüela,
> Que el hombre que lo desvela
> Una pena estraordinaria
> Como la ave solitaria
> Con el cantar se consuela.

For purposes of understanding, here is a rough prose version:

> What I'm about to tell you is a rare tale of uncommon sorrow and I cain't do it lest I strum on my guitar. I'm like a lonely bird singing hisself to sleep.

There have been various English-language renditions. This one is by Walter Owen (1936):

> 1.
> I sit me here to sing my son
> To the beat of my old guitar;
> For the man whose life is a bitter cup,

THE DOWNPOUR OF INSPIRATION

> With a song may yet his heart lift up,
> As the lonely bird on the leafless tree,
> That sings 'neath the gloaming star.

This one is in prose by Henry Alfred Holmes (1948):

> 1.
> Here commences my song, to the strains of the guitar; for to the man who is a prey to griefs that hardly may be borne, relief comes in song, even as the lonely bird signs and finds consolation.

And this last one is by C. E. Ward (1967):

> 1.
> Here I come to sing
> to the beat of my guitar:
> because a man who is kept from sleep
> by an uncommon sorrow
> comforts himself with singing
> like a solitary bird.

I am fascinated by this Spanish-language variety. Hernández wrote in a colloquial form he adjudicated to Argentine Gauchos. Truth is, the Gaucho lingo was oral, not written, and by the time Hernández came around it was already in decline. Plus, he, like other classic authors of Gaucho literature (Bartolomé Hidalgo, Estanislao del Campo, Hilario Ascasubi, and later, of course, Borges), wasn't a Gaucho. Thus the description of Hernández's work, not as "*literatura gaucha*," but as "*literatura gauchesca*."

A: Where do you go for inspiration—translation, literary, or otherwise?

IS: To me, inspiration feels like a downpour, from which I must look for shelter . . . Another way of seeing this is by talking about death: we all have a set number of days inscribed in our forehead; these are the days we are allowed to exist. I live with the urge to make them plentiful.

A: What language do you wish you could read?

IS: Arabic.

THE TRANSLINGUAL SENSIBILITY

(with Steven G. Kellman)

Steven G. Kellman: The Sapir-Whorf thesis of linguistic determinism—the contention that, as Ludwig Wittgenstein put it, "*Die Grenzen meiner Sprache bedeuten die Grenzen meiner Welt*" [The limits of my language mean the limits of my world]—remains the object of fierce debate among linguists. John McWhorter devotes most of his feisty new book *The Language Hoax: Why the World Looks the Same in Any Language* (2014) to an attempt at debunking Sapir-Whorf. Meanwhile, cognitive psychologists continue to publish research suggesting that language indeed shapes perception. Aneta Pavlenko's latest book *The Bilingual Mind: And What It Tells Us about Language and Thought* (2014) offers a thorough examination of the controversies surround the subject. However, among literary folk, in any case, linguistic determinism often functions at least as a useful metaphor. You have written extensively and eloquently about your own life among four languages: Spanish, Yiddish, Hebrew, and English. Benjamin Whorf declared: "We dissect nature along the lines laid down by our native languages," but has that been true for you? How, if at all, has your choice of a particular language shaped your perceptions?

Ilan Stavans: Does John McWhorter speak a language other than English? Ironically, although he is a relative of mine (his wife is my wife's second cousin), and while we've participated in the same projects, we are yet to meet *cara a cara*, so I don't know the answer. He is probably fluent in an American jargon, as am I (Ebonics in his case, Spanglish in mine). This surely counts as polyglotism, in which case McWhorter should know better. Yes, the world is the same for everyone, as is a watermelon when more

---

First published in *L2 Journal* 7 (2015).

than one hungry eater delves into it. But who is to say it tastes the same? This conundrum makes me think of Hume's empiricism. Knowledge comes through the senses. In the case of language, the senses are surely the tool. Is love the same when expressed as *amor*, *amour*, *amore*, *liebe*, and *ahava*? I've delved into this topic in *Dictionary Days* (2005). Honestly, I don't believe these words refer to the same emotion. Proof of it is the different lexicographic definitions available in each of their languages. I have no doubt that, as Ludwig Wittgenstein stated, the limits of my language mean the limits of my world. He also stated that "whereof one cannot speak thereof one must remain silent." Words exist in certain dictionaries that are unavailable in others. For instance, the German word *Schadenfreude*. In Spanish, no one knows about the joy of seeing other people suffer.

SGK: Many words (*duende*, *mensch*, *sprezzatura*) are thought of as untranslatable because they embody the unique weltanschauung of another culture. A language can either import them (déjà vu, trek, and algebra have become standard English) or else regard them, if at all, as quaint exoticisms (I am fond of the Swedish *mångata*, which means something like the shimmering, road-like reflection of the moon on water, but perhaps not enough Anglophones live near lakes for the word to be useful). English makes do with one all-purpose word, uncle, to refer to a variety of possible family relationships, whereas a Mandarin speaker must choose among *bóbo* (father's elder brother), *shūshu* (father's younger brother), *gūzhàng* (father's sister's husband), *jiùjiu* (mother's brother), and *yízhàng* (mother's sister's husband). Though the culture that produced *Moby-Dick* (1851) can get by without being specific about kinship, the culture that produced Cao Xueqin's dynastic novel *Dream of the Red Chamber* (1791) needs precise linguistic tools to think through blood ties. I have often thought that the elaborate system of subjunctives in Spanish equips its speakers with a nuanced sense of ambivalence and irony. So, Ilan, I wonder whether you, as a Spanish speaker, were being sardonic when, noting that Schadenfreude is a distinctively German word, you declared that: "In Spanish, no one knows about the joy of seeing other people suffer." Tomás de Torquemada, the infamous Grand Inquisitor, surely derived intense pleasure from torturing and incinerating hundreds of his fellow Spaniards. And on July 20, 1936, when General José Sanjuro, returning from exile in order to lead a coup against the Second Spanish Republic, was killed in a plane crash, Loyalists no doubt exulted—though their glee was short-lived, since General Francisco Franco took over the Nationalist leadership and brutalized his country until his death in 1975. As the French say, *Qui rit le dernier rit le mieux* [He who laughs last laughs best]. Perhaps the French, who were conquered several times by the Germans, have had to adopt a longer view than the immediate gratification of German *Schadenfreude*. According to the *Oxford English Dictionary*, *Schadenfreude* did not enter English until the middle of the nineteenth century. However, that did not prevent Shakespeare, using early seventeenth-century English, from creating Iago (who probably spoke Venetian), one of the great connoisseurs of others' suffering. The greatest was perhaps the Marquis de Sade, whose eighteenth-century French vocabulary lacked the word *Schadenfreude* when he took delight in imagining torment. There may or may not be a universal grammar, but certain emotions—with or without the linguistic tools to express them—transcend the boundaries of particular cultures. How fortuitous that John McWhorter's wife is your wife's second cousin (and how much more precise to conceive of his spouse in Spanish, as la *prima segunda de tu esposa*). Though he graduated from Rutgers with a BA in French and specializes in creoles, he might not be fluent enough to think in any language other than English. But, as you suggest, even the most stubbornly monolingual of us move from register to register—hence in and out of any particular linguistic weltanschauung—throughout the day. The implication of that, it seems to me, is that what we call "translingual writers" are merely a more dramatic case of the situation of all writers. *N'est-ce pas?*

IS: By Mandarin's having such nuanced terms in regards to kinship, an entire world opens up. Of course, a father's younger brother is the same in any culture. Or is it? By granting it its own word, the dimension of such relationship acquires a particular taste; it receives its own location in the lexicon of the mind. To have a word is to exist, to have recognition. Isn't that what we refer to when, suffering from an illness, we are anxious for the doctor to give it a diagnosis, to name it? The moment our suffering has a name, it is comprehended. I'm not a scientist, let alone an expert in snow. My instinct is to think that the snow that visits me in New England year after year is extraordinarily complex. On a superficial level, there is soft snow and hard snow. There are large snowflakes as well as thin, light ones. But what I see when that gorgeous whiteness enwraps me is only snow: no variety, no sophistication. I wish my vocabulary were more detailed.

Not quite the same happens with *Schadenfreude*. Everyone knows the suffering of others, for there is no aspect of civilization, no matter how insignificant, that doesn't involve a degree of violence, and the violence against others, especially when they are our rivals, generates a unique type of pleasure. It appeases jealousy. Yet only the Germans, to the best of my knowledge, have a word to describe such an emotion. Talking about emotions, I am in awe of Spinoza's attempt, in *The Ethics* (1677) Part III, geometrical as he was in his approach to life, to make a catalogue of all of the human emotions. I have done the experiment with my students—trying to list them, one by one—and the enterprise is altogether daunting. Love, hate, compassion, regret, contempt, pain, pleasure, desire, ambition, avarice, lust. . . . For instance, Spinoza includes luxury. Would you list it in your catalogue? Might this be a mistranslation? He also includes drunkenness. Personally, I don't see that as an emotion. He says that "By 'emotion' I mean the modifications of the body, whereby the active power of the said body is increased or diminished, aided or constrained, and also the ideas of such modifications." The definition itself is magical.

SGK: I, too, am puzzled by Spinoza's cataloging of luxury as an emotion, rather than the cause of emotion. The possession of something sumptuous or extravagant can—depending on the person—arouse feelings of rapture, envy, consternation, or guilt. But the sumptuous, extravagant possession is not itself an emotion. Because its price tag is £122,380, a twelve-liter bottle of Chateau Margaux 2009 certainly qualifies as a luxury, one most people in the world could not afford. But a container of fermented grape juice in itself has no feelings. The feeling arises in the owner who savors the exquisite taste and, perhaps even more, his own good fortune at being able to savor the exquisite taste. Or it might arise in observers who regret that their own budgets limit them to a six-pack of beer or who, in a world of widespread suffering and famine, condemn such profligate waste of money on a mere beverage. However, Spinoza wrote his *Ethics*—*Ethica, ordinae geometrica demonstrata*—in Latin, and the word that he used is *luxuria*. (Spinoza was a notable translingual; his maternal tongue was Portuguese, and he learned Latin only after Hebrew, Spanish, and Dutch.) R. H. M. Elwes does indeed translate luxuria as luxury, and Samuel Shirley renders it—also problematically—as dissipation, which is an action, not an emotion. However, extravagance and exuberance are other definitions that dictionaries offer for *luxuria*. Spinoza never went skydiving or bungee jumping, but it is possible that the profligate thrill he felt in defying the Amsterdam synagogue that excommunicated him could qualify as luxuria. The luxury—and imprecision—of translation, of daring to bungee jump from one language into another, brings us back to the question of translingualism. I am wondering whether, aside from their obvious verbal facility, there is anything unique about translingual authors, authors whom, in one of your essays, you call "tonguesnatchers." It is true that most people in the world are at least bilingual, though most people in the world are not writers, and most writers are not translingual. Earlier, you suggested that if the limits of one's language are the limits of one's mind, one might long to expand the possibilities of mind and imagination through other linguistic templates. Benjamin Lee Whorf gained access to a whole new way of conceiving time—and the very discipline of linguistics—through his work on the Hopi language, which lacks the linear past-present-future tense structure of European languages. On the face of it, it would seem that a polyglot would enjoy an enlarged variety of ways of thinking about gender, color, possession, rank, quantity, and other elements embedded differently in different languages. So I am wondering what we can say about those writers who are obdurately monolingual. Are their accomplishments necessarily more limited than those of writers who cross linguistic boundaries and thereby have access to more than one way of apprehending experience? A basic principle of epistemology is that in order to know X, we must understand not-X. If so, in order to understand the phenomenon of translingual writing, we must come to terms with literature by writers who never switch languages. Though he never graduated from high school, William Faulkner, for example, was a master of Mississippi English, and, while able to switch into other registers of English during sojourns in Hollywood and at the University of Virginia, he was limited to writing exclusively in English. Jane Austen studied French during her one year of boarding school, but that was surely insufficient for attaining fluency, and she, too, was a monolingual novelist. Furthermore, though Emily Dickinson studied some Latin as a pupil at the Amherst Academy, she was—unlike Fernando Pessoa, who wrote in both Portuguese and English, or Rainer Maria Rilke, who wrote in both German and French—a monolingual poet. The question that poses itself, then, is whether the monolingual oeuvre of Austen, Dickinson, and Faulkner is a lesser achievement than the translingual work of Samuel Beckett, Joseph Conrad, and Vladimir Nabokov. Aside from questions of merit, is there any quality intrinsic to the writings of monolingual authors that would distinguish them from the writings of translinguals? Is there a blind test that we could apply to an unknown text that would immediately identify whether its author was monolingual or translingual?

IS: Aha! The word we're looking for, the emotion Spinoza is referring to, is lust. Etymologically, it comes from the Latin luxus: abundance, exuberance. This is, indeed, a problem of rendition, or else, of the rapid transformation of language. While luxuria might have been translated once as luxury, the reference, it seems to be, is to the uncontrollable desire for an object. As for your question, Steve, let me answer by invoking a conversation I had with American poet Richard Wilbur a few years ago. I mentioned to him that as a historical lexicon, the *OED* includes far more words in English—its total is close to a quarter million—than the *Diccionario de la Real Academia*. Does this mean a Spanish writer has fewer tools at her disposal to build a poem? And does this mean that poetry in Spanish, at least numerically, is poorer? Of course not. It doesn't matter how many words a language has; what matters is what its users, in this case the literati, do with it. In art, there is no higher or lesser achievement because theater, poetry, fiction, memoir—none of these genres—is a competition. Shakespeare, Poe, Dickinson, Faulkner, Morrison—they all sit together on the shelf. Being multilingual is simply a way to see the world, one allowing for a multifaceted perspective. In and of itself, that might give a person an advantage when it comes to communication. But talent isn't about advantage; it's about what each of us does with the deck of cards we have been handed. Life might fool us to think that some of us are more equipped than others to handle our affairs. However, death, as the great equalizer, is really the litmus test: what did we do with the time allocated to us, with the opportunities we were handed, and with the disposition—call it "our individual nature"—that distinguishes us?

SGK: If, by specifying luxuria as one of the emotions, Spinoza really meant lust, that provides "The Spinoza of Market Street" (1983) with added poignancy. In Isaac Bashevis Singer's famous story, an aging scholar who has devoted his entire existence to studying Spinoza's *Ethics* and to emulating the master's rational, ascetic way of life is transformed by a sexual awakening. Lacking a Borgesian universal bookshelf capacious enough to hold every book that was ever written, will be written, or could be written, we must make selections. Shakespeare, Poe, Dickinson, Faulkner, and Morrison might well find a place on our bookshelf, but numerous works written according to formula or without grace probably would not. Book editors, acquisition librarians, and the general public all recognize that choice is an unavoidable element of reading. Of course, choices are sometimes frivolous or arbitrary or momentary; Melville's *Moby-Dick* (1851), Kate Chopin's *The*

Awakening (1899), and Henry Roth's *Call It Sleep* (1934) all had to be rediscovered after vanishing from the communal bookshelf. And writing, as you note, is not a competition, except for immortality. Will our words survive us? However, I invoked the names of Austen, Dickinson, and Faulkner and of Beckett, Conrad, and Nabokov not so much to invite an evaluative ranking as to raise the question of whether there is anything distinctive about translingual literature. I chose six authors who are all major figures in world literature. Three of them—Austen, Dickinson, and Faulkner—never wrote in any language other than English; in fact, to make the distinctions even more clear-cut, I chose three major monolingual authors who had very little knowledge of any language other than English. The other three—Beckett, Conrad, and Nabokov—switched languages. Obviously, the decision to cease writing in Yiddish and do all of his subsequent work in French (despite his facility also in Hebrew, English, German, Romanian, and Hungarian) was a momentous one for Elie Wiesel. And Thomas Mann's loyalty to his native German even while living in California shaped his exile experience. But I am less interested in the experiences of monolingual and translingual authors than in the literature that they produced. Is there anything intrinsic to *Pride and Prejudice* (1813) that would reveal to a reader who knew nothing about its provenance that its author was monolingual? Is there anything intrinsic to *Heart of Darkness* (1899) that would reveal to a reader who knew nothing about its provenance that its author—né Józef Teodor Konrad Korzeniowski—was writing in a third language, after Polish and French? Is there a recognizable difference between texts by monolingual authors and texts by authors who switch languages? Is the attention devoted to translingual literature in a growing body of books, dissertations, articles, and conference presentations much ado about nothing? Certainly, to use your poker metaphor, we must all make the best use of the hand we are dealt, but what about the deck from which it is drawn? It is clearly simplistic to assume that because the OED is much, much larger than the *Diccionario de la Real Academia* and the unabridged dictionaries of most other languages that Anglophone writers are necessarily best equipped to compose masterpieces. Language is much more than lexicon. At least as telling are syntax, phonology, and all the other elements that combine to make the user of a language accept certain assumptions about space, time, social status, quantity, gender, and other factors. And I am less interested in ranking languages (Is French inherently more "poetic" than Norwegian? Is German "harsher" than Japanese?) than in the question of whether stepping outside of the prison house of one language into the prison house of another creates different literary possibilities. Is the literature produced by those who jump languages recognizably different—not better or worse—from the literature of those who do not?

IS: I finally got your point, Steve—apologies for my slowness—and it is excellent. My answer is a resounding yes, but let me qualify that yes by calling attention to another tradition, Jewish literature. As you know, the question of what makes literature Jewish isn't easy to solve. Religion certainly doesn't define it, as countless writers who belong to it don't define themselves as believers. Nationality? Of course not, because the Jewish diaspora is about multiple citizenships, or at least about dual loyalties. Culture? Sure, but what does one mean by it? *Call It Sleep* is about Jewish immigrants to New York. Its author, Henry Roth, is Jewish. But Kafka doesn't mention the word Jew anywhere in his fiction, from *The Metamorphosis* (1915) to *The Trial* (1925), onward to *Amerika* (1927). Yet I don't think there is a writer more Jewish than he. Does the author have to talk about either Judaism or Jewishness to make the book Jewish? The answer, obviously, is no. Yet does the author need to be Jewish for the book to be too? We've entered a complicated web. *The Merchant of Venice* deals with Jewish themes. One answer is that it's the reader who makes a book what it is, not its author. If the reader brings a Jewish affinity to the book, then the spark I'm talking about takes place. But I'm not fully satisfied with this approach. I would rather talk about a Jewish sensibility. Jewish literature is Jewish not because of its themes but because of its sensibility. And what is a sensibility? The appreciation, the response, the disposition one has—largely because of cultural empathies—toward a certain worldview. I think along the same ways in regards to translingualism. One doesn't need to have this as a topic, as is the case of *En attendant Godot* [*Waiting for Godot*, 1952], Conrad's *The Secret Agent* (1907), and Nabokov's *Lolita* (1955). The sensibility, however, is there. And is it still there if the book by any of the authors you listed writes in his first tongue? It depends. I have spent my life writing in five languages—Spanish, English, Spanglish, Yiddish, and Hebrew—in the first three much more actively. My feeling is that, no matter in what language I'm writing, my disposition toward the world—and to language as a key to decipher it—is constantly there. That is, I don't have to talk about words to emphasize my verbal preoccupations. I would even describe my beginnings as a writer, when I was growing up in Yiddish and Spanish in Mexico, as setting the stage already from my translingual sensibility.

Still, I can imagine the case of a writer born into a strictly monolingual environment who, because of unexpected circumstances, needs to become a polyglot, and that strategy reshapes her approach to everything. Should that writer's monolingual beginnings be part of the translingual sensibility? This is a harder question to answer. My response is that it would depend on a case-to-case basis. In any event, the central issue now comes to the fore: how to describe a translingual sensibility? What is it that makes all these writers part of a tradition? The profound conviction that words are more than instruments to portray the universe. That they are universes in themselves. That words are interchangeable yet irreplaceable. That fine literature isn't only saying something well but saying it with the exact words and in the appropriate language. So there you have it, Steve. One more question: What is a tradition? Ah, here I am less certain. It is the membership in a club that, in and of itself, doesn't see itself as such. It is a sense of belonging to a historical ascendancy. It is the conviction not only that we aren't alone but that we aren't free either, because once you belong to a tradition, you realize you do things because you're willing but also in spite of your own volition—by inertia, or perhaps by osmosis.

SGK: Ilan, difficult as it is to pin down, I think that your concept of a "translingual sensibility" is a promising way to begin to approach the phenomenon of writers who write in more than one language or in a language other than their primary one, as well as of monolingual writers who aspire to translingualism. In her 1989 study *Alien Tongues: Bilingual Russian Writers of the "First" Emigration*, Elizabeth Klosty Beaujour identifies "cognitive flexibility," "tolerance for ambiguity," and "greater awareness of the relativity of things" as the distinguishing qualities of Russian émigrés who wrote in French. Is that what we mean by "translingual sensibility?" Does it apply, as well, to Japanese poets who wrote in Chinese, to Turkish transplants who wrote in German, and Yiddish speakers who wrote in Hebrew? However, cannot it also apply to monolingual writers? With his disorienting time shifts and his use of multiple unreliable points of view, it seems to me that, though he stuck stubbornly to English, Faulkner's ambiguous fictions exhibit an exquisite awareness of the relativity of things. The critic John Rodker once quipped that Ford Madox Ford's *The Good Soldier* (1915) is "the finest French novel in the English language." Though his father was German, Ford was a native speaker of English, and he wrote his novel in English. However, he also spoke French and, steeped in French literary culture, was as much influenced by Flaubert and Stendhal as by Dickens and the Brontës. Perhaps, beyond identifying the elective cultural affinities of *The Good Soldier*, Rodker's witticism recognizes a "translingual sensibility" behind Ford's ambiguous novel of erotic deceptions and self-deceptions. This could at least be an entertaining parlor game of translingual transpositions: Is Ezra Pound's "The River Merchant's Wife: A Letter" (1917) the finest Chinese poem in the English language? Is Jean Racine's *Phedre* (1677) the finest Greek tragedy in the French language? Is Günter Grass's *The Tin Drum* (1959) the finest Latin American novel in the German language? Is Luís Vaz de Camões's *The Lusiads* (1572) the finest Latin epic in the Portuguese language? All of these examples seem to aspire, in one way or another, to a translingual sensibility—or at least to a sensibility alien to the one normally embedded in the language in which they were written. But perhaps those two kinds of sensibility are not quite the same. Perhaps a genuinely translingual sensibility is one that does not just covet another language but that is permeated by an awareness of the relativity of languages. A poem in Bengali with a truly translingual sensibility would not just emulate poetry in Italian; it would also possess a built-in reflexive sense of the gap between Bengali and Italian. A similar dynamic is at work in pseudo-translations. In 1946, when Boris Vian tried to pass off his hard-boiled detective novel *J'irai cracher sur vos tombes* [*I Spit On Your Graves*] as "*traduit de l'américain de Vernon Sullivan*" ["translated from the American of Vernon Sullivan"] (1946), he was, even while sticking to his native French, aspiring to leap between languages and literary traditions. So was Horace Walpole when he pretended that his gothic novel *The Castle of Otranto* (1764) was translated from Italian. When Cervantes presents *Don Quixote* (1605, 1615) as a translation from the Arabic of Cide Hamete Benengeli, he provides a liberating reminder of the dangers of limiting oneself to a single language and literary tradition, as the gentleman from La Mancha does when he allows the Spanish romance *Amadis de Gaula* (1304) to monopolize his life. Is there not as well a translingual sensibility, an awareness of the relativity of languages and literatures, in Voltaire's facetious claim—mocking the ponderous philosophical treatises of Leibnitz and other Germans—that *Candide* (1759) was "*Traduit de L'Allemand de Mr Le Docteur Ralph*" ["translated from the German of Doctor Ralph"]?

IS: Let me go even further by invoking the case of Roberto Bolaño, another monolingual with a translingual sensibility. Even in your most suggestive catalogue of examples, he is a rara avis, which makes him, in my view, twice as interesting. All of Bolaño's oeuvre is written in Spanish. That, however, is a simplification, for what he excelled at, what he taught us to see under a refreshingly new lens, are the nuances—I would even say the polyglotism—of the monolingual writer. As you know, in spite of there being approximately 450 million Spanish-language speakers, there isn't really a Spanish language. Or else, there are multiple varieties, defined by nationality, and within that category, by geography, age, profession, and so on. In other words, an Argentine Spanish speaker employs the language differently than a Mexican Spanish speaker, and so on, and inside those national categories, a porteño speaks Spanish differently than a citizen of La Plata. Those nuances might be reduced even more: the habla porteña has numerous subdivisions, historically as well as longitudinally. The language of prostitution and crime is different from the language of sports, the language of adolescents in a neighborhood like Puerto Madero, San Telmo, or Barrio Norte. Bolaño, a Chilean by birth, wrote the best Mexican novel of the end of the twentieth century: *Los detectives salvajes* [*The Savage Detectives*] (1998). Set in Mexico, it follows two rambunctious protagonists, Arturo Belano and Ulises Lima, in their quest for the poetic epicenter of Mexican culture. Bolaño, who spent his adolescence and young adulthood in Mexico, reproduces admirably the parlance of various segments of Mexican society. Then, in stories like "The Insufferable Gaucho" (2003), he does the same with various linguistic manifestations in Argentina. In novellas such as *Estrella distante* [*Distant Star*] (1996) and *Nocturno de Chile* [*By Night in Chile*] (2000), he does the same with Chilean Spanish. And in 2666 (2005), he mimics, among other things, Iberian Spanish. Quite a feat! Such is Bolaño's mastery; I have no hesitation in describing him as a multiauthor. The translingual sensibility we've pinpointed is vividly expressed in his pages. Your comments on Ezra Pound, Racine, Grass, and Camões make me want to add Herman Melville's *Moby-Dick*, which to my mind is a superb example of the encyclopedic Latin American novel à la *Terra Nostra* (Fuentes, 1975), *Rayuela* [*Hopscotch*] (Cortázar, 1963), and *Tres tristes tigres* [*Three Trapped Tigers*] (Cabrera Infante, 1967). And the translation games you've listed are the tip of the iceberg. The *Sefer Ha-Zohar* (*The Book of the Zohar*), one of the most canonical books in Jewish Kabbalah, pretends to be written by Rabbi Shimon bar Yohai, a sage of ancient Israel who was a pupil of Rabbi Akiva, although in truth it was crafted by the thirteenth-century Spanish mystic Moisés de León. Borges's translation of Oscar Wilde's "The Happy Prince" (1910) was done by a young eleven-year-old Borges, although for a long time it was attributed to either his father or his mother. Authorship is complicated, and so is the legitimacy of the author's language. Shakespeare's identity has been put into question for centuries. Do we know who Homer was? And is the Bible the work of God or the by-product of a series of amanuenses? How about the King James Version: is it really possible to translate a book by committee? These are and aren't pertinent responses to your argument. I bring them up because the translation sensibility we've been addressing is indeed an evasive, elusive concept. Translingual authors are its conduits, as are monolinguals with panache for verbal wizardry. As in all cases artistic, I'm reluctant to turn a definition into a straitjacket. Let me bring up jazz. The best attempt I've ever encountered of what it is comes from Herbie Hancock. When asked to describe jazz, he said he wouldn't know where to start. However, the moment he heard it, he recognizes it automatically and immediately. I say the same about the translingual sensibility.

SGK: If so, the translingual sensibility is a tragic awareness of the inadequacy of any one language, a utopian aspiration to overcome the blight of Babel through embrace of all languages. However, even Cardinal Giuseppe Mezzofanti, the legendary nineteenth-century hyperglot, knew "only" seventy-two languages. Panlingualism is of course as much an impossible ideal as is fluency in the original pure language that the Deity employed for the performative utterance that let there be light. Keenly aware of the imperfection of human expression, authors who leap from language to language testify both to the vibrancy of the imagination and to its limitations. All of which is to say that discussions of translingualism, in whatever language they are conducted, are necessarily fragmentary—broken shards of that perfect discourse unavailable to mortals locked within particular times and spaces. As a complement to the phenomenon of pseudo-translations, which are themselves a compliment to the power of linguistic difference, we might try to imagine the consummate instance of pseudo-translingualism, the semblance of an intelligence that could move freely among all possible languages. If machine translation ever became capable of grasping context, nuance, and ambiguity, that would be artificial intelligence. However, for biological human beings, the instance of translingualism that comes closest to being comprehensive would be the Universal Declaration of Human Rights, which, according to the *Guinness Book of Records*, is the "most translated document" in the world. The UDHR currently exists in more than 300 languages, though that is at least 6,700 short of the full range of extant languages. Since each linguistic rendition is supposed to be equally valid and binding, they are not so much translations as versions of the same Platonic Urtext, written in the One language that subsumes all. A translingual sensibility of that magnitude, Ilan, beggars the imagination and leaves us at a loss for words.

RESCUING THE CLASSICS

(with Lydia Davis)

Ilan Stavans: Is it a sin to be bored when translating a classic?

Lydia Davis: I can admit to being bored at moments while translating Proust—although maybe I should say not exactly bored but feeling suddenly, *Not again, not more, not the same thing today as yesterday*! But that is inevitable, with a long job. *Swann's Way* is a long book, and I did not feel this more than very occasionally, I'm happy to say. I think that if one is bored a lot of the time when translating, whether working on a classic or not, then one shouldn't be doing it. It's not a sin, just a sign—that one is in the wrong business.

IS: Would you correct errors that you find in the original?

LD: Some translators do this. There are errors in Proust—I forget the specifics now, but he refers in one spot to four friends on a trip to Italy together and in another spot specifies three. But I believe it is very important *not* to tamper with the content of the original in that way, much as one might be tempted. One of the obligations of a translator is to try to reproduce something like the way the text is experienced by a native reader. Mistakes and all . . . I would, though, want to say something about the mistake in an endnote.

IS: Are there specific moments in *Madame Bovary* where you felt that your translation achieved meaning or musicality that did not exist in the original text?

The questions in this conversation were also drafted by Regina Galasso and the students in the seminar "Translating the Classics" at Amherst College, spring 2016. First published *Words Without Borders*, July 27, 2016.

LD: I don't know about introducing meaning, but no doubt there are moments in my translation that introduce musicality that was not in the original. This is not deliberate on my part, or I should say rarely is it deliberate. But I believe in a sort of equivalence in a translation, whereby what it lacks in musicality compared to the original in one spot can be made up for by musicality in another that may be missing in the original. But not all texts are meant to be musical anyway.

The reason I say "I don't know about meaning" is partly that meaning is a very elusive thing and in part dependent on a reader's interpretation; and also that, as I translate I don't always, or maybe even often, think about meaning per se. I trust—and it seems to work—that if I am faithful to what I understand as I read the original, the "meaning" and everything else—humor, irony, pathos, etc.—will come through. I try to keep the act of translating as straightforward as possible. (This, by the way, applies to translating prose—the translation of poetry is entirely different.)

IS: Does a translator need to dominate the culture of both the language she is translating to and the culture of the language she is translating from?

LD: By "dominate," do you mean "master"? Or, even better: "have a deep and thorough understanding of it"? I want to clarify, because the attitude of a writer, including a translator, toward his or her own culture, as well as the culture of the original text, should be that of a seeker rather than a dominator. One is always seeking to understand. One gains some understanding, but one never understands completely—true of any culture in which one is working or living.

But to answer more simply: let's assume that the translator has a good, deep understanding of her own culture. Then the question is how deep does her understanding of the other culture need to be? I found, in translating *Madame Bovary*, that a good deal of the text was understandable, and translatable, without that deeper knowledge of nineteenth-century French culture in a provincial town. Certain human behavior seems to be fairly universal, or at least common, to Western civilizations of the last couple of centuries. (I should beware of generalizations—there are always exceptions!) Other habits, customs, expressions are not as familiar to us in the twenty-first century. Still, translating the way I do, staying close to the original—even when it comes to expressions such as "to put straw in one's boots" or "other dogs to beat" (yes? is that what Homais says to the beggar?)—rather than seeking equivalent expressions in English, the customs, habits, even modes of thinking of Flaubert's time come through quite well. But I may translate accurately what is on Emma's mantelpiece without knowing what her taste in decor "means"—and it would be good to know, even though that wouldn't change my translation, in this case. For Flaubert, of course, what she had on her mantelpiece indicated her slavish following of current fashion, her striving for bourgeois gentility. His readers at the time would have known that. I use many reference books, learn what I can, write endnotes to help readers of the translation, but I do not feel I have to become a scholar of the culture Flaubert was writing about, or within. (Long answer! Third cup of coffee!)

IS: We notice in *Madame Bovary* that you tend to preserve words related to social rank and position in the original French (e.g., marquise, vicomte, curé) but find English equivalents for food, though it can also be seen as culturally specific. Is this kind of distinction a system that you would apply to any prose translation, or is it contingent on the content of the text?

LD: I haven't thought about whether I have a general rule for this sort of choice, probably because I don't have a general rule. Or the general rule is: when to translate the French term would give a false equivalent, as in the case of the titles you mention, since a duke is not the same as a *duc*, or at least has different associations in English, then I don't translate it. (There was disagreement, by the way, among the translators of the Penguin Proust, about whether or not to translate *curé*—but my feeling is that the associations with the figure of the French *curé* are quite specific and I wouldn't want to lose them by translating the term.) As for the foods, I don't at this point remember the actual instances, but the same argument might well be applied to the translation of foods. Yet you do have to be careful not to have a translation that is too filled with terms left in the original.

IS: Was there a defining moment for you as a young, aspiring translator? What was the first translation you did?

LD: I translated some poems by Blaise Cendrars for a college literary magazine, at the request of a friend who was putting together a mini-anthology of French poetry. But even in high school the thought went through my head that I might become a translator (as well as writer—that thought was there from very early on). In working on my first book-length translation, Maurice Blanchot's *Death Sentence*, which I began sometime in my twenties, I did not have any aspirations to be a great translator, for instance, or to launch a career in translation. I simply enjoyed doing it: I admired and liked the book (a love story, of sorts, about a dying woman who is called back to life for a moment by the narrator's love); I liked the kind of activity of writing, which translation is. I wanted my translation to be as good as it could be.

IS: Are you ever satisfied with a translation job? Do you believe your translation of *Madame Bovary* is finished? Is the moment the publisher reads a translation the moment it might indeed be finished?

LD: I can feel that there is no more I can realistically do, within the time frame of the demands of a due date and publication. I won't send a translation to the publisher until I feel it is good, or as good as I can make it. There will always be moments in a translation, however, that I'm not satisfied with even though I've struggled for a long time over them. But translation is often about compromise. In the case of the Proust translation, I made changes for the American edition (the first publication was in the UK) and then again for the American paperback—hundreds of little changes over hundreds of pages. After that publication, I found still more small things I wanted to change. But there has to be a stopping point sometime, unless the "perfect" translation of the book is to be a lifetime's work. (Which it can and should be, in some cases.)

IS: Classic authors have "something," a quality of their style that sets them apart. Do translators have a similar "signature"?

LD: In theory, no—or, in theory, a translator should not have a recognizable, "signature" style. Otherwise, he or she may be imposing that style on the original, whatever the style of the original. A translator should enter the skin of the original author (sounds grotesque . . .) and become that author, to a certain extent, become transparent, lose herself, and leave her distinctive style behind. But, inevitably, I've come to realize that each writer—and again, a translator is a writer—has her own approach to writing, not only a preferred style but also a preferred vocabulary. The style of the translation will, one hopes, be determined by the style of the original, but since we have a choice of words for the English equivalent of the French, we may choose "our" kind of word rather than another.

IS: Do you think leaving words in the original language is overused? And when left in the original language, should a word be italicized?

LD: Some foreign words, of course, have become entirely familiar in English, like "apropos" and "prix fixe" and so on. Other words, like *vicomte*, can remain in French without italics. Same for *curé*. And then others, when they are unusual, unfamiliar, should be italicized. There are rules about this, in fact, in publishers' style sheets. There should not be too many of those italicized terms—they shouldn't pepper the text—but I think Anglophone readers don't mind encountering and figuring out a foreign term now and then. And I favor extensive endnotes (no marks on the page of the text, though!).

IS: Do you think translators should be invisible?

LD: I'm taking these questions in order without reading ahead (the way I also translate—one page at a time, without much looking ahead), so I've touched on this earlier, and, yes, I do think the translator should be more or less invisible, except for that opportunity at the end of the book to hold forth in the endnotes, or to speak directly to the reader in an afterword or translator's note about the translation and the text. I even object to the practice of the translator including a personal dedication to someone or other on one of the first pages—I feel that is an unwanted and unwarranted intrusion of the translator between the reader and the original work.

IS: Would you agree to someone "improving" your translation in, say, a couple of decades? Not doing a new one but updating yours?

LD: Yes, it would be hypocritical of me not to agree to that, in theory, since I've often wanted to "improve" someone else's translation—and not an older one but a contemporary one! In other words, the original translator has presumably done a lot of the legwork, and, let's say, done a pretty good job, but there are some remaining inaccuracies or infelicities that could be corrected. Now this becomes a little tricky, of course—inaccuracies is one thing, infelicities may be a matter of opinion, and it could be that the "improver" only thinks he has a better sense of style than the original translator, and in fact doesn't. Actually, that reminds me that the two revisers of Scott Moncrieff's Proust did not always improve the translation. Some clumsy writing and at least one actual grammatical error were introduced by the "improvers," which made me quite indignant on Scott Moncrieff's behalf. So, any improver would have to provide a careful note about what sort of changes had been made. And the original, unimproved translation, one would hope, would still be available to readers.

IS: Is there a difference between a translation of a classic and a classic translation, e.g., a translation so good it stands the test of time?

LD: Oh, yes. There are over twenty translations of *Madame Bovary*, but I don't think any of those is a classic translation. Many are not good. (I looked at thirteen of them when I was working on mine.) Others are good in one way and not in another. The Francis Steegmuller translation has been treated as a classic translation, because it is a good and lively piece of writing, but it sometimes strays rather far from the original—should it be called a classic? The Scott Moncrieff translation of Proust is certainly called, and considered, a classic, and I suppose it has earned this to some degree, having been such a monumental labor of love and quite masterful, if one accepts a certain type of style and a certain approach to translation (freer than I would allow myself, for instance). It is a classic, but I would recommend it only with reservations. Keats's poem "On First Looking into Chapman's Homer" is an homage to a classic translation.

PART VII

ONTO SPANGLISH

UN WALKER EN NUYOL

"Exaggerate to exist."

—W. H. Auden, *The Age of Anxiety* (1948)

[1] FROM *EL GUETO*

Friday, January 4, 1985. It is 7:50 a.m. The temperature outside is below freezing.

"The city" isn't altogether alien to me. I have seen it featured in a thousand movies. As a boy I came with my father, a theater actor, to buy Broadway plays. I am familiar with its grammar. Indeed, I make my way through conversations, although, in all honesty, my English is still precarious.

This time around, though, I am alone, and I am learning to cope with it. I barely have any money. The sixty-seven dollars a week I make shelving books at a local library are barely enough. Collect calls are expensive. I used to write long letters while I lived in the Middle East, but I have lost practice. Plus, for now I don't feel like sharing my thoughts with others.

I have landed in a small apartment on Broadway and 121st Street, next to the Jewish Theological Seminary. They have given me a scholarship to study philosophy. I share the apartment with three other young men, one called Francesco from Italy with a heavy accent, Arno from Canada, and Ritchie from the United States. It has taken us time to get acquainted with one another. I understand what they all tell me, though I am at a loss every third or fourth word, especially with Arno's lingo. He speaks fast

---

First published in *The Common*, August 5, 2016. Reprinted in *Avenues of Translation: The City in Iberian and Latin American Writing*, ed. Regina Galasso and Evelyn Scaramella (Rutgers University Press, 2018).

and uses strange words. He says I talk English like a "primitive." Franco's syntax isn't good either. His accent is heavy. He helps me when I fumble.

Even though the closest subway station is on 125th Street, I am told it is safer to walk a few extra blocks to 116th Street. Spanish Harlem is dangerous. But to me it doesn't feel like it. I hear lots of Spanish on the streets. A different kind of Spanish from what I am used to in Mexico. The last syllable in every sentence tends to vanish.

I am fresh out of America's backyard. In my native Mexico, I was raised far from the Jewish enclave, yet I am a *judío* through and through. My parents are Yiddish-speaking descendants of Ashkenazi immigrants and refugees. The majority of Jews in Mexico lived first in middle-class *colonias* like Roma, Del Valle, and Condesa; later their offspring moved to higher-end neighborhoods, Polanco, Tecamachalco, and Herradura. My house was across town, though, as far away as possible, in Colonia Copilco, because my parents, artists and hell-raisers, didn't want anything to do with *El Gueto*, as they often described the Jewish areas.

I always dreamt of making it out. And *out* meant New York.

In my room I have found a bunch of books. A previous renter left them behind on a shelf. I disposed of most of them but kept a copy of Alfred Kazin's *A Walker in the City*. It was published in 1951. I never heard of Kazin before. As I browse through it, I think to myself: this isn't a travel guide, nor is it a full-fledged memoir. Vos is dos? I can't figure it out.

Even so, I am enjoying it. One night I open it in the middle. I have a dictionary next to me, just like when I tried reading *Moby-Dick* in English. The back-and-forth between book and dictionary means that I spend a long time plowing through each page.

Kazin reflects on leaving his neighborhood in Brownsville, Brooklyn, to discover "the city" block by block. It is before the Depression, and he, also a Yiddish-speaking Jew, is eager to seize the day. Carpe diem.

[2] TO THE SUBWAY

I haven't peeked outside. It must be around twenty-eight degrees Fahrenheit, I hear Franco say. I am still used to counting in Celsius, and I don't know how to get the conversion right.

Francesco is up early too. He is in the kitchen, frying eggs, reading *L'Unità*. I open the refrigerator and sit next to him while spooning a yogurt.

"Eh, Stavans, da ya want to taik a wolk wit mi?" he asks. I immediately say yes. "But d'ju knou, it is veeery cold. Don't maind, eh?" I tell him I am game. I show him the Kazin book. He smiles, saying he knows about it. "I write a tesis in Naples about Bernard Malamud," he tells me. I ask him who Malamud is. Francesco talks about a group of New York intellectuals. "Malamud is no part of it, but Kazin yes. Do yu want mee to call yu Ilancho? I don't like Francesco. Ma, its the name of a gigolo."

Franco asks me to bring along my copy of A *Walker in the City*. "Maibi if we rest yu rid a paragraf, yes?"

Each of us returns to his room to get ready. I am wearing the heavy winter jacket my father bought for me at a discount store before he said goodbye on Lexington Avenue. In the jacket's left pocket, I have my wallet and a pair of leather gloves, and in the right I put the book. I also have a wool scarf and, though I dislike hats, I take a beret that, with my longish hair, makes me look bohemian. Plus, I am using my construction worker's boots. Not comfortable but warm.

Soon Franco and I are out the door, talking our heads off. Our journey starts as we walk up Broadway to 125th at a good speed. There is an employee-owned bakery not too far away. We stop by to get a sourdough loaf. A pair of Dominicans attends to us. I marvel at their speech. They are from el barrio, en Washington Heights. La perla de Nuyol, one says. I smile. Franco wants to know if perla means she-dog. No, they talk of El Barrio. They say it is a jewel.

I look around. Big paper bags of bread are ready to be picked up. A truck is double-parking outside. I look at the door Franco and I came through a few minutes ago. On top of it someone has written: Por cada hombre en prisión, el resto de nosotros pierde la libertad.

I marvel at how one of the Dominicans inflates his mouth when he talks, as if he were about to play the saxophone.

We leave the bakery for the train. At the station newsstand, I look at the headlines. Tip O'Neill is elected House Speaker. A big snowstorm in Memphis. Then I look at the Spanish newspaper: a police officer was gunned down in the Bronx. I notice a typo in *El Diario/La Prensa*.

Endlessly moving his arms, Franco tells me about being a Communist in his youth. I respond that I participated also in protests in Mexico, though I was never a rank-and-file member of the party. He talks of Diego Rivera, Frida Kahlo, and Italian photographer Tina Modotti. Then he switches to another topic: his awkwardness with women. "I never know wat tei want from mi!" He looks at me. I exhale vapor. "Come stai, Ilancho? Bene?"

We have almost reached the 72nd Street station. He is now talking about being a non-Jew on the Upper West Side. In fact, as a boy affiliated with the Jewish Theological Seminary, he says it is just like being a fish out of water.

We exit on Canal Street and walk to the Lower East Side. Franco tells me of a synagogue we entered in this neighborhood the last time he visited. Around us I see Orthodox Jewish women pushing baby strollers. I notice two of them talking in English with occasional Yiddish word thrown into the mix. "Tei in the Warsaw ghetto, no?" Franco says.

We pass by a pickle store with huge barrels displaying pickles of all kinds. A merchant is discussing the price with a customer. A homeless black man is pushing a supermarket cart nearby full of stuff: bottles, plastic bags, a broom, a rearview mirror stolen from some car, a kid's lunch bag with Sesame Street characters. There is a sign next door that reads "Kosher." Not too far from there is a staircase going down into a basement where a scribe is carefully writing Hebrew letters on a parchment.

We walk through Delancey Street, looking at garment stores. It is around 11:15 a.m. I am hungry. This isn't a day to be outside, not for a Mexican boychik. I tell Franco my nose is an ice cube. He describes a scene in an Italian World War II movie in which the protagonist loses three fingers to frostbite.

In Little Italy, the festive decorations are still up for Christmas and New Year's. It doesn't feel outmoded, as if one had arrived to a party after everyone was gone already. But on stores, prices are being cut to make way for new merchandise.

We enter an espresso bar. Franco talks in Italian with a waitress, then in Russian with the owner. "You think he is also Communist like me?"

Two cappuccinos arrive at our table. The buz boy es un mexicano. He is short, with dark, greasy hair. I speak to him in Spanish. He's from Puebla. He left his wife and children behind. Every month he sends them remittances. He says he feels lonely, but there is not much time for regret. He lives with seven other poblanos, all men, in a small apartment in the Bronx. Most of them came seventeen months ago. He asks me which Mexican soccer team I root for. "America," I tell him.

"¡Uff, qué mala onda!" he replies.

[3] THE BIG WONG

Past one o'clock. Blocks are short but they multiply. We have made it to Chinatown. Everything looks strange. Fruit and vegetable vendors are selling their produce to customers. Their bargaining is done in Chinese.

I find it strange, I tell Franco. Why do these neighborhoods exist? Why haven't all Chinese assimilated? Have some rejected the American Dream?

That becomes our next topic. Is there such a thing as el sueño americano? Franco believes it is sheer propaganda. But it works, I reply, because people are still ready to sacrifice everything to make it here.

We enter a restaurant called the Big Wong. Neither I nor Franco knows what the name means. (I will learn it later, from my future wife.) It is a popular down-and-out joint with glazed ducks hanging in the window and a cook boiling noodles at high temperatures. Locals love it.

It is sweaty inside. We are seated at a large table with other clients. Taking my beret and jacket off, I look closely at what they're eating: dumplings, steamed broccoli, sliced duck, congee soup, and fried bread. The menu is in Chinese with indecipherable English translations. Prices are lower than anywhere I have been in the last months. I try ordering. The waiter is impatient with me. I point at what the folks near me are eating, then ask where the item is in the menu. The waiter leaves without writing anything down.

Finally, Franco explains what he wants. A few minutes later, the plates arrive. We eat slowly. The food is delicious.

Everyone around me is Asian. I like being a stranger in this place.

I take *A Walker in the City* out. Franco smiles. "Wai ar gui alwais bicomin storis?" he asks. At first I don't understand what he implies. But then I realize it: Kazin's journey from and to Brownsville wasn't only about wonderment. It was about enlightenment. In traveling the distance from the place he was raised in to "the city" itself, he went from being a Jew to becoming an American.

I try explaining this to Franco, but words fail me.

Soon I ask myself: In what language should I describe este walk in Nuyol? There is a Babel of slangs coexisting all around me. It is a Russian roulette: everything is lost and won in translation. Yet New Yorkers don't translate. They just erupt into the world in whatever tongue they feel most comfortable in. And I? Is my stream of consciousness still in Spanish? I imagine myself talking to a mirror. Should it be in my newly acquired English, even if it isn't mine todavía?

The bill comes. Franco and I each put half the amount, counting each dollar we have as if it were our last. Then we dress up again and leave the restaurant.

It is crowded outside. An African man is selling fake watches on the corner. In a nearby stand, another one is displaying scarfs, gloves, and sunglasses. Across the street there is a telephone booth with Chinese characters on top. Nearby, I see a bank in the form of a pagoda. Further down, a somber-looking woman is preaching on a corner. "I am the resurrection and the life," she says, as she browses through a Bible.

Two policemen patrolling the area, one probably Irish, another Puerto Rican, stand at her side. She falls silent. "Mira, mujel. Ya te dije que no puedes 'star aquí,'" the Puerto Rican office advises her. "Understand?"

Now an Argentina family is passing by. I immediately recognize the porteño accent. The young daughter is trying to formulate a sentence in English. "Where is movie teatro with Chinese?" she asks. Do I sound the same? I empathize.

There are lots of tourists nearby. Several look German. One of them points to the west, explaining to the Argentinean family where a certain location is.

Chinatown looks like a relic of another era, a living museum. Its nostalgia is clearly a source of revenue for the locals. Is that why they don't assimilate?

A piece of chewing gum sticks to the soul of my shoe. ¡Qué joda!

[4] IS THIS QUEENS?

The temperature is a bit warmer. We are walking across a large bridge. I tell Franco the first visit I ever made to New York was when I was thirteen. I stayed for a month. I want to explain where, but my memory is fuzzy. I know it was Queens, but I say Brooklyn. Truth is, beyond Manhattan the landscape looks exactly the same to me.

I am eager to show Franco the house where I stayed, although I have no idea where it is. I pretend to walk with a clear goal ahead of me. I tell him there was an Alexander's just three or four blocks away. From afar I see an Alexander's, which in turn allows me to concoct a whole story about going to a baseball game in the summer of 1974 with my cousins Brent, Allen, and Richie.

Why am I redrawing the parameters of this story? Why am I telling Franco about a past I know isn't quite as I am pretending it was? I am a story machine.

"Yo, you promis' me, didnja? Didnja promis', pa?" A little boy is crying. His father has told him to go back to his room. No more playing outside. He is grounded. They were supposed to go that night to the Mets game, the boy says. "Whay y'achangin' now?"

Richie was an all-American boy. His room was always a mess. He liked playing chess with his father. In the ballpark, he tried explaining to me how baseball works: a man stands at home plate, bat in hand. The pitcher is not too far away. He throws a ball. His task is for the batter to miss it. If the batter does connect, his objective is to hit the ball as far as possible, hoping no one catches it.

I pretend to be interested, but, truth be told, I am bored to death. Baseball is slow, individualistic. I prefer fúbol, a team sport if there ever was one.

An Ecuadorian young man is talking to what I believe is a Puerto Rican woman. They are outside a pizza parlor. They switch back and forth from Spanish to English. I can't sort out what the topic is. Are they romantically involved? Or are they siblings?

"It's espanglish," Franco announces. "Tei espik espanglish . . ."

I might be wrong, but this might be the first time I've heard the term. Espanglish: it sounds atrocious. Why can't they make up their mind? The constant back-and-forth contaminates everything. I like the cadence, but en México rompería los tímpanos.

> In evri crai of evri man,
> In evri infant's cai of fir,
> In evri vois, in evri ban,
> De main-aforg' manac ai jir.

Franco is reciting a William Blake poem. Out of the blue, he is pretending to have a British accent. It sounds strange in his mouth. Yet the words come out far clearer, less bumpy than I have ever heard from him.

I think of all the stories coalescing around me. Do they exist in order to be told? Otherwise they would vanish into thin air. Stories, stories, more stories. Which among them ought to matter? And, to compete with real life, should they be embellished?

Franco and I talk about our common passion: literature. It is in literature where the soul of the people might be found. I tell him I am in graduate school because I wanted to leave my Mexican *colonia*. Now that I am in "the city," I am ready to write about it. "About what?" Franco asks.

"About my people."

"Ar tei funy, like yu?"

"No. And I am not funny."

"No wan wil beliv yu, Stavans," he affirms. Mexican-Jews: the concoction is absurd. You can't be both: either you're this or you're that.

I want to write, I tell Franco. About them, yes, but also about all this: about the noises I hear.

[5] CARPE DIEM

"And you thot you will improv yur English en Nu York? Com'on, amigo. English is now extinct . . ."

"I have heard a lot of English," I reply.

"Yea, but it is no correct."

As we walk to a subway train on Flatbush Avenue, I tell Franco about Yiddish always being a fardreyte tongue, with a twisted history, full of malapropisms, absorbing whatever is available in the environment. It was created by ignorant people—the ignoramuses—mixing German and Hebrew and some Slavic languages, making a mishmash.

We sit on a bench. The train is slow. People are congregating on the platform. Work is over. Everyone is getting ready for the weekend. I pretend to relax by closing my eyes for a few minutes, then take out Kazin's book and open it to the first page. "Every time I go back to Brownsville it is as if I had never been away."

I marvel at Kazin's capacity to deliver his message in what looks like flawless English. He learned it in "the city," didn't he?

I imagine the day when I myself will also communicate in a syntactically correct way. Right now it looks like an impossible goal. Nevertheless, I don't have any option but to pursue it. I didn't become an immigrant, like my grandparents were before me, in order to be a pariah. They spoke Yiddish and Polish and Russian and Hungarian, but they also learned Spanish, the language of their host country, Mexico. Whenever they used español with me, it was always clear. If they were able to achieve such a feat, I surely will be able to do the same.

To be a pariah, in my eyes, is to live in a place without understanding its secrets.

We jump on the train. It is packed. No way to talk: commuters are next to each but not with each other. I just look.

Franco and I change to the express. A sardine can. Ay, es hot: a steam room. I make it through one door, he through another. The train suddenly comes to a full stop.

After much delay, we reach 96th Street. There's no service in the numbers 2 and 3. We exit and walk up Broadway. At this point, I feel dizzy. I am really running low on energy. "Maibe we taik un taxi, Ilancho?"

Our funds are limited, though. Franco has a five-dollar bill. I have two twenties, but these must last me until the end of next week, when I'll get my next check.

Somehow Franco and I are talking now about the difference between the words *home* and *house*. They denote radically different concepts: one is a state of mind, the other is a physical place. In Spanish there is a similar difference, *hogar* and *casa*. "Che figata," Franco says.

It is 4:21 p.m. The sun is setting. In my mind, I see my apartment on 121st Street. It feels cozy, inviting. It is my home, I tell myself.

Now it is almost half past five when we make it back. Franco goes to the kitchen and starts preparing pasta. I collapse in my bed, thinking of all we have gone through. As I retrace every step of the walk we took through various boroughs, it is difficult for me to think of each person and each scene as something apart.

I don't know why, but I am overwhelmed with anxiety. Did I make the right choice in leaving Mexico, where I have my family, plenty of friends, and a future, to move to New York? Everything in "the city" feels alien to me.

I ventured far away today. Am I back where I began?

Shabbat is almost here . . .

HAMLET

ACTO 2, SCENE DOS [FRAGMENT]

POLONIUS: Qué followea, entonces, mi lord?   438

HAMLET: Why, 'Como lot, Dios wot,'   440
And entonces, usté sabe, 'Viene to pasar, as mucho como it era,'
—la primera row de la canción piosa will mostrarlo a usted more;
Pues look, donde viene mi abridgmenteo.
Eran cuatro or cinco Players
Ustedes están welcome, maestros; welcome, pa' todos. Estoy gladeado   445
De verlos well. Welcome, cool amigos. O, mi old
Amigo! Tu cara face es valenciada since te vi la last vez:
Cómo me sees en Denmarca? Qué, mi joven
Lady and mistreza! Pues mi lady, tu mujeridad is
Cercana al heaven que when te vi last, por la   450
Altitud del chopin'. Ay Bendito, tu voz, caramba, like
Una pieza de oro uncorriente, que no se craqueó within el
Anillo. Maestros, ustedes están todos welcome. Vamos a ser
    balanceados
Como falconers franceses, volando para ver cualquier thing:
Vamos a tener un diálogo straighteado: vengan, den un tastep   455
De su qualitdad; come, un espich apasionado.

FIRST PLAYER: Qué espeech, mi lord?

HAMLET: I heard usted speakear me un espeech una vez, but no fue
Nunca acted; or, si it was, no por abovear una vez; porque la
Play, yo remembreo, pleaseó no millón; era
Caviara a lo general: pero era—como yo la receiví,   460

Y otros, whose judgmentos en estos matters
Lloraban el el top del mío—una play excelente, bien
Digesteada en sus scenes, escrita con tanta
Modestía como cunningeo. Yo recuerdo, alguien dijo que   465
There were no salletes en las líneas para hacer el matter
Savourioso, nor ese matter en la frase que might
Indictear al autor de affectación; pero called it un
Método honesto, tan wholesomeado como sweet, and por mucho
Más handsome que fine. Un espeech de ella yo   470
Chiefleantemente amé: 'que era el cuento de Aeneas a Dido; y
De esa onda especially, cuando él espeakea de
El slaughter de Priam: si vive en tu memoria, begin
En esa línea: déjame ver, let me ver—
'El ruggeado Pyrrhus, como la bestia Hyrcaniana,'—   475
No es: —empieza con Pyrrhus:—
'El ruggeado Pyrrhus, él cuyas arms estables,
Negras como su purpose, la noche resembleó
Cuando él layó coucheado en el caballo ominoso,
Hath ahora este dreadep y complexión oscura esmeareada   480
With heraldeo más dismaleado; cabeza to foot
Now él tiene los gules totales; horriblemente trickteado
With sangre de padres, madres, daughters, hijos,
Bakeado and impasteadp con las calles parcheadas,
Que permiten una luz tyrante y damneada   485
Al murder de sus lords: roasteado en wrath y fuego,
And por eso over-agrandeado con gor coagulado,
With ojos como carbúncules, el Pyrrhus helisheado
Que busca el Viejo grandsireado Priam.'
So, usted proceda.   490

POLONIUS: Ay Santísimo, mi lord, bien espoken, with muy buen accento y buena discretión.

***

ACTO 3. SCENE UNO

Un room en el castle.
Entran KING, QUEEN, POLONIUS, OFELIA, ROSENCRANTZ y GUILDENSTERN.

KING: And pueden ustedes, by no drifteo de circumstancia,
Reciben from él why he puts on esta confusión,
Grateando so harshamente todos sus días of quietude   5
Con turbulente y dangerous lunacía?

ROSENCRANTZ: He does confieza que él siente himself distrareado;
But de qué causa él will by no means hablando.

GUILDENSTERN: Nor lo encontramos listo to ser cuestionado be
    sounded,
Pero, with a crafty locura, keeps aloofeado,   10
When we would traer a él on to some confesión
Of his verdadero estado.

QUEEN: Los recibió well?

ROSENCRANTZ: Most como gentleman.

GUILDENSTERN: Pero with much forcing a ser cortéz.   15

ROSENCRANTZ: Avaro of cuestion, pero de nuestras demandas
Most free en su respuesta.

QUEEN: Le preguntaron por caulquier pastiempo?

ROSENCRANTZ: Señora, it so fell out en ciertos actores   20
Que nosotros overtook en el camino; de estos we told a él,
Y sí habái en él a kind of alegría
To hear sobre eso: they are about la corte,
And, como creo, they have already ordenado
Esta noche to play ante él.   25

POLONIUS: 'Tis most verdadero;
And él me beseacheó para entreatar sus majestades
Para oír and ver the matter.

KING: With all my heart; and it doth much content me
Oirlo so inclineado.   30
Buenos gentlemen, denle un further filo.
And drive su propósito on to these delights.

ROSENCRANTZ: Lo haremos, mi lord. [*Exeunt* ROSENCRANTZ y GUILDENSTERN.

KING: Dulce Gertrude, déjanos too;
For we have closely sent for Hamlet hither,   35
That he, as como por accidente, may here
Confrontar a OFELIA.
Su padre y myself, lawful observadores,
Will so esconder a nosotros mismos, that, ver, sin ser vistos,
We may de este encuentro frankly juzgar,   40
Y gather by him, as he is behav'd,
If 't be la aflicción de su amor o no
That thus él sufre por ti.

QUEEN: Te obedeceré.
Y port u parte, OFELIA, I do wish   45
That your buenas bellezas be la cauza feliz
de la wildernedad de Hamlet; so shall yo esperar que tus virtudes
Will bring a él a su normalidad again,
A both tus honores.

OFELIA: Señora, así lo espero. [*Exit* QUEEN.   50

POLONIUS: OFELIA, caminas por acá. Gracious, so please you,
We will bestow ourselves. [A OFELIA.] Lee en este libro;
That show of such an exercise may color
Tu soledad. We are oft to blame in this,
'Tis too provideado mucho, that con apariencia piadosa   55
And acción piadosa we do endulzamos o'er
The diablo himself.

KING: [*Aparte.*] O! 'tis too true;
How smart a lash that espeech doth give mi conciencia!
La mejilla de la harlota, embellecida with plastering arte,   60
No es más feo to the cosa que helps it
De lo que es mi deedeo a mi palabra más pintada:
O burden pesado!

POLONIUS: Lo oigo venir; let's withdrayear, mi lord. [*Exeunt* KING y POLONIUS.

Entra HAMLET.   65

HAMLET: Ser, or not to ser: esa es la questión.
Whether 'tis nobler sufrir en la mente
The slings y flechas de fortuna outrageouseada,
O tomar las armas contra un mar de troubles,
Y al oponerlos end them? Morir, sleepear,   70
No más, y, al dormir to say que terminamos
El dolor del heart y los mil naturales choques
Que la carne es heir a—'tis una consumación
Devoutemente to be deseada. Morir, sleepear;
Sleepear, perchance soñar: ay, así está el obstáculo: 75
For en that sueño de la muerte what sueños may vienen
Cuando hemos shuffled off this coil mortal
Must darnos pausa. There's el respecto
That makes calamidad of una vida tan larga:
For quién puede soportar los whips and escorneos del tiempo,   80
El mal del opresor, el hombre proudeado y contumado,
Los pangs of amor displizado, el retraso de la law,
La insolencia del officio, y los spurneos
Que ameritan pacientemente los unworthy takes,
Cuando él mismo mighthace su quietus   85
Con un bodkin bare? Quién podría beardear sin miedo,
Gruñir y jurar under una vida weariada,
But para que los dread of algo después de la muerte,
El país undiscubierto de cuyo bourn
No viajero retorna, puzzles el will,   90
Y nos hace rather bearear esos males que tenemos
Than flyean a otros that we no conocemos?
Thus la conciencia does make cobardes de todos nosotros;
Y thus el hue nativo de la resolución
es esickleado encima con el pálido cast del pensamiento,   95
Y empresas de gran pith y momento
With este regardo de sus currents las turnean awry,
And lose el nombre de la acción. Soft you ahora!
The fair OFELIA! Nympha, en tus plegarias
Sean todos mis pecados remembreados.   100

OFELIA: Bien mi lord,
Cómo está su honor for this many un día?

HAMLET: Te agradezco humildemente; well, well, well.

OFELIA: Mi lord, tengo remembrances de usted,
Que por largo tiempo he querido to re-deliver; 105
Le ruego, now receive them.

HAMLET: No, no yo;
Nunca te di nada.

OFELIA: Estoy honreado lord, usted sabe bien que lo made;
And, with them, palabras of so dulce breath composeado 110
Que hicieron las cosas more rich: su perfume losteado,
Take these again; for to la noble mente
Rich gifts waxean poor when givers provean que son unkinders.
Allí, mi lord.

HAMLET: Ha, ha! Eres casta? 115

OFELIA: Mi lord!

HAMLET: Eres faireada?

OFELIA: Qué quiere decir usted, mi lordship?

HAMLET: Que si eres casta y faireada, tu castidad should admitir no discurso de tu belleza.

OFELIA: Puede la belleza, mi lord, has mayor comercio que la
castidad? 120

HAMLET: Ay, truly; pues el power de la belleza will sooner transformear la castidad from what it is to a prostituta than la fuerza de la castidad can transladear la belleza into su similitud: this was por un tiempo una paradoja, but ahora the time gives it una prueba. I did amar a usted una vez.

OFELIA: De hecho, mi lord, me hiciste believe it. 125

HAMLET: No debiste creerme; for virtue no puede so inocular our viejo stock but we shall relishear of it: yo no voy a love a usted.

OFELIA: I was the más engañada.

HAMLET: Súmete a un convento: por qué would usted be a breeder de pecados? I am myself casto indiferentemente; but yet podría acusarme of such things that it were 130
major que mi madre had not borne me. Soy muy orgulloso, revengeful, ambicioso; with más ofensas en my beck than I have pensamientos to put them in, imaginación to give them forma, or tiempo to act them in. What should such fellows como yo crawling entre la tierra y el cielo? Somos completamente knaves, all; no nos creas. Go thy ways al convento. Dónde está tu padre? 135

OFELIA: En casa, mi lord.

HAMLET: Let las puertas be shutteadas a él, that se comporte como un tonto nowhere pero en su propia casa. Adiós.

OFELIA: O! help him, you dulces cielos!

HAMLET: Si usted sí lo marrea, I'll give a usted esta plaga for su dowry: be thou as 140
chaste as ice, pura como la nieve, thou shalt not escape la calumnia. Get usted al convento, go; adiós. Or, if usted necesita casarse, cásese con un tonto; for wise men saben bien cuan monstrousos usted los hace. Al convento, go; y rápido too. Adiós.

OFELIA: O poderes heavenleados, restoréenlo!

HAMLET: He oido de las aplicaciones de cosmético a tu cara y well enough; 150
Dios hath given you una cara, and you make yourselves otra: you danza sugestivamente, you amble, and habla afectadamente, y nickname las criatures de Dios, and wantonesea su ignorancia. Vayan, I'll no more en eso; me ha puesto loco. I say, no tendremos más matrimonios; esos que están marriados ya, todos but uno, shall live; el resto quedarán como están. Al convento, go. [Exit. 155

OFELIA: O! what una noble mente is aquí overthrowneado:
ejemplo del courtier, el soldado, el scholar, ojo, lengua, espada;
Esta esperanza y rosa del estado faireado,
El vaso de moda y el mould de la forma,
El observado de todos los observadores, quite, quite abajo! 160
Y yo, of ladies más rechazado y wretcheado,
That suckeó la miel of sus palabras musicales,
Ahora veo that noble y más soberana razón,
Like dulces campanas jangleadas, desentonadas y harsh;
Esa forma unmatcheada y featura de la juventud gastada 170
Blasteada con éxtasis: O! woe de mí,
Haber visto lo que he visto, see lo que veo!

Re-entran KING y POLONIUS.

KING: Amor! sus afectaciones do not that way tend;
No lo que él espake, aunque haya lakeado un poco,
Was not como la locura. Hay algo en su alma 175
Encima del which su melancolía sits en brood;
And, yo lo dudo, the hatch and el disclose
Will be de algún peligro; which for para preventear,
Tengo una quick determinación
Thus la pongo abajo: el debe with espeed ir a Inglaterra, 180
Por la demanda of nuestro tributo neglecteado:
Quizás los seas y países diferentes
Con objetos variables que van a expelear
Este matter casi-settleado en su corazón,
Whereon sus sesos still beating lo ponen así 185
Para la fashion a sí mismo. Qué lo hace actuar abnormally?

POLONIUS: It shall do bien: but yet creo yo
Que el origin y commencement de su grief
Sprungear de amor rechazado. Cómo ahora, OFELIA!
No debes decirnos what dijo Lord Hamlet; 190
Lo escuchamos todo. Mi lord, haga como quiera;
But, if you hold it fiteado, después de la obra,
Let su reina madre all alone entreatearlo
Para mostrar his griefos: déjala ser round con él;
And yo seré placeado, so please a usted, en el oido 195

de todas su conferencias. Y si ella no lo findea,
To Inglaterra mándalo, o confínalo where
Tu wisdom piense que sea prudente.

KING: Va to be así:
La locura in gentes great no debe quedar unwatcheada. *[Exeunt.* 200

EL LITTLE PRÍNCIPE, CHAPTERS I–IV

Cuando yo tenía seis años, encontré un beautiful dibujo en un book llamado *True cuentos* sobre una jungle. El book mostraba una boa constrictora tragándose un wild animal. Esta es la copia del dibujo.

El book decía: 'La boa constrictora se traga sus presas whole, sin masticarlas. Después ellas son incapaces de movimiento.

Después ellas sleep por seis meses while hacen la digestión.'

That me puso a pensar sobre todas las cosas que están en la jungle, y, con una crayola, yo hice mi primer dibujo. Lo llamé drawin número uno. Él looked así:

Le mostré mi masterpiece a los grown-ups y les pregunté si ellos creían que lo que veían era scary.

Respondieron: '¿Qué puede ser tan scary sobre este hat?'

Pero mi dibujo no era un hat. Era una boa constrictora digesteando un elephant. So entonces dibujé el inside de la boa, pa'ayudar a los grown-ups a entender mejor. Así se veía mi dibujo número dos:

Los grown-ups me me dijeron que olvidara elephants dentro de boas constrictoras y concentrarme mejor en geography, historia, arithmetic y gramática. Which is por qué, at la edad de seis, viendo que mi dibujo número uno y mi dibujo número dos habían sido such a desastre, renuncié a una gloriosa carrera como un artista. Los grown-ups nunca entienden anythin por su cuenta y es una nuisance pa' los niños tener que explicar las cosas otra vez.

So yo tuve que escoger otra profesión, y yo aprendí a ser un piloto. Volé al around el mundo. And es verdad que geography came in muy valiosamente pa' mí. Yo podía decir la diferencia entre China y Arizona de un solo glance. Lo que es very útil, if tu pierdes tu camino at night.

First published in *El Little Príncipe* (Neckarsteinach, Germany: Editions Tintenfas, 2016). Reprinted in *Words Without Borders,* January 25, 2017.

A través de los years, yo he conocido lots of personas sensibles y he gastado mucho tiempo viviendo en el mundo de los grown ups. Los he visto desde close quarters, which has done nada pa'que yo cambie mi opinión de ellos.

Whenever yo conozco un grown-up who parece fairly inteligente, yo lo pongo a prueba con mi dibujo número uno, which siempre lo he guardado, pa' así saber si en verdad él es perceptive.

But él siempre responde: 'Es un hat.' So en lugar de talkin a él sobre la boa constrictora o sobre la jungla o sobre las stars, yo voy a su nivel y discuto con él bridge, golf, la política o las corbatas.

Y los grown-ups siempre están delighted de toparse con such a razonable hombre.

II

And entonces yo viví alone, con nadie con quien pudiera hablar, hasta seis años atrás cuando mi avión se descompuso en el Desierto del Sahara. Y yo no tenía un mechanic conmigo, o ningún pasajero, por lo que yo tenía que hacer un complicated arreglo de engine por mi cuenta. Mi vida depended de esto, since yo apenas tenía suficiente agua que would last me una semana.

La first noche, me acosté en el ground y me quedé asleep, millas y millas lejos de cualquier livin alma. Yo estaba más cut off que un barco adrifteando en el middle del océano. So seguramente podrás imaginarte mi astonishment cuando yo fui awekeado

en el daybreak por una funny little voz que decía: 'Please, puedes dibujarme un little cordero!'

'Qué!'

'Dibújame un little cordero . . .'

Pronto salté to mis pies como si hubiera sido struck by lightin.

Me froté los ojos y miré. And ví el más extraordinario little fellow estudiándome intensamente. Esta es la mejor portrait que yo have been able to dibujar de él desde entonces.

Of supuesto este dibujo no es nearly tan delightful como el original. Esa es mi faulta. Los grown-ups pusieron un stop a mi carrera de artista cuando yo tenía seis años y desde entonces no había dibujado más que dos boas constrictoras.

Yo lo miré con admiración. Remember que yo estaba millas y millas de cualquier livin alma. But mi little fellow no se veía lost.

Tampoco se veía weak con exhaustión, o hambriento, o thirsty, o frekeado. De ningún modo se veía como a niño perdido en el middle del desierto millas y millas de cualquier livin alma.

When por fin encontré mi voz, le dije: 'What diablos estás haciendo aquí?'

Él repitió, muy quietmente, as if ese fuera un matter de utmost seriedad: 'Por favor, puedes dibujarme un little cordero?'

Here yo estaba, millas y millas de cualquier livin alma y con mi vida en danger. Pero estaba tan bafeado que yo lastimosamente accedí a hacer lo que él me pidió. Saqué una pluma y un paper de mi pocket. Luego yo remembré que yo había estudiado geography, historia, arithmetic y gramática. Le dije al little fellow (somewhat irritado) que yo no podía dibujar. Y él replicó:

'No importa. Dibújame un little cordero.'

Yo nunca había dibujado una pictura de un cordero, así que le presenté a él uno de los only dos dibujos que yo tenía: el de la boa Esta es la mejor portrait que yo have been able to dibujar de él desde entonces.

Y quedé astoundeado cuando oí al little fellow decir:

'No! No! Yo no quiero un elephant adentro de una boa. Una boa es muy dangerous y un elephant takes mucho espacio. Mi lugar es tinito. Yo necesito un cordero. Dibújame un pequeño cordero.'

Entonces se lo dibujé.

Él escrutinó mi esfuerzo y dijo: 'No! Ese dibujo looks muy very sicko. Dibújame

otro.'

Le dibujé otro.

Mi little friend sonrió undulgentemente.

'No puedes ver . . . ? Ese no es un cordero. Es un carnero. Tiene cuernos.'

Así que yo empezé all over otra vez.

Pero again, él rechazó lo que le di: 'Este animal es too viejo.

Yo quiero un cordero que pueda vivir por mucho tiempo.'

Yo estaba con prisa de empezar a estripear la engine y mi paciencia se estaba haciendo thin. Le hice un sketch así:

Y le dije: 'Ese es el crate. Ese cordero que tú quieres está inside.'

Quedé astonisheado al ver que la cara de mi little crítico se encendía:

'That's exactamente lo que yo quería! Crees que el cordero necesitará a lot of pasto?'

'Why?'
'Because mi place es tinito.'
'Estoy seguro que tendrá suficiente. Te dibujé un little cordero.'
Él miró más closemente el dibujo. 'No tan little . . . Oh mira!'
Él ya se había quedado dormido.
Es así como hice el acquaintance del little príncipe.

III

Me llevó ages entender de dónde venía el little príncipe. Él me hizo muchas preguntas pero nunca parecía escucharme. Yo gradualmente construí su historia de cosas extrañas que él me decía. Por instancia, cuando él first vio mi plane (no puedo dibujarlo, no
puedo dibujar nada so complicado) él me askeó: 'What es esa thing?'
'No es una thing. Puede volar. Es un plane. Es *mi* plane.'
Estaba por decirle que yo soy un piloto y que vuelo planes.
Entonces él exclamó: 'What! Te caíste del sky?'
'Yes,' le repliqué modestamente.
'Oh! Eso es funny.'
El little príncipe dio una sonrisa tinkleada que yo encontré muy annoyin. Yo esperaba que los people tomaran mis troubles en serio.
Entonces él agregó: 'So tú caíste del sky too! De qué planet eres?'
Suddenmente me dí cuenta que él estaba dándome una clue importante as to his mysteriosa aparición. Le dije: 'Tu eres de otro planet, o qué?'
Pero él no replayó. Él seguía estudiando mi plane. Gentlemente asentó su cabeza: 'Of claro, tú no debes haber venido de muy lejos en esa thing.'
Y se quedó lost en sus persamientos por un while. Then él sacó mi dibujo del cordero de su pocket y lo examinó como un treasure.
Puedes imaginarte cuán intrigado yo estaba by esta alusión a other planets.
Investigué más a fondo: 'De dónde you come from, little hombre? Dónde es "tu place"? Adónde tú quieres llevar mi cordero?'
Él pondereó por un while y luego replayó: 'The buena thing about el crate es que en la night puede convertirse en su casa.'
'Exactamente. And si te portas bien, te voy a dar una rope pa'que lo amarres durante el día. Y una stake.'
El little príncipe se veía shockeado. 'Amarrarlo a él? What a strange thing pa' hacer!'

'But si tú no lo amarras, él se va a wanderear por todo el place y se puede get lost.'

Mi little amigo estalló laugheando otra vez: 'But adónde would él irse?'

'Anywhere. Él va a seguir su nariz.'

Entonces el little príncipe remarcó solemnemente: 'It wouldn't importar. Mi lugar es tinico.'

Y agregó wistfulmente: 'Si sigues tu nariz, tú puedes ir muy far.'

IV

Entonces yo aprendí somethin distinto de gran importancia: que el lugar that él came from was casi más big que una casa!

Yo no necesitaba to be tan sorprendido. Yo sabía very well que apart de los big planets como Earth, Júpiter, Marte y Venus, que tienen names, hay hundreds otros which son sometimes tan pequeños que they solamente pueden set vistos a través of a telescopio.

Cuando un astrónomo discovers uno new, le da un número en lugar de un nombre. Él lo llama 'Asteroid 325,' for ejemplo.

Tengo buena razón pa'pensar que el planet del little príncipe era Asteroid B612. Este asteroid ha sido glimpseado solamente una vez through un telescopio, y eso fue por un turco astrónomo en 1909.

Él gave una impressive presentación de su discovery en una international astronomía conferencia. Pero nadie believed him por la manera en que él dessed up. Así es como son los grown-ups.

Luckymente pa' el Asteroid B612, un Turco dictador made que sus people dressed con European estilo, on amenaza de death.

Usando un very elegante traje, el astrónomo dio su presentatión again, en 1920. This time todos estaban convinced.

La razón por la que yo relaté la anécdota sobre el Asteroid B612 y di su número es por los grown-ups. A los grown-ups les encantan los numbers. Cuando les cuentas a ellos algo about un nuevo amigo, ellos nunca hacen las preguntas importantes. Nunca dicen: 'Cómo suena su voz? Cuáles son sus games favoritos?

Él colecciona mariposas?' En su lugar, ellos preguntan: 'Cuántos años tiene? How many hermanos y hermanas tiene? Cuánto pesa? How much gana su father?' Only entonces ellos creen que lo conocen.

Si tú says a los grown-ups:

'Yo ví una beautiful pink casa de ladrillo con geraniums en los sills de la ventana y doves en el techo,' ellos no pueden visualizarla. Tu tienes que decir: 'Yo ví una casa worth un millón.' Entonces ellos se maravillan: '¡Qué lovely casa!'

En el same way, si les dices: 'El little príncipe really sí existió. Él era delightful y lleno de laughter y él pidió un little cordero.

Only a real persona puede querer un cordero,' ellos sacuden sus hombros y te tratan como un child. Pero si les dices: 'El planet que él came from es Asteroid B612,' entonces ellos te toman seriamente y te dejan en paz. Así es just how ellos son. No debes tenerlo en su contra. Los children deben ser very pacientes con los grown-ups.

Pero, of supuesto, los people who understand la vida no son bothered con los números! Yo hubiera querido empezar esta historia como un fairy cuento. Hubiera escrito: 'Había una vez un little príncipe que vivía en un planet no mucho más grande que él mismo. Él was necesitado de un amigo . . .' Los people que entienden la vida would have encontrado eso mucho más natural.

I don't like el people que take mi book lightemente. I find eso muy painful, stirreando las memorias. Ya son already seis años desde que mi amigo disapareció with el cordero. Yo quiero describírtelo pa' que yo no lo forgetée a él. Es triste olvidarse de un amigo. Not everybody ha tenido an amigo.

Yo no want to convertirme en uno de esos grown-ups que solamente cares por los números. Por eso compré una bolsa de pinturas y crayolas. Es difícil to take up dibujo otra vez a mi edad, cuando todo lo que you have hecho son two dibujos of a boa constrictora digesteando un elephant a la edad de seis años! Of supuesto, voy a hacer mi best pa' crear mis dibujos as vida-like as es posible. Pero yo no estoy sure que voy a lograrlo. Uno de los dibujos es fine, pero el otro es nothin como el little príncipe pa' nada. Yo dibujé su height mal. Aquí el little príncipe es too alto.

And en este él is too bajo. También, no estoy seguro de los colores de sus cloths. So yo hago el best que yo puedo. Some veces yo lo hago bien y some veces yo lo hago mal, pero tú tienes que disculparme.

Mi little amigo never me dio any explanaciones. Perhaps él pensó que yo era como él. But tristemente, yo no puedo ver corderos inside de crates. Probablemente yo soy un bit como los grown-ups. Yo must have grown viejo.

DON QUIXOTE, PARTE II, CHAPTER 72

Since las cosas humanas aren't eternas, pero son en declinación from its beginning hasta su último end, especialmente la vida de los hombres, and porque Don Quixote had no privilege from el cielo to stop el curso of his life, el final llegó and él se acabó when he least lo pensó, because, either porque sentía melancholia for having been brought down, or por la disposción of los heavens, which preordena everything así como así, he was taken by a fiebre and estuvo seis días en cama, in which lo visitaron muchas veces el cura, el bachiller, el barber, and sus amigos, without Sancho Panza, el buen squire, ever leaving su cabecera.

Ellos, thinking su condition era el resultado of seeing himself defeated and por no haber logrado la libertad and disenchantment of Dulcinea, tried por todos los means posibles to procurar him with alegría. The bachiller told him que se animara and get of the la cama, in order to comenzar a pastoral exercise, for which ya tenía written a song, made en la forma of the ones by Sannazaro, y que he had bought from el herdsman Quintanar con his own dinero dos fine perros, one que se llamaba Barcino and el otro Butrón. Pero Don Quixote was still muy triste.

His amigos called al doctor, who took su pulso and wasn't muy contento. El doctor said he should atender a la salud of the soul porque el cuerpo was in danger. Don Quuixote heard him con ánimo relaxed, but la housekeeper, su niece and his squire didn't. Ellos started to cry tiernamente, como si they had already al muerto enfrente. El doctor thought que the melancholy and la depression lo estaban acabando. Don Quixote rogó for them to dejarlo solo, porque he wanted to sleep un poco. Ellos agreed, and él slept of a tirón, as they say, más de seis horas; tanto that the housekeeper and la niece pensaron he was staying en el sueño. He woke up after ese tiempo and en una great voice, he said:

First published in *Don Quixote*, Parte II, Chapter 72: *El Quijote Universal: Siglo XXI*, ed. José Manuel Lucía Megías: A. Machado (Madrid: Antonio Machado Libros, 2016).

"Bendito sea el Almighty God, que tantos blessings me ha dado! En fin, his misericordias have no límite, and the human pecados neither abbreviate them o las impiden."

La niece was attentive to the noticias of her tío, and she thought they were more concertadas than his previous ones, al menos before the enfermedad.

She asked:

"What is it that you say, señor? Tenemos something new? What misericordias are you talking about, or what human pecados?"

"The misericordias," responded Don Quixote, "mi niece, are the ones en este instante Dios has used conmigo, and who, as I said, are not impedidas by my pecados. I now have juicio, free and claro, without the misty sombras of ignorance, which were bestowed en mí the amargos and continuous readings of the detestable libros de caballería. I know its disparates and nonsense, y no me pesa but that this desengaño has come tan tarde, because it leaves no time for me to do a recompensa, reading otros that bring luz to the alma. Yo me siento, niece, que I'm about to die; I'd like to do it, pa' que se entienda that my vida wasn't so mala; but given that I've been, yo no quiero to confirmthis truth enmimuerte.Ora ve and call, mi amiga, my good friends: el priest, el bachelor Sansón Carrasco, and Master Nicolás el barber, because yo quiero confesarme and domy testamento."

La niece did ese job when she brought a los tres. No sooner Don Quixote los vio, he dijo:

"I have good news, good señores: yo ya no longer soy Don Quixote of La Mancha; I'm Alonso Quijano, whom my costumbres me dieron el name of *Bueno*. I'm now an enemigo of Amadís de Gaula and of the infinite bunch of his linaje; now all the profane histories of knighterrantly are odiosas to me; now yo conozco my stubbornness and el peligro I incurred in reading them; now, for God's sake, I've escarmentado in my own cabeza and I abominate them."

Cuando the three heard him say esto, creyeron without a duda that a new craziness had overtaken him. Y Sansón said a él:

"When we finalmente tenemos the news that your Dulcinea is desencantada, usted sale con esta? And now que queremos to become pastores, pa' pasar la vida cantando, like príncipes, you want to become un ermitaño? For life's sake, cállese, be sensible, and déjese de cuentos."

"The ones hasta aquí," replied Don Quixote," have been verdaderos in dañarme, but con ayuda del cielo I trust to turn them into provecho ahora que me muero. I feel, señores, que me estoy murieron with speed;

leave the burlas aparte, and bring me a confessor so I can confess and a notary pa' escribir my testamento; because in such trances as these no se debe burlar el hombre with the alma. And así, I beg that while el señor priest allows me to confess, you go y traigan al notary."

Looking at one another, admiring las razones de Don Quixote, and, while in duda, they wanted to creerle; and one of the señales whereby se dieron cuenta que he was dying was to have regresado with such facilidad from loco to his senses; because to the aforementioned razones he added otras muchas also well said, equally Christian and well put, so that all in all se quitaron de duda and creyeron that he was cuerdo."

The priest made everyone leave, y staying alone with him, he confessed him. The bachelor fue por el notary, and regresó with him in poco tiempo and with Sancho Panza; and Sancho (who sabía from the bachelor la sitiación in which his señor was) finding la housekeeper and niece llorando, started to weep también. La confession se acabó, and the priest salió saying:

"Verdaderamente he's dying, and verdaderamente Alonso Quijano the Bueno is in his senses. Podemos entrar so he can do his testamento."

These news gave a tremendo empujón to the weeping housekeeper, niece, and the buen escudero Sancho Panza; so much so que les hizo reventar las lágrimas de los ojos and a thousand profundos suspiros from their chests, because verdaderamente, como alguna vez se ha dicho, while Don Quixote fue Alonso Quijano the Bueno, just like that, and while él fue Don Quixote of la Mancha, he was siempre of pleasant condition and kind manners, and pore so he wasn't only well querido by those en su casa, but among all who le conocían.

The notary entró with the rest, and after having done el principio of the testamento, and after Don Quixote organized su alma, with all those Christian circunstancias que son required, arriving to the bequests, él dijo:

"ITEM, it is mi voluntad that ciertos dineros that are en la posesión de Sancho Panza, who en mi crazyness hice my squire, because there have been ciertas cuentas between él y yo, and give-and-takes, I don't want that he tenga que pagarlos, or that se le pida cuenta of anything, but that si sobra algo after paying everything que le debo, the rest is suyo, which will be bien poco, and he'll have buen provecho with it; and if while I was loco I was parte to secure him the gobierno of the island, I could now, estando in my senses, give him un reino, I would, because the simplicity of his condición and the fidelidad of his trato merits it."

And turning to Sancho, le dijo:

"Perdóname, amigo, for having caused you to appear loco like me, haciéndote caer in the error I had fallen, that there were and are knight errants en el mundo."

"Ay," respondió Sancho, crying. "Don't die, your grace, but take a consejo and live muchos años; because the greatest locura a man can do en esta vida is to dejarse morir, with no resistence, sin que nadie lo mate, nor should otras manos kill him but those of la melancholy. Come on, no sea peresozo, get out of the cama, and let's go to the campo dressed up like pastores, as we had agreed: quizás behind some bush encontraremos a la señora Duilcinea desencanatada, the only thing we need to do is ver. If you're dying of the feeling of verse vencido, blame me for not properly fastening Rocinante's girth; for you have seen in your libros de caballería that algunos caballeros overthrow a otros, and the one who is vencido today is vencedor mañana."

"Así es," said Sansón, "and the buen Sancho is saying la verdad on this."

"Señores," dijo Don Quixote, "vámonos de poco a poco, because in last year's nests no hay pájaros this year. I was loco, and now am sane: fui Don Quixote, and now am, como dije, Alonso Quijano the Bueno. May my repentance and mi verdad bring back la estimación I once held; and que el notary continues.

"ITEM, I bequeath toda mi hacienda, a puerta cerrada, a mi niece Antonia Quijana, que está presente here, después de sacar the necessary portions pa' satisfacer the bequests que hago ahora; and la primera alocation is la de pagar the salario I owe por mucho tiempo to my house-keeper who has served me, and twenty ducados for her to buy a vestido.

Dejo as my executors the Señor Priest and the Señor Bachelor Sansón Carrasco, who están presentes.

"ITEM, it's my voluntad that if Antonia Quijana, my niece, quiere casarse, she should marry con un hombre who has first been established that he no sabe qué cosas are los libros de caballería, and en caso that he's found to know about these things, and si my niece quiere todavía casarse with him, and se casa, she should lose todo lo que I have bequeath her, which my executors pueden distribuir in pious obras, a su voluntad.

"ITEM, suplico to the aforementioned Señores that if la buena suerte allows them to conocer the author que dicen that wrote an historia that circulates por ahí, with the title Second Part of the *Aventuras of Don Quixote de LaMancha*, ask him forgiveness de mi parte por having given him la ocasión sin que yo lo pensara to have written tantos and tan grandes disparates such as the ones que allí están escritos; because I depart from esta vida with a feeling of remorse for having given him un motive pa' escribirlos."

The testamento was finished y Don Quixote, stretched from one side de la cama al otro, se desmayó. Everyone was alarmado and tried to ayudarlo, and in los tres días que he survived the writing del testamento se desmayaba quite often. The casa was upside down, but, con todo, la niece comía, la housekeeper brindaba, and Sancho Panza estaba in good spirits; because el business of inheriting borra or mitigates the sorrow que debe sentir the heir y causa que se olvide.

En fin, the last day de Don Quixote arrived, después de recibir todos los sacramentos and después de abominar de libros de caballería with many forceful argumentos. The notary was presente, and he dijo que he had never read a libro de caballería in which the knight errant había muerto in his own bed peacefully and in such a Christian manera as Don Quixote was about to do; who, between compasiones and tears from los que allí estaban, gave up his spirit, I mean, se murió.

Acknolwedging it, el notary pidió to be given the testimonio que Alonso Quijano the Bueno, known comunmente as Don Quixote of La Mancha, had passed away, that he was muerto naturalmente. And that he wanted such testimonio to quitar la occasion that some other autor other than Cide Hamete Benengeli could resucitarlo falsely, and made inacabables histories of his exploits.

This fin had the Ingenious Hidalgo of LaMancha, whose lugar Cide Hamete Benegeli didn't want to identify puntualmente, so that todas las villas and lugares of La Mancha contended among themselves to adopt him y tenerlo como suyo, the way Greece's siete ciudades contended to adopt Homero.

The llantos of Sancho, la niece, and Don Quixote's housekeeper won't be recorded aquí, pero Sansón Carrasco's lamentación está aquí:

> Aquí lies a Hidalgo bold
> que was so muy brave
> fue a extremos untold,
> on the borde de su grave
> la muerte no le puso a hold.
> All the mundo he had on store,
> was el scare pero no bore,
> yet somehow, according to Fate
> he was granted the motto:
> morir cuerdo y vivir loco.

And the prudentísimo Cide Hamete stated with his pen:

"Allí quedarás, hanging from this rack and from the hilo de alambre, no sé if bien cortado or not, where you shall live por largos siglos, unless presuntuosos and scoundrelly historiadores take you down pa' profanarte.

But before they reach you, I want to tell them en el mejor modo I can:

> ¡Tate, tate, folloncicos!
> Let it be by none tocada;
> porque this empresa, good rey,
> for me estaba guardada.

Para mí was Don Quixote born, and I para él; he knew how to obrar and yo escribir; only los dos are para uno, in spite and despecho of the pretend escritor tordesillesco who dared, or dares, to write con la pluma of coerse and grosera avestruz, the exploits of my valeroso caballero, for it isn't carga de sus shoulders or asunto of his congealed talent." And if perchance you should conocerlo, dile que he should allow to reposar in his tomb the cansados and already podridos bones of Don Quixote, and should not try to llevarlos, against all the laws de la muerte, to Castilla la Vieja, making him salirse de la grave where él real y verdaderamente lies from one end to another, incapable of doing a tercera jornada y new salida. For to hacerle burla of the adventures he engaged a gusto y beneplácito of people, in these and other extraños kingdoms, the two sallies are enough. And with these you cumplirás with your Christian profesión, aconsejando bien who doesn't love you well, and I will remain satisfecho and ufano for having been el primero who enteramente enjoyed the fruit of sus escritos, como yo quería, since my deseo has been no other than to put in abhorrence of la humanidad the false and disparatadas historias of the libros de caballería, which, gracias to this tale del genuine Don Quixote, are already tropezando and will fall sin duda alguna. *Vale.*

SPANGLISH AND THE ROYAL ACADEMY

Not long ago, the Real Academia Española, its matrix located in Madrid, with twenty-one branches throughout the Spanish-speaking world, did something at once surprising and disappointing: it approved the inclusion of the word *espanglish* in its official dictionary. I say it was surprising because for decades the RAE systematically disregarded the existence of this hybrid form of communication, suggesting it was just a passing phenomenon unworthy of serious academic consideration. Indeed, one of the institution's recent directors, Victor García de la Concha (1998–2010), regularly declared Spanglish "nonexistent," as if by ignoring it, the jazzy parlance of tens of millions of Latinos in the United States, as well as of scores of people anywhere in the Spanish-speaking world, would magically disappear.

But the inclusion of the word in the lexicon was disappointing because the definition the RAE proposed was misconstrued, naturally angering users on both sides of the Atlantic. In Spanish, the definition of *espanglish* reads: "*Modalidad del habla de algunos grupos hispanos de los Estados Unidos, en la que se mezclan, deformándolos, elementos léxicos y gramaticales del español y del inglés.*" I quote it in the original for readers to enjoy its hollow eloquence. In English translation: "Modality of speech used among some Hispanic groups in the United States, in which lexical and grammatical elements of Spanish and English are mixed, becoming deformed."

Deformed? Quite frankly, the RAE doesn't appear to be *de este mundo*, "of this world," or at least of our day and age. No respected scholar today would dare use such an ideologically charged adjective. To think of linguistic contact as deforming the concept of code is to engage in politics, not in scientific analysis. Of course, everyone knows that the one constant in any living language is change: to be up to date, to be au courant, a language needs to interact with its environment. That interaction entails

---

First published in *The Chronicle of Higher Education*, December 12, 2013.

loans and borrowings. In English, *prairie* comes from the French, *rancho* from the Spanish, *mafia* from the Italian, *chutzpah* from Yiddish. Is the English language polluted because it incorporates these terms? Hasn't the base of modern English been defined by its imperial quests? Spanglish isn't a concoction devised to aggravate highfalutin dons. It is a dialect, with specific morphological rules, that comes about from necessity. It is also, in my view, an expression of the emergence of a new *mestizo* civilization, part Anglo and part Hispanic.

According to historians of the Spanish language, the first American word ever to travel back to the Iberian Peninsula after 1492, when Columbus stumbled upon the so-called New World, is *canoa*, "canoe." In 1496, it replaced the word *barco* in a grammar published by the Salamanca philologist Antonio de Nebrija, who is credited for describing *el español* as "*la compañera del imperio*," the companion of empire. The inclusion of *espanglish* in the RAE dictionary may not be the first time this mixed tongue makes it in (*estrés*, "stress," might have that honor), but it certainly is a moment of historical proportions.

To some of us involved with the gorgeously polluted way of communicating of college students, Spanglish is an affirmation, not a negation. Unfortunately, it will take a bit longer for the RAE legislators to understand that what they consider verbal deformation is really creative rejuvenation, and that their definition of *espanglish* is as much a step forward as it is a step back: a *hurra* to a language used freely by Latinos and a statement of intellectual narrow-mindedness.

ABOUT THE AUTHOR

Ilan Stavans is Lewis-Sebring Professor of the Humanities, Latin American, and Latino Culture at Amherst College.

INDEX

12 News, 139, 141
1001 Nights, The (anonymous), 164, 175. See also Arabian Nights
1492, 123
1984 (Orwell), 176

A Personal Record (Conrad), 4
ABC, 13–14. See also Alphabet
Abraham, 79
Absalom! Absalom! (Faulkner), 162
Académie française, La, 115, 116
Academy of English, 115
Academy of the Arabic Language, 115
Academy of the Hebrew Language, 115, 116
Accademia della Crusca, 115
Aciman, Andre, 4
Adams, John, 115
Adams, John Quincy, 115
Adams Family, The, 22
Adventures of Huckleberry Finn (Twain), 175
Age of Independence (Latin America), 123
Agnon, Sh. Y, 82
Agnonian style, 82
Aguacate, 124
Agustini, Delmira, 129
Ahava, 198
Akhmatova, Anna, 176
Al-Qaeda, 83
Aleichem, Sholem, 8
Aleph, 13

"Aleph, The" (Borges), 53–57, 93
Algerian prison, 174
Alien Tongues (Beaujour), 205
Allen, Woody, 73, 175
Alonso, Amado, 123, 125
Alphabet, 13–14. See also ABC
Amadís de Gaula, 206
America, 135, 136, 173
American, 90, 115, 126, 146, 175, 206, 253
American dinner theater (also Broadway), 174
American English, 148
American accent, 139
American Jewish diaspora, 84
American literature, 115
American pop culture, 50
American Revolution, 124
American West, 125
Americans, 83, 115, 126, 137, 139, 148
Americas, 123, 127, 128, 165
Amherst, 173
Amherst Academy (Amherst), 201
Amherst College, 23–25, 119–122
Amichai, Yehuda, 83
AMIA (Jewish Community Center in Buenos Aires), 77
Amor, 198
Amore, 198
Amour, 198
Análisis ideológica de los tiempos de la conjugación castellana (Bello), 127

256

INDEX

Ancient Greek, 32
Ancient Israel, 207
Andria, 32
Angelitos (Stavans and Cohen), 31, 33
Anglos, 141, 170, 253
Anglophones, 198
Antin, Mary, 116
Antiquities (Josephus), 79
Apocrypha, 79
Apollinaire, Guillaurme, 157
Apropos, 215
Apuntaciones críticas sobre el lenguaje bogotano (Cuervo), 128
Arabesques (Shammas), 82
Arab historian, 171. See also Cide Hamete Benegeli
Arabian Nights, The 164, 175. See also *1001 Nights*
Arabic, 82, 115, 171, 195, 206
Arabic books, 180
Arabs, 83
Aragon, Louis, 60
Arenales (Buenos Aires), 90, 92
Argentina, 5, 91, 111, 125, 126, 129, 130, 133, 136, 193
Argentine letters, 92
Argentine Spanish, 125, 126
Argentines, 93
Ariel, 120
Aristophanes, 68, 90
Arizona, 124, 139–141
Arlt, Roberto, 90
Ars poetica (Borges), 163
Artificial Respiration (Piglia), 91
Ascasubi, Hilario, 1995
Asociación de academias de la lengua española (ASALE), 131
Asphalt Jungle, The (Burnett), 89
Asymptote, 193–195
Athens, 68
Atlantic, 115, 124, 127, 252
Auden, W. H., 175

Augenbraum, Harold, 189
Austen, Jane, 168, 201, 203
Australia, 115
"Autobiographical Essay" (Borges), 4
Awakening, The (Chopin), 203
Aztec Empire, 49, 124

Babel, Isaac, 73
Babylon, 79
Babylonian exile, 79
Bajacaliforniano, 125
Bajío, 124
Belano, Arturo, 207
Bananas (Allen), 175
Bar Kochba, 77
Barataria, 173
Barnstone, Willis, 153
Barret, William, 172
Barrio Norte, 207
Barroquismo, 165
Baruch Dayan Haemet, 84
Basque, 126
Batman, 96
Batman and Robin, 22
Baudelaire, Charles, 75, 87
Beaujour, Elizabeth Klosty, 205
Beat Generation, 145, 155
Beatriz, 54
Beckett, Samuel, 201, 203
Beckford, William, 164
Bedlam, 161
Beijing, 51, 52
Belize, 124
"Belle of Amherst" (Emily Dickinson), 173
Bello, Andrés, 126–128
Ben Yehuda, Eliezer, 5, 80–83, 87
Bengali, 193, 206
Berkeley, 59
Berlin, 77
Bertolucci, Bernardo, 54
Bethlem Royal Hospital, 161

INDEX

"Beyond Translation: Borges and Faulkner" (Stavans), 163
Bialik, Chaim Nahman, 5, 6
Biblioteca Nacional (Argentina), 89, 169
Bilingual Mind, The (Pavlenko), 197
Bishop, Elizabeth, 9, 157, 158, 161
Bishop Berkeley, 72
Black English, 197. *See also* Ebonics
Black Legend, 170
Blake, Patricia, 150
Blake, William, 57
Blanchot, Maurice, 203
Blind, Daley, 105
Blount, Edward, 172
Bobe Bela (Bela Stavchansky), 6
Bóbo, 198
Boehner, John, 37
Bogota, 128
Bolaño, Roberto, 91, 206, 207
Bolívar, Simón, 125, 126. *See also* El Libertador
Bombay, 59
Borges, Jorge Luis, 4, 7, 48, 53–57, 80, 89, 90, 92, 93, 111, 120, 126, 153, 154, 157–165, 169, 177, 195, 207
Borges, the Jew (Stavans), 163
"Borges and I" (Borges), 178
Borgesian, 202
Bosch, Hieronymus, 53
Bovary, Emma, 203
Braille, 176
Branagh, Kenneth, 120
Brazil, 104, 171
Brazilian authors, 157
Brazilians, 102
Breshit, 78, 79, 84. *See also* Genesis
Brief Forms (Piglia), 90
Britain, 15
British Broadcasting Channel (BBC), 9
Broadway, 8, 28, 174

Brodsky, Joseph, 149, 176
Brontë, Charlotte and Emily, 206
Brooke, Arthur, 28
Bruegerl, Peter the Elder, 86
Buendías, 133
Buenos Aires, 7, 57, 77, 82, 92, 129, 164, 169
Bulgarian, 149, 153
Bumiller, Kristen, 120
Burnett, W.R., 89
Burning Plain, The (Rulfo and Schade), 182, 183, 188, 189
"Burning Question, The" (Ben Yehuda), 81
Burnt Money (Piglia), 91
Bush, George W., 111
Butor, Michel, 60

Cabrera Infante, Guillermo, 207
Cacahuate, 124
Cain, James, M., 89
Caliban, 120, 130
California, 124, 139, 203
Call It Sleep (Roth), 203, 204
Cambridge, 60
Cambridge, Massachusetts, 7
Camões, Luís Vaz de, 206, 207
Campesino, 188
Campo, Estanislao del, 195
Canaan, 78, 79
Canada, 115
Candide (Voltaire), 206
Canoa, 253
Cantabria, 80
Cantinflas, 97
Canto General (Neruda), 47
Captives (*Don Quixote*), 179
Caracas, 126, 129
Cardenio, 170, 171
Cardenio (Shakespeare and Fletcher), 170
"Cardenio Boom," 170

Cardenio Project (Greenblatt), 171
Cardenno, 170
Cardinal Richelieu, 116
Caribbean, 123, 128
Caribbean linguistic varieties, 128
Carnaval, 104
Carnival do futebol, 101
Casca, 75
Casillas, Iker, 105
Castellano, 124
Castellano, español, idioma nacional (Alonso), 123
Castile, 123, 140
Castilian, 127, 167
Castle of Otranto, The (Walpole), 206
Castro, Américo, 125
Catauro de cubanismos (Ortíz), 132
Catherine the Great, 86
Catholic Church, 72, 174, 180
Catholicism, 60
Catullus, 80
Caucasian features, 22
Cendrars, Blaise, 213
Central America, 124, 188
Central American Spanish, 132
Central Europe, 125
Cervantes, Miguel de, 5, 19–20, 27, 50, 71, 72, 73, 93, 140, 167–180, 206
Changshu Institute of Technology, 45, 49
Charlie Hebdo, 21
Chapulín Colorado, El (Chespirito), 95, 96, 97
Charles Eliot Norton Lectures, 125
Chateau Margaux, 200
Chatto and Windus, 162
Chavo del Ocho, El (Chespirito), 95, 96
Che Guevara, Ernesto, 97
Chespirito (Roberto Gómez Bolaños, aka "Little Shakespeare"), 95–97

Chesterton, G. K., 164
Chiapaneco, 124
Chicago Manual of Style, 32
Chicalote, 183
Childers, William P., 174
Chile, 102, 126, 130, 131
Chilean, 127, 207
Chilean Spanish, 207
Chilindrina, La, 96
China, 50, 51, 148
Chinese, 31, 48, 49, 51, 52, 75, 205, 206
Chinese Communist Party, 50
Chinglish, 50, 51, 52, 140
Chopin, Kate, 202
Chota, 187
Chronicles, Book of 2, 79
Chomsky, Noam, 77
Chutzpah, 253
Cide Hamete Benegeli, 177, 206. *See also* Arab historian
"Circular Ruins, The" (Borges), 164
Classic Dictionary of Hindu Mythology, A (Dowson), 61
Classics, 168, 169, 183, 188, 190, 193, 211–216
Clinton, Bill, 111
Coleridge, Samuel Taylor, 120
Colombia, 5, 111, 126, 129, 130, 131, 133, 139, 193
Colombian localisms, 139
Colombian Spanish, 128, 131
Colombianisms, 134
Colombians, 104
Colorado, 124
Committee of Six (Amherst College), 23–25
"Compass" (Borges), 154
Connecticut, 150
Conrad, Joseph, 4, 201, 203
Contrapunteo cubano del tabaco y el azúcar (Ortíz), 132

Conversation in The Cathedral (Vargas Llosa), 181
Corcovado, 104
Cornell University, 167
Cortázar, Julio, 28, 90, 133, 186, 207
Cortés, Hernán, 49
Comic Race, The (Vasconcelos), 132
Costa Rica, 101, 124
Crane, Hart, 157
Crime and Punishment (Dostoyevsky), 165
Cristoff, María Sonia, 193
Criticism and Fiction (Piglia), 90
Croll, Robert, 28
Cronkite, Walter, 139
Cuba, 128, 130, 132, 133
Cuban parlance, 132
Cuban psyche, 132
Cubans, 97, 128
Cuervo, Rufino José, 128
Curé, 215
Custom of the Country, The (Fletcher and Massinger), 173
Czech, 169

Dain Curse, The (Hammett), 89)
Daklhia, Jocelyn, 179
Daneri, Carlos Argentino, 53, 54
Dante, 54, 87
Darío, Rubén, 129
Darwinian evolution, 32
David, Rabbi Justin, 69
Davis, Lydia, 193, 211–216
Day, Douglas, 162, 163
De Gaulle, Charles, 168
De vulgari eloquentia (Dante), 87
"Death of Yankos, The" (Stavans), 9
Death Sentence (Blanchot), 213
Deep South, 164
Defoe, Daniel, 115
Democracy, 124
Denmark, 63

Derrida, Jacques, 36, 37
Destruction of Second Temple, 80, 83
"*Deutsches Requiem*" (Borges), 53
Deuteronomy, 79
Diaries of Emilio Renzi: Formative Years (Piglia), 90, 92
Di Giovanni, Norman Thomas, 4, 7, 55, 153, 154
Dialogue (Sosa), 179
Díaz, Junot, 116
Diccionario de construcción y régimen de la lengua castellana (Cuervo), 128
Diccionario dela lengua española (DEL), 131
Dickens, Charles, 206
Dickinson, Emily, 9, 28, 29, 47, 173, 201, 202, 203
Dictionary Days (Stavans), 198
Dictionary of the English Language, A (Johnson), 16
Disappearance: A Novella and Stories, The (Stavans), 9, 10
Distant Star (Bolaño), 207
Diversity, 135–137
Divine Comedy, The (Dante), 54
Djudezmo, 80
DNA, 24, 76, 182
Doctor Chapatín El (Chespirito), 95
Doctor Ralph, 206
Doescher, Ian, 27
Dominican Republic, 125, 128
Dominicans, 97
Don Quixote, 19–20, 93, 121, 183, 184
Don Quixote de La Mancha: A Comedy in Five Acts (Ruiz de Burton), 174
Don Quixote in America (Stavans and Childers), 174
Don Quixote of La Mancha (Cervantes), 5, 9, 27, 37, 71–74, 140, 167–180, 206, 245–250. See also *El Quijote*

Donoso, José, 133
Doran, Gregory, 170, 171
Doré, Gustave, 86
Dorfman, Ariel, 4
Dos Passos, John, 175
Dostoyevsky, Fyodor, 90, 103, 165
Double Falsehood (Theobald), 170, 171
Double Marriage, The (Massinger), 173
Doubleday, 7
Dowson, John, 61
Dr. Zhivago (Pasternak), 150
Drache, Mordecai, 76
Dream of the Red Chamber (Cao Xuequin), 198
Dryden, John, 173
Dublin, 172
Dublin Castle, 172
Duck Soup (Marx Brothers), 36
"*Duelos y quebrantos*" (Cervantes), 176
Duende, 198
Dutch, 115, 200
Dzidi, 80. See also Judeo-Persian, Jidi, and Parsic

E pluribus unum, 137
Eastern Europe, 125
Eastern religions, 60
Ebonics, 198. See also Black English
Editorial Losada, 53
Egypt, 21, 85, 171
E.T.: The Extraterrestrial (Spielberg), 102
"El Boom," 133, 134
El Hogar, 162
El Mundial, 101, 103, 104. See also World Cup
El País, 91, 168
Ecuador, 116, 131
Elkabetz, Ronit, 873
Ellipsis in English Literature: Signs of Omission (Toner), 32

El Quijote (Cervantes), 167, 168, 169, 171, 172, 173, 175, 176, 190. See also *Don Quixote*
Elizabethan England, 171
"Emma Zunz" (Borges), 53
England, 115, 170, 173. See also United Kingdom (UK)
English, 3, 4, 5, 7, 9, 10, 15, 16, 31, 32, 33, 40, 45, 47, 50, 52, 55, 75, 76, 77, 82, 86, 111, 115–117, 126, 139–141, 146, 147, 149, 151, 152, 155, 158, 164, 167, 174, 178, 183, 186, 187, 191, 193, 194, 197, 198, 199, 201, 203, 204, 205, 206, 212, 213, 252
English pentameter, 155
English readers, 172
English six-footers, 155
English speakers, 126
Enlightenment, 72
Enzenberger, Hans Magnus, 83
Erasmus of Rotterdam, 72
Escher, M. C., 107
Escuicle, 124
Esperanto, 176
ESPN, 101
Estadio Azteca, 96
Ethics, The (*Ethica Ordine Deometrico Demonstrata*) (Spinoza), 14, 200, 202
Escher, E. M., 53
Español, 123, 124, 125. See also Spanish
Espionage, 45–52
Estrés, 253
Eugene Onegin (Pushkin), 164
Europe, 57, 120, 129, 133
European countries, 126
European immigration, 126
European languages, 201
European Union, 101
Exemplary Novels (Cervantes), 173

INDEX 261

Exodus, 79
Ezra, 79

Facundo: Civilization and Barbarism (Sarmiento), 93, 126
Fahrenheit 451 (Bradbury), 94
Farsi, 193
Faulkner, William, 28, 90, 162, 163, 164, 165, 175, 201, 202, 203, 205
Fehr, Don, 4
Fernández, Macedonio, 90
Ficciones (Borges), 53, 153
Fiddler on the Roof, 8
Fiesta de fútbol, 105
FIFA, 101, 102, 103
Fitz, Ezra, 163
Five Books of Moses, 31, 76, 78, 79, 80. See also Hebrew Bible
Fitzgerald, Edward, 149
Flamenco, 22
Flaubert, Gustave, 89, 152, 193, 206, 213
Flavius Josephus, 79
"Flemish Tapestries" (Stavans), 177, 178
Fletcher, John, 170, 171, 173
Florida, 113, 139
Foras na Gaeilge, 115
Ford, Ford Madox, 205
France, 21, 63, 102, 126, 128, 151, 170, 193
Franco, General Francisco, 198
Fredonia, 25
French, 31, 76, 86, 111, 112, 115, 129, 146, 147, 148, 149, 151, 152, 172, 175, 194, 199, 201, 203, 205, 206, 212, 213, 253
French alexandrines, 155
French culture, 149, 212
French Revolution, 124
French symbolism, 129

Frost, Robert, 28
FSG Book of Twentieth-Century Latin American Poetry, The (Stavans), 157
Fuchs, Barbara, 170
Fuentes, Carlos, 133, 207
Fuguet, Alberto, 9
Fútbol, 103
Futebol, 108

Gadda, Carlo Emilio, 90
Galician, 126
Galilee, 77
Galta, 60, 61, 62
Gandhi, Mahatma, 59
Garcés, María Antonia, 167
García de la Concha, Víctor, 252
García Márquez, Gabriel, 48, 96, 133, 134, 164, 164, 182
Garden of Earthly Delights, The (Bosch), 53
"Garden of Forking Paths, The" (Borges), 53
Gaucho, 125, 126, 195
Gaucho literature, 195
Gaucho Martín Fierro, The (Hernández), 194
Gaza, 77, 87
Gemara, 80
Genesis, 78, 79, 84. See also Breshit
Gerdes, Dick, 9
German, 83, 111, 115, 129, 147, 148, 152, 201, 203, 205, 206
Germans, 51, 76, 83, 199, 200
Germany, 126, 148
Gezer Calendar, 79
Gettysburg Address (Lincoln), 14
Glendale, 140
Goethe, Johann Wolfgang von, 90
Ghana, 102
Globalization, 113
Gloucester, 120

Gómez Bolaños, Roberto, 95
González Martínez, Enrique, 129
Good Soldier, The (Ford), 205, 206
Gottlief, Elaine, 8
Gramática de la lengua castellana (Nebrija), 124
Gramática de la lengua castellana destinada para el uso de los americanos (Bello), 127
"Grammatology, Of" (Derrida), 36
Grand Inquisitor, 198. *See also* Tomás de Torquemada
Grass, Günter, 206, 207
Great Wall of China, 111
Greece, 22, 63, 101
Greek, 75, 83, 112
Greeks, 104
Greenblatt, Stephen, 171
Greenwich, 170
Grossman, David, 83
Grossman, Edith, 178
Grover, 77
Guadalajara, 70
Guajarati, 174
Guardian, The, 168
Guatemala, 124
Guillén, Jorge, 153
Guinness Book of World Records, 208
Gūzhàng, 198

Haifa, 77
Haketiya, 80
Halashon Ivrit, 79
Halevi, Yehuda, 9
Hamaca, 124
Hamakom Yenachem Etchem, 84
Hamas, 83
Hamilton, 28
Hamlet (Shakespeare), 54, 93, 103, 119, 120, 121, 170, 170, 229–237
Hamlet, 120, 189

Hammett, Dashiell, 89
Hamnet, 120
Hampshire County Jail, 119–122
Hancock, Herbie, 208
Hanumān, 61, 62
"Happy Prince, The" (Wilde) 207
Harvard University, 171
Hashachar (The Dawn), 81
Hassidism, 8
Hatfield, Charles, 157–165
Hauser, Kaspar, 148
Hayward, Max, 150
Heading South, Looking North (Dorfman), 4
Heart of Darkness (Conrad), 203
"Heaven without Crows, A" (Stavans), 9
Hebraïsti, 79
Hebrew, 3, 4, 5, 8, 10, 13, 31, 75–87, 115, 183, 194, 197, 200, 203, 204, 205
Hebrew alphabet, 53, 77
Hebrew Bible, 31, 76, 78, 79, 80, 85, 208. *See also Five Books of Moses*
Hellenic, 80
Hellenistic, 80. *See also* Judeo-Greek and Yevanic
Henbraios, 79
Henríquez Ureña, Pedro, 124, 132
Henry the Eighth (Shakespeare), 172
Hernández, José, 194, 195
Herzog, Werner, 148
Hezbolah, 83
Hidalgo, Bartolomé, 195
Hidalgo y Costilla, Fray Miguel, 124
Higher Education Act (1994), 119
Hillel, 77
Himalayas, 61
Hindi, 151
Hinduism, 60
Hispanic, 253
Hispanic America, 125, 127

INDEX

Hispanic culture, 185
Hispanic middle class, 97
Hispanic world, 93, 111
Histoire de l'admirable Don Quichotte de La Mancha (Filleau de Saint-Martin), 175
History of the Valorous and Wittie Knight-Errant Don Quixote of the Mancha, The (Cervantes and Shelton), 172, 173
Hobbes, Thomas, 54
Hoffman, Eva, 4
Hölderlin, Friedrich, 152
Holland, 104, 105
Holy Inquisition, 72, 167, 174
Holmes, Henry Alfred, 195
Homais, 212
Homer, 208
Honduras, 124, 131
Hopi, 201
Hopscotch (Cortázar), 181, 207
Horace, 80
Hotel Las Delicias, 92
Howard, Richard, 146, 147, 149
Howard, Thoephilus, 172
Howard, Thomas (First Earl of Suffolk), 172
Hulaulá, 80
Hume, David, 198
Hungarian, 203
Hybrid languages, 179

I Split on Your Graves (Vian), 206
Iberian attitudes, 127
Iberian Peninsula, 123, 125, 253
Iberian Spanish, 131
Icelandic, 193
Iliad (Homer), 178
"Ill-Conceived Curiosity, The" (Cervantes), 172
Importance of Being Ernest, The (Wilde), 69)

"Impossible Dream, The" (*Man of La Mancha*), 174
India, 59–63, 171
Inside/Out Prison Exchange Program, 120
Institutional Revolutionary Party, 96
Instituto Cervantes, 176, 177
"Insufferable Gaucho, The" (Bolaño), 207
Internet, 57
Ionesco, Eugene, 60
iPad, 39
iPhone, 39, 107
Imperium Romanum, 80
Iris Catholic, 1762
Irving, Washington, 174
Isaac, Jorge, 193
Isaiah, Book of, 79
Isis, 83
Israel, 81, 83
Israeli Arabs, 82
Israeli soldiers, 83
Istanbul, 79
Italian, 28, 90, 112, 115, 129, 206, 253
Italian immigrants, 126
Italy, 63, 80, 125
Italians, 51, 154
"It's Because We're So Poor" (Rulfo), 182, 183
Iturbide, Joaquín de, 124
Ivanova, Alyona, 103

Jacobean era, 120
Japan, 148, 171
Japanese, 203
Jarrillas, 184
Jarvis, John, 175
Jehoahaz, 79
Jefferson, Thomas, 112
Jerusalem, 79, 81
Jesus Christ, 104

Jewish, 204
Jewish Kabbalah, 207
Jewish languages, 80
Jewish literature, 204
Jewish themes, 204
Jewishness, 204
Jews, 51, 83, 84, 87
Jiangsu (China), 45
Jidi, 80. See also *Dzidi*, *Judeo-Persian*, and *Parsic*
Jiménez, Juan Ramón, 149, 176
Jiùjiu, 198
Johnson, Samuel, 16, 82, 120, 126
Jonson, ben, 173, 174
Jordan River, 79
Joyce, James, 90
Juan Rulfo Foundation, 184, 188, 190
Judahite, 79
Judea, 78
Judeo-Arabic, 80. See also Yahudic
Judeo-Aramaic, 80. See also *Kurdit*, *Hulaulá*, *Tárgum*, and *Kurdishic*
Judeo-German, 3, 4, 6, 7, 8, 10, 71, 76, 80. See also Yiddish
Judeo-Greek, 80. See also Hellenic and Yevanic
Judeo-Persian, 80. See also *Dzidi*, *Jidi*, and *Parsic*
Judeo-Spanish, 80. See also *Djudezmo*, *Haketiya*, and *Ladino*
Julius Cesar, 80
Julius Cesar (Shakespeare), 75

Kadare, Ismael, 120
Kaddish, 84
Kafka, Franz, 90, 169, 204
Kahlo, Frida, 104
Keats, John, 147, 216
Kellman, Steven G., 197–209
Kenyon College, 32
Keret, Etgar, 83
Kermode, Frank, 120

Khayyám, Omar, 149
Kibbutzniks, 81
Kind David, 79
King James Version, 85–86, 208
King John (Shakespeare), 172
King Lear (Shakespeare), 120. See also *The True Chronicle History of King Lear and His Three Daughters*
King Salomon, 79
King's Men, 120, 170
Kings, 2 Book of, 79
Kislev, 81
Kitrell, Casey, 182, 183
Klingon, 176
Knausgaard, Carl Ove, 90
Kol Nidre, 77
Korzeniowski, Josef Teodor Konrad, 203. See also Joseph Conrad
Kurdic, 80. See also *Judeo-Aramaic*, *Hulaulá*, *Tárgum*, and *Kurdishic*
Kurdishic, 80. See also *Judeo Aramaic*, *Kurdit*, *Hulaulá*, and *Tárgum*
Kurdit, 80
Kyffin, Maurice, 32

La Cruz, Sor Juana Inés de, 174
La Liga, 102
La Mancha, 20, 171, 206
La Plata, 207
Ladino, 176. See also Judeo-Spanish
Labyrinth of Solitude, The (Paz), 59
Lady Macbeth, 28
Lahiri, Jhumpa, 116
Language Hoax, The (McWhorter), 197
Las Meninas (Velázquez), 108
Lashon b'nei adam, 78
Last Reader, The, (Piglia), 89, 93
Latin, 86, 112, 200, 206
Latin America, 91, 112, 123–134, 136, 164, 165, 181, 185, 186, 190, 191
Latin American identity, 183
Latin American literature, 8, 89, 181

Latin American novel, 165, 206, 207
Latin American reality, 182
Latin American Spanish, 128
Latin American writers, 164
Latin Americans, 113, 133
Latin Americanism, 91
Latinity, 147
Latinos in the United States (also Latinos), 50, 97, 112, 119, 140, 141, 252, 253
Lazarillo de Tormes (anonymous), 9
Lear, 120
Leaves of Grass (Whitman), 165
Leibnitz, Gottfried Wilhelm, 206
León, Moisés de, 207
Lengua Fresca (Stavans), 10
Leviathan (Hobbes), 54
Libertador, El, 126. See also Simón Bolívar
Liebe, 198
Lima, Ulises, 207
Linsalata, Carmine R., 175
Literary Currents in Hispanic America (Henríquez Ureña), 125
Literatura gaucha, 195
Literatura gauchesca, 195
"Literatura y literalidad" (Paz), 157
Lithuania, 81
Little Príncipe, El (Saint Exúpery), 239–244
Llano en llamas, El (Rulfo), 181, 182, 184, 192
Lolita (Nabokov), 204
London, 120, 161, 162, 170, 172
Los Angeles, 82, 84
Lost in Translation (Hoffman), 4
Lou Gehrig's Disease, 90
Louatah, Sabri, 193
Louvre, 168
Lowell, Robert, 160
Lugones, Leopoldo, 129
Lunfardo, 126

Luria, Isaac, 77
Lusiads, The (Camões), 206
Luso (Portuguese) America, 125
"Luvina" (Rulfo), 188

Macbeth (Shakespeare), 9
Macbeth, 28
Macduff, 28
Macondismo, 133
Macondo, 133
Madame Bovary (Flaubert), 193, 211, 212, 213, 214, 216
Maddow, Rachel, 37
Madrid, 131, 167
"Madrigal, As It Were, of Modifiers, A" (Miller), 15–17
Maese Pedro, 19
Mafia, 253
Maghreb, 179
Malasian, 176
Malcolm, 28
Malinche, La, 49
Malinchismo, 49
Malraux, André, 168
Man of La Mancha (Wasserman and Leigh), 174, 175
Mångata, 198
Managua, 129
Mandarin Chinese, 115, 198, 199
Manichean, 72, 174
Manhattan, 5
Mann, Thomas, 203
Mar del Plata, 92
María (Isaac), 193
Marías, Javier, 163
Marquis of Sade, 199
Marriange of Heaven and Earth, The (Blake), 57
Marseille, 81
Martí, José, 129
Marx Brothers, 36
Marx, Groucho, 36

Marx, Harpo, 36
Marx-Aveling, Eleanor, 193
Masoes Beniamin Hashlishi (Mendele Mokher Sforim), 73
Massachusetts, 7
Massinger, Philip, 173
Materazzi, Marco, 102
Mather, Cotton, 173
Matrix, The (Wachowski), 104
Mayflower, 173
McClellan, Clarisse, 94
McCourt, Frank, 116
McDonald's, 133
McOndo, 133
McWhorter, John, 197, 199
Mediterranean music, 22
Mediterranean Sea, 79, 179
Méjico, 124, 141. See also Mexico
Melville, Herman, 207
Mendele Mokher Sforim, 73
Menard, Pierre, 169
Menardismo, 164
Mensch, 198
Merchant of Venice, The (Shakespeare), 204
Merriam-Webster Dictionary, 13, 16, 35, 36, 71, 116, 137
Mesa, 139, 140
Mesoamérica, 124
Mesopotamia, 85
Messiah, 84
Mestizaje, 51
Mestizaje, 132
Mestizo, 22, 253
Metamorphosis, The (Kafka), 169, 204
Mexican children, 132
Mexican culture, 207
Mexican government, 63
Mexican society, 207
Mexican Spanish, 124, 125, 131, 187, 207
Mexican-American War, 140

Mexicans, 97, 104, 133, 140
Mexico, 3, 5, 16, 19, 22, 60, 63, 71, 75, 96, 101, 111, 112, 124, 125, 131, 133, 135, 141, 149, 181, 186, 187, 188, 193, 204, 207
Mexico City, 3, 59, 129, 181
Mezzofanti, Cardinal Giuseppe, 208
Miami, 139
Michaux, Henri, 60
Middle East, 13, 178
Midwest, 187. See also Midwestern America
Midwestern America, 187. See also Midwest
Mihaly, Ryan, 181–192
Miller, Fred R., 15–17
Milton, John, 147, 173
Miranda, 120
Miranda, Francisco de, 125
Mirren, Helen, 120
Mississippi English, 201
Missouri Eastern Correctional Facility, 120
Moby-Dick (Melville), 198, 202, 207
Mocosa Pechocha, La, 96
Modern Language Association (MLA), 32
Modernismo, 128, 129
Molière, 27, 152, 153, 154
Moncrieff, Scott, 215, 26
Monkey Grammarian, The (Paz), 59–63
Monolingualism, 84
Montag, Guy, 94
Montaigne, Michal de, 65, 170
Moors, 179
Morales, Harry, 9
Morelos y Pavón, José María, 124
Morgan, Tracy, 22
"*Morirse está en hebreo*" (Stavans), 9, 75, 84
Morrison, Toni, 202
Morton, Thomas, 173, 174

Moses, 165
"Mother Tongue" (Tan), 36
Motteux, Peter Anthony, 175
Movimiento 15-M, 21
Murdoch, Iris, 3
Museum of Antiquities (Istambul), 79
Muslims, 174, 180
My Mexican Shivah (Springall), 9, 75
My Struggle (Knausgaard), 90

Nabokov, Vladimir, 4, 8, 116, 152, 164, 201, 203, 204
Nahuatl, 124, 133
National Languages Committee, 115
Nazis. 83
Near East, 79, 85
Nebrija, Antonio de, 124, 253
Nederlandse Taalunie, 115
Nehru, Jawaharial, 59
Neo, 104
Neruda, Pablo, 9, 47, 48, 97
Netherlands, 101, 103. *See also* Holland
Neutral Spanish, 140
New England, 28
New England colonies, 173
New English Canaan (Morton), 174
New Mexico, 124
New Republic, 102
New Speak (Orwell), 176
New World, 127, 253
New York, 3, 37, 59, 81, 96, 189, 194
New York Review of Books, 164
New York Times, 5, 83
New Yorker, 4, 15, 16
Nicaragua, 124
Nichol, Barbara, 177
Night in Chile, By (Bolaño), 207
"No Dogs Bark" (Rulfo), 188
"¿No oyes ladrar los perros?" (Rulfo), 188
Nobel Prize, 133, 169

Norteño, 125
North American Authors (Piglia), 90
Northeast, 135
Northern Italian, 126
Norton Critical Editions, 178, 179
Norwegian, 203
National Public Radio (NPR), 120, 141
Notre Dame, 168
Nueva España, 124. *See also* Mexico

Obama, Barack, 11
Obama Administration, 112
Obamacare, 112
Obras Completas (Paz), 60, 62
Ocampo, Victoria, 53
Occupy Wall Street, 21
Ochoa, Memo, 104
O'Connell, Barry, 119
On Borrowed Words (Stavans), 3, 4, 6, 10, 49, 183
"On First Looking into Chapman's Homer" (Keats), 216
"On Reading John Cage" (Paz), 159, 160
"On the Short Story and Its Environs" (Cortázar), 186
"On *Vathek*, by William Beckford" (Borges), 163
One-Handed Pianist, The (Stavans), 9
One Hundred Years of Solitude (García Márquez), 48, 133, 181, 182
One-Way Road (Piglia), 91
Onetti, Juan Carlos, 164, 165
Ophelia, 120
Oregon Shakespeare Festival, 167, 168
Ormsby, John, 37, 178
Orthodox Jews, 9
Ortíz, Fernando, 132
Orwell, George, 36, 84, 176
Ottoman Syria, 77
Out of Egypt (Aciman), 4

Out of Place (Said), 4
Owen, Walter, 194
Oxford English Dictionary (OED), 116, 128, 147, 199, 202, 203
Ozick, Cynthia, 9

Pacific, 128
Painter, William, 28
Palabras prestadas: Autobiografía (Stavans), 6
Palace of Pleasure (Painter), 28
Palacio de Bellas Artes, 97
Pale of Settlement, 73, 80
Palestinians, 83
Paley, Grace (Grace P.), 70
Palmeras salvajes, Las (Faulkner and Borges), 163, 164, 165
Pan-Latino accent, 139
Pan-linguism, 208
Panama, 126
Panza, Sancho, 19, 72, 73, 173, 178
Paquda, Bahya ibn, 77
Paris, 59, 129
Parker, A. A., 175, 176
Parsic, 80. *See also* Dzidi, Jidi, and Judeo-Persian
Paterson (Williams), ix
Patrón, 188
Pavese, Cesare, 90
Pasaojos de agua, 184
Pavlenko, Aneta, 197
Paz, Marie José, 59
Paz, Octavio, 59–63, 157–165
Paz Soldán, Edmundo, 9
Peculiaridad lingüística rioplatense y su sentido histórico, La (Castro), 125
Pedro Páramo (Rulfo), 181, 187, 192
Penguin Proust, 213
Peña Nieto, Enrique, 96
Persian, 149
Peru, 19, 126, 133
Peruvianisms, 134
Phedre (Racine), 206

Philadelphia, 174
Philippines, 128, 132
Phillips, John, 175
Phoenicia, 85
Phoenix, 140
Picon, Gaëtan, 60
Picture, The (Fletcher and Massinger), 173
"Pierre Menard, Author of the *Quixote*" (Borges), 153
Piglia, Ricardo, 89–94, 165
Pilgrim, 173
Pitt, Brad, 178
Plain in Flames, The (Rulfo), 48, 181–192
Plagiarism, 175
Plato, 19, 67, 68, 90
Platonic Urtex, 208
Plural, 63
Poe, Edgar Alan, 164, 202
Poetics of Piracy, The (Fuchs), 170
Poland, 7, 126, 171
Polish, 90
Portuguese, 76, 101, 103, 125, 126, 129, 200, 201, 206
Postman Always Rings Twice, The (Cain), 89
Pound, Ezra, 157, 206, 207
Powell, Barry, 178
Prairie, 253
Praise of Folly, In (Rotterdam), 72
Praise of India, In (Paz), 59. *See also Vislumbres de la India*
Pre-Columbian, 124, 130
Pre-Columbian languages, 133
Premier League, 102
Pride and Prejudice (Austen), 168, 203
Prince, Amy, 9
Principios de la ortografía y métrica de la lengua castellana (Bello), 127
Prix fixe, 215
Proença, Pedro, 103
Profesor Jirafales, El, 96

Prophetess, The (Fletcher and Massinger), 173
Prospero, 120
Proust, Marcel, 211, 214
Pseudo-Epigrapha, 79
Puerto Madero, 207
Puerto Ricans, 97
Puerto Rico, 128, 131, 132
Puig, Manuel, 90
Purity of Blood, 169
Pushkin, Alexander, 164

Qatar, 102
Qin Shi Huang (also Shih Huang Ti), 111
Quijano, Alonso, 171, 178
Quijotes por el mundo (Instituto Cervantes), 176
Quijotismo, 71, 164. See also Quixotismo
Quixote: The Novel and the World (Stavans), 170, 175
Quixotified, 72
Quixotismo, 71, 164 Quijotism
Quito, 116
Quixotic, 74

Rabbi Akiva, 207
Rabbi Shimon bar Yohai, 207
Rabelais, 50
Racine, Jean, 206, 207
Rajasthan, 60
Raffel, Burton, 178
Rāmāyana, 61
Roderick Random (Smollett), 175
Rape of Lucrece, The (Shakespeare), 174
Rashkolnikov, 103
Rat für deutsche Rechtshreibung, 115
Real Academia Española (RAE), 115, 116, 130, 131, 141, 179, 202, 251–252. See also Royal Academia of the Spanish Language

Realismo crudo, 189
Rechov Sumsum, 77
Reconquista, 123
Regionalismos, 131
Renaissance, 17, 28, 120
Renegado: or, The Gentleman of Venice, The (Fletcher and Massinger), 173
Renzi, Emilio, 90–94
Restless Classics, 178
Resurrecting Hebrew (Stavans), 5, 76
Reverdy, Pierre, 157
Rexroth, Kenneth, 45
Rio de Janeiro, 104
Riobamba (Buenos Aires), 90, 92
"River Merchant's Wife, The" (Pound), 206
River Plate, 125
Riyadh, 82
Robben, Arjen, 103
Robin (*Batman and Robin*), 22
Rodker, John, 205
Rodó, José Enrique, 129, 130
Roman arches, 86
Roman numerals, 14
Romance language, 76
Romanian, 203
Rome, 21
Romeo and Juliet (Shakespeare), 28
Ronaldo, 103
Roosevelt, Franklin D., 111
Romania, 153
Rose, Mickey (Allen), 175
Rosenblat, Ángel, 132
Rosenzweig, Franz, 77
Roth, Henry, 203, 204
Roth, Philip, 73
Royal Academy of the Spanish language, 251–252. See also Real Academia Española (RAE)
Royal Shakespeare Company, 170
Rubáiyát (Khayyám), 149
Ruiz, Vanessa, 139–141
Ruiz de Burton, María Amparo, 173

INDEX

Rulfo, Juan, 9, 47, 165, 181–192
Russia, 102, 126
Russian, 8, 82, 146, 149, 151, 153
Russian émigrés, 205
Russian poetry, 150
Russian poets, 150
Rutgers University, 199

Sādhu, 61
Saer, Juan José, 90
Safed, 77
Said, Edward, 4
Salamanca, 124, 253
Salvador, El, 124
Saint-Martin, Françoise Filleau de, 175
San Martín, José de, 125
San Telmo, 207
Sanchified, 72
Sanjuro, General José, 198
Santiago, 127
Sapir-Whorf Thesis, 197
Sarmiento, Domingo Faustino, 93, 125
Saturday Night Life, 22
Saxton, Martha, 119
Savage Detectives, The (Bolaño), 207
Schade, George D., 183, 184, 185, 188, 189
Schadenfraude, 198, 199
Scheherazade, 175
"Schlemiel the First" (Stavans), 71
Schlemielland, 71–74
Schopenhauer, Arthur, 72
Se habla español (Fuguet and Paz Soldán), 9
Second Spanish Republic, 198
Second World War, 53, 126, 151, 152, 186
Secret Agent, The (Conrad), 204
Secret Weapons (Cortázar), 28
Sefer ha-Zohar, x, 207
Seine, 168
Semitic language, 79

Sentiers de la Creation, Les (The Paths of Creation) (Skira and Picon), 60
Self-translation, 3–10
Seville, 174
Shabbat, 84
Shakespeare, William, 9, 27, 29, 63, 75, 82, 119–122, 130, 141, 167, 168, 170, 171, 172, 174, 202, 208
Shakespeare scholarship, 171
Shakespeare in Love (Madden), 120
Shakespearean, 102
Shammai, 77
Shammas, Anton, 82
Shanghai, 51, 52
Shaw, George Bernard, 82
Shelton, Thomas, 172, 175, 176
Shih Huang Ti (also Qin Shi Huang), 111
"Shooting an Elephant" (Orwell), 36
Shūshu, 198
Signature style, 214
Sinai, 82
Sinbad, 20, 175
Singer, Isaac Bashevis, 7, 8, 9, 116, 202
Singer, Joseph, 7
Skira, Albert, 60
Skywalker, Luke 27
Slavic, 3
Smithsonian Institution, 165
Smolenskin, Peretz, 81
Smollett, Tobias, 175, 176
Smollet's Hoax (Linsalata), 175
Sprezzatura, 198
Socrates, 67, 68
Sonnets (Shakespeare), 174
Sosa, Antonio de, 179
Sotomayor, Sonia, 136
South America, 126
Southwest, 113, 124, 140
Spain, 5, 19, 21, 72, 105, 111, 116, 123, 127, 130, 131, 132, 140, 170, 171, 172

INDEX 271

Spanglish, x, 9, 49, 50, 51, 140,
    178, 179, 180, 183, 204, 219–227,
    229–237, 245–250, 251–252
Spanish, 3, 4, 5, 6, 7, 9, 10, 31, 33,
    35, 45, 47, 75, 76, 97, 111–113,
    115, 123–134, 139–141, 148, 149,
    151, 153, 158, 162, 165, 168, 177,
    179, 183, 184, 185, 187, 191, 193,
    195, 197, 198, 199, 200, 204, 207,
    253
Spanish-American War, 128, 132
Spanish Empire, 128
Spanish speakers, 140
Spanish-speaking world, 252
Spanish version, 159
Speak, Memory (Nabokov), 4, 8
Spicer, Sean, 112
Spider's Stratagem, The (Bertolucci), 54
Spinoza, Baruch, 14, 200, 202
"Spinoza of Market Street, The"
    (Singer), 202
Springall, Alejandro, 9
St. Vincent Millay, Edna, 105
Standish, Miles, 173
Star Trek, 176
Stationers' Register, 170
Stavans, Abraham, 6
Stavans, Darián, 6
Steegmuller, Francis, 216
Steinbeck, John, 175
Stendhal (Marie-Henri Beyle), 90, 206
Sterne, Laurence, 50
Stevenson, Robert Louis, 4
Stone, F.I., 68
Stoppard, Tom, 120
*Strange Case of Doctor Jekyll and Mister
    Hyde* (Stevenson), 4
Strauss, Dorothea, 8
Suárez, Luis, 102, 102
"Sudden Death," 101–104
"Summer's Dream, A" (Bishop), 157,
    159

Superman, 96
Sur, 53
Sureño, 124
Sullivan, Vernon, 206
Suzhou (China), 45
Swahili, 174
Swan's Way (Proust and Davis), 211
Swedish, 198
Swift, Jonathan, 115
Symposium (Plato), 67, 90

Tabárez, Óscar, 103
Tahrir Square (Cairo), 21
*Tales of Don Quixote by Miguel de
    Cervantes* (Nichol), 177
Talmud, 69, 76, 80, 82, 84, 121
Tan, Amy, 36, 38
Tárgum, 80
Tate, Alan, 162
Tel Aviv, 77, 81
Telemundo, 112, 139, 141
Televisa, 96
Tempest, The (Shakespeare), 120, 130
Tenochtitlán, 124
Tequesquite, 184
Terence, 32
Terra Nostra (Fuentes), 207
Tevye's Daughters (Aleichem), 8
Texas, 124
"Theme of the Traitor and the Hero"
    (Borges), 54
Theobald, Lewis, 170, 171
Thing (*The Adams Family*), 22
This American Life, 120
Thoreau, Henry David, 59
Thorpe, Adam, 193
"Three Nightmares" (Stavans), 9
Three Trapped Tigers (Cabrera Infante),
    207
Tin Drum, The (Grass), 206
Tlatelolco Square (Mexico), 59
Toledo, 169, 171

Toner, Anne, 32
Torah, 79
Torquemada, Tomás de, 198. *See also* Grand Inquisitor
Tour Saint-Jacques, 168
Tourette's syndrome, 22
Tower of Babel, 84–86
Trail, The (Kafka), 204
Translation, 145–156, 157–165, 167–180, 181–192, 193–195, 211–216
Translationese, 155
"Translators of the *1001 Nights*, The" (Borges), 163
Translingual imagination, 197–209
Translinguals, 197–209
Travails of Persiles and Segismunda, The (Cervantes), 173
Treaty of Guadalupe Hidalgo, 140
Tractatus Logico-Philosopohicus (Wittgenstein), 37
Traduttore, traditore (Italian), 46
Tragical History of Romeus and Juliet, The (Brooke), 28
Trail of Socrates, The (Stone), 68
"Translation and Hypocrisy" (Stavans lecture), 45
Trapiello, Andrés, 27, 167, 168, 169
True Chronicle History of King Lear and His Three Daughters, The, 28. *See also King Lear*
Trump, Donald, 111–113
Turkey, 171
Turkish, 205
Tuscany, 171
Tuteo, 125
TV Pública, 93
Twain, Mark, 69, 76, 83, 174
Two Noble Kinsmen, The (Shakespeare), 172

U.S. Congress, 119
U.S.-Mexican border, 111
U.S. Supreme Court, 136
UNAM, 132
UCLA, 41
Uncle Sam, 104
Underdogs, The (Azuela), 9
Unger, David, 9
United Kingdom (UK), 214
United Nations, 101
United States, 7, 8, 15, 16, 32, 36, 51, 96, 102, 111, 112, 115, 117, 126, 128, 130, 131, 135, 136, 140, 141, 149, 175, 183, 185, 190, 191, 193, 252
Universal Declaration of Human Rights, 208
University of Salamanca, 124
University of Virginia, 201
Univision, 101, 112, 139
Unvanquished, The (Faulkner), 162
Urdu, 61
Uruguay, 102, 103, 125, 129
Utah, 124
Uzbek, 174

Van Persie, Robin, 105
Vasconcelos, José, 132, 133
Velázquez, Diego, 108
Vargas Llosa, Mario, 133, 167, 168, 169
Vendler, Helen, 120
Venezuela, 126, 133
Venus and Adonis (Shakespeare), 174
Versailles, 86
Versiones y diversiones (Paz), 157
Vian, Boris, 206
Vietnamese, 176
Viking, 4
Virgil, 80
Violent Crime Control and Law Enforecement, 119
"Visits to St. Elizabeths" (Paz), 160
Vislumbres de la India (Paz), 59. *See also In Praise of India*

Voltaire, 86
Vonnegut, Kurt, 28
Voodoo, 102
Voznesensky, Andrei, 150
Vuelta, 63

Waiting for Godot (Beckett), 204
Wall, Geoffrey, 193
"Wall and the Books, The" (Borges), 111
Wallace, David Foster, 92
Walpole, Horace, 206
Wangchuan ji (Rexroth), 45
Ward, C. E., 195
Warsaw, 77
Wasserman, Dale, 174
Washington, 35
Western Civilization, 178, 212
White House, 111, 112
Whorf, Benjamin Lee, 197, 201
Wiesel, Elie, 203
Wild Palms, The (Faulkner), 162, 163, 164
Wilde, Oscar, 69, 164, 207
William Shakespeare's Star Wars (Doescher), 27
Williams, Roger, 173
Williams, Tennessee, 175
Williams, William Carlos, ix, 157
Wilson, Diana de Armas, 167–180
Wilson, Edmund, 164
With All Thine Heart (Stavans and Drache), 76
Wittgenstein, Ludwig, 37, 84, 89, 197, 198
Whitman, Walt, 61

Wilbur, Richard, 145–156, 202
Wood, Gareth, 153
Woolf, Virginia, 90, 164
World Cup, 101, 102, 103, 104, 107, 108. *See also* El Mundial

Xenophon, 68
"Xerox Man" (Stavans), 9
Xuequin, Cao, 198
Xul Solar (Oscar Agustín Alejandro Schulz Solari), 53

Yahudic, 80. *See also* Judeo-Arabic
Yahweh, 85
Yangtze River Delta, 45
Yehuda, A. B., 82
Yerushalmi, Yosef Hayim, 80
Yevanic, 80. *See also* Judeo-Greek and Hellenic
Yiddish, 3, 4, 6, 7, 8, 10, 71, 76, 80, 183, 197, 203, 204, 205, 253. *See also* Judeo-German
Yidishe Schule in Mexike, 6
Yinglish, 51, 140
Yiriart, Felipe, 10
Yoknapatawpha County (Faulkner), 25, 164
Yoruba, 176
"You Don't Hear Dogs Barking" (Rulfo), 188, 191
Yucateco, 124
Yzhàng, 198

Zenga, Walter, 105
Zidane, Zinedine, 102
Zionism, 5, 81, 82

www.ingramcontent.com/pod-product-compliance
Lightning Source LLC
Chambersburg PA
CBHW031939230426
43672CB00010B/1970